It's *Probably* Nothing

More Adventures of a Vermont Country Doctor

It's *Probably* Nothing

More Adventures of a Vermont Country Doctor

BEACH CONGER, MD

Chelsea Green Publishing
White River Junction, Vermont

Project Manager: Patricia Stone
Developmental Editor: Susan Warner
Copy Editor: Laura Jorstad
Proofreader: Helen Walden
Designer: Peter Holm, Sterling Hill Productions
Printed in the United States of America
First printing August, 2011
10 9 8 7 6 5 4 3 2 1   11 12 13 14 15

Our Commitment to Green Publishing

Chelsea Green sees publishing as a tool for cultural change and ecological stewardship. We strive to align our book manufacturing practices with our editorial mission and to reduce the impact of our business enterprise in the environment. We print our books and catalogs on chlorine-free recycled paper, using vegetable-based inks whenever possible. This book may cost slightly more because it was printed on paper that contains recycled fiber, and we hope you'll agree that it's worth it. Chelsea Green is a member of the Green Press Initiative (www.greenpressinitiative.org), a nonprofit coalition of publishers, manufacturers, and authors working to protect the world's endangered forests and conserve natural resources. *It's Probably Nothing* was printed on FSC®-certified paper supplied by Thomson-Shore that contains at least 30% postconsumer recycled fiber.

Library of Congress Cataloging-in-Publication Data is available upon request.

Chelsea Green Publishing Company
Post Office Box 428
White River Junction, VT 05001
(802) 295-6300
www.chelseagreen.com

To the folks at Temple.
They let me think I knew what I was doing.

and

To Trine.
She doesn't.

CONTENTS

INTRODUCTION

· · · · · · · · · · ·

This is a book of stories. Most of them are about Dumster, a small town in Vermont where I have lived and worked for most of the past thirty-five years. The stories of Dumster are those of simple, hard-working, no-nonsense folks and the picturesque land in which they live. They are told with deep affection and homespun humor. The stories are the kind that, if you didn't live here, would make you wish you did. They are stories that will make those of you who do live here scratch your heads, and to you I beg forgiveness. But if I hoped anyone outside of Vermont would read the book, I had no choice but to write them that way. Knowing what a small state we have, I ask you to accept that choice.

The other stories are about Philadelphia, where my wife, Trine, and I lived for five years. It was not easy to talk about Philadelphia with affection and homespun humor. Although the time I spent there was long enough to give me a grasp of the foibles and peccadilloes of the natives, it was not nearly enough to understand that they were, after all, just people—some good, some less good, and in the aggregate no better or worse than anywhere else.

Furthermore, Philadelphia is not picturesque. Not that there aren't pretty parts. There are. We lived in one of them, Chestnut Hill, which is a very pretty place, especially in the spring, first with the azaleas, and then the tulips and the rhododendrons. There are beautifully manicured lawns in Chestnut Hill and large stone mansions and plenty of green open spaces. I have to concede that Philadelphia can be a very pretty place. It's all a matter of having The Money.

They didn't have The Money in the part of Philadelphia where I worked. I call it Other Philadelphia, even though there is no such place, because to me it was a completely different world. This is how different: You are likely familiar with that yellow barricade tape that sprouts up on sidewalks and streets everywhere, whenever you are in a hurry to get somewhere. In Dumster this tape is particularly ubiquitous in the spring, marking the places where the town highway crew is thinking about fixing the worst of the worst frost heaves—when they get around to it. Or it can be seen on Main Street on Old Home and Alumni Days to close off the street for parades. To a car it can present quite a nuisance, but to a cyclist like me it's no barrier at all. I just slip under it and wend my way past whatever it is that would not be good for a larger vehicle to encounter.

The first time I saw yellow tape in Other Philadelphia, I did what I usually do: I ducked under and kept riding. I had barely started down the street when three policemen suddenly appeared with guns drawn and wanted to know what on earth I thought I was doing. I was about to say, *Oh, just saving the planet,* or some equally clever rejoinder when I saw the two dead men lying in the middle of the street.

The people who live in Other Philadelphia struggle for those things that we in Dumster take for granted—food, shelter, and safety. Health care was a luxury they could not afford. In Dumster, being a good doctor is very easy. In Other Philadelphia, it was impossible.

There's also the fact that I am from New York, and so it's difficult for me to give the city the respect it deserves. At any rate, after struggling with trying to describe our years in Philadelphia for some time, I decided it might be best to leave that part out altogether. But my daughter, Nadya, said I shouldn't.

"It's part of your perspective," she said. Nadya teaches history, and she knows a lot about perspective. So in this area I pay the strictest attention to what she has to say. At least as much as I can with the threadbare remnants of paying-attention-to-others that is left after forty-some years of doctoring.

She also pointed out that at first blush you might think it wouldn't be of much use to anyone in Vermont to hear about Philadelphia. But, she explained, you would have to blush again, because there are always people in Vermont who are thinking of moving to greener pastures. Some might be considering a place like Philadelphia, and telling them about my experiences could be very helpful to them.

I told her Philadelphia didn't have much to offer in the way of green pastures, and besides there's no place *like* Philadelphia other than Philadelphia itself. She said that didn't really matter, because, never having been there, the readers wouldn't know that.

Trine also said she thought writing about Philadelphia was a good idea. Not, she explained, simply to be a supportive wife, support not being on her list of What Every Good Spouse Provides for Her Husband When That Husband Is a Doctor. As far as she could see, doctors already got far more support than they needed and, if she might add her own two cents' worth, than they deserved. No, she said it was a good idea because she believed in the principle that good ideas should be encouraged. Whether, she added, a good idea would produce a good book was another matter altogether, and on that she would reserve judgment. So I'll have to leave that up to you, dear reader. I'll only add that if you don't give a hoot about anything south of Brattleboro, you can still read the book. Just start at chapter 11. And for those few Philadelphians who may have bought the book by mistake, you should know better than to expect a fair shake from a Giants fan.

If you have read my previous book, *Bag Balm and Duct Tape*, which I heartily recommend, as it will enhance your perspective on this work, you will see that several of the characters—Hiram Stedrock, Fusswood, Sunrise Holbode, Samantha Sticklethwaite—reappear in these pages. I do not want to give the impression that these are the only patients in my practice, as that is certainly not the case. It's just that the nature of being a doctor in a small town like Dumster is such that you have your patients for a long time, usually until they die— unless the doctor does first. And so for those of you who might have one of those migratory primary care providers, this seemed to be the best way to point that out.

There is one last subject I must address before I can allow you to start reading. It is a personal one. I suffer from a chronic affliction. It is one to which physicians are particularly susceptible. The condition is *seriosity*. Seriosity produces an irresistible compulsion always to take oneself seriously. It is accompanied by the expectation that others will do the same. It is a most disagreeable condition, not only for those who are affected, but for everyone around them.

I have attempted several treatments to rid myself of seriosity. I have giggled in important meetings. I have sung nursery rhymes in hospital corridors. I have even paraded down Main Street dressed in outlandish outfits. None of these measures has succeeded. This book is my last hope, and it falls upon you, dear reader, to effect the cure that has so long eluded me. I hope you will not fail.

AUTHOR'S NOTE

············

I'm often asked whether this is a work of fiction or of nonfiction. The crux of the matter, in the eyes of those who rule on such matters, apparently hinges upon whether or not such facts as are contained in said work are, in fact, factual. I am sure that those who engage in such determinations have perfectly good reasons for so doing, although I, for one, cannot imagine what they might be. Perhaps it has to do with some repressed trauma in childhood. Everything these days seems to hinge upon that. At any rate, the whole concept is absurd. The only important question in a work is whether or not the author, in telling his tale, has told the Truth. And I would submit that the relationship between Truth and Facts was best described by Henry Adams, who said in his *Education*,

> if [the historian] values truths, he is certain to falsify his facts.

Pursuant to this, I will only say that I have done my best not to write an intentionally false word, and I will leave the question of fictionality to those more qualified than I.

Nat's Lunch

···········

Thirty-five years ago, almost to the day, Trine and I were sitting at our home in Berkeley having our evening tea. Almost simultaneously, we heard the dripping of a faucet and the ringing of a phone. Trine got up to attend to the faucet while I went for the phone. That neither of us succeeded in our task was no fault of ours. It was due to the fact that the phone that rang belonged to our neighbor Phil on the left, and the faucet that dripped was that of our neighbor Melody on the right.

We were very close to our neighbors. And as people do who are close to one another, there was much that we shared. When we returned to our tea, we talked about this closeness and sharing. It was quite something, we agreed, that they should both be so close that they could share afternoon tea with us without actually being present. Something in fact that seemed to be an omen—the interpretation of which, we also agreed, suggested that it was time to move.

Being pretty methodical in our decisions, we started off by making a list of what we would want wherever we made our new home. We weren't very fussy, so the list wasn't very long. There were only four items.

1. A hospital
2. A law school
3. Snow
4. A Chinese restaurant

After much searching about, the place we finally decided upon was Dumster, Vermont. It had a hospital that needed someone to replace the retiring general practitioner, which would suit me very nicely. Trine was finishing her first year at law school, and Vermont's only law school was just up the road a bit. And, as a Norwegian, she needed her snow. Dumster didn't have a Chinese restaurant, but we figured it was only a matter of time before that changed. (We were right. Thirty years later a Chinese family arrived in Dumster and opened up a restaurant called Yummy Tummy. It featured the usual fare: egg rolls, sweet-and-sour soup, fortune cookies. But mostly it they sold was burgers and fries.)

I am what is called an internist. Although in name similar to those newly graduated from medical school, internists bear them no relation. Once we were the elite of the profession, those to whom everyone turned when no one else could figure out what was going on. Relying almost exclusively on our hands and our heads, the diagnostic dishes we served up were without equal. We were the Master Chefs of medicine.

But that was back when mostly what doctors could do was give a name to things, without being able to do much about them. All that has changed with the Age of Specialization. We now have experts in every field of medicine you can think of, and even some you probably can't. Now, not a problem exists about which we can't do something, and most of the time the something is even something good. This is particularly so at the most elite of medical facilities, the academic medical centers. While we were living in Berkeley, I was working at one of the finest, the University of California Medical Center.

In such a grand establishment an internist has a more modest, though no less important, role than that which once we held. I was a maître d'. My job was to ensure that those who entered our doors had a fully satisfying experience—one that would guarantee their continued patronage. Were I to perform my job but indifferently, almost certainly the next time the issue of dining at the table of one's complaints came up, the vote would be, not for us, but rather for the Chiropractor, the Homeopath, or perhaps even to stay at home and sup on Herbs and Grasses.

I would greet the customers and find them seating suitable to their desires. I would determine their needs and preferences, as well those items on the menu to which they might be especially averse. I would make suggestions as to the specialties of the house, and then I would leave them to their just desserts. With respect to the actual food, whether it was preparing, serving, or tidying up afterward, I played no role whatsoever.

Such was my life in California. At Emmeline Talbot Memorial Hospital, as I was to discover rather more quickly than I was prepared for, things were quite different. Even by small-hospital standards, Emmeline Talbot was quite small. Only a thirty-bed facility, it was built solely from money raised by the people of Dumster. The town had applied to the federal government for the funds from the Hill-Burton Act of 1946, the principle of which was to ensure that small towns like Dumster would not go without a hospital just because they didn't need one. At the time they applied in 1972, however, the rules of the act had changed, and the townspeople were told they would need first to get approval from the State Comprehensive Heath Planning Agency. The people from the state did some studies and hired some consultants and made some projections and determined that, based on the population it would serve, and taking into account various factors, conditions, and considerations that such bodies always took into account, the town was entitled to funding for a hospital of 3.6 beds. The townspeople were very appreciative of the effort, but told the state that a 3.6-bed hospital was not quite what they had in mind, so they would just build one themselves. Which they did.

Were there such a guide, you would not find Emmeline Talbot Memorial Hospital listed in the Michelin Hospital Guide as a three-starred medical dining establishment. Emmeline Talbot was more along the lines of Dumster's signature restaurant, Nat's Lunch.

And accordingly, I would become more along the lines of Nat.

Except for the irregular assistance of a stream of itinerant adolescents, Nat ran the place by herself. She was owner, operator, cook, server, and bottle washer. Nat was Nat's Lunch.

Nat was born Natalie Contremond, but for as long as anyone could remember, and for reasons unknown to anyone except to her parents, she had been called Nat. Nat was the daughter of Elmer Contremond, a descendant of the merchant branch of the Contremond family tree, the patriarch of which was Elmer's grandfather Stanley. Stanley was one of the nine children of Maurice and Louisa Contremond, who came down from the Eastern Townships of Quebec in 1850 to the more forgiving and fertile farmlands of the Upper Connecticut River Valley. There were seven daughters, all of whom were married off, and two sons, Stanley and his older brother, Ezra. When Maurice died, he left most of the farm in equal portions to the two sons. He reserved a section near the ferry at Sumner Falls to be sold off, the resulting income from which would be divided equally among his daughters.

Ezra, who was honest, hardworking, and unimpaired by any imagination, took up his share without a second thought. His father had farmed, and so would he. He expected nothing different from his brother—expectations, however great or small, being reserved for a very different world than that in which he lived—excepting the expectation that the way things always had been was the way they most likely would be—barring the unexpected.

Which was exactly what happened. For no sooner was the earth shoveled over his father's grave than Stanley approached Ezra with an offer to sell his share of the farm. Stanley was just as well endowed with work ethic as his elder brother, but he was somewhat differently equipped in the distribution of the resources of honesty and cleverness: Most of the supply of the former had been diverted to the latter. Not that anyone would go so far as to say Stanley ever attained Snopesian proportions, but he was, by general agreement among the townspeople, a shrewd one. Ezra accepted his offer. Stanley took the money and opened Contremond Dry Goods in the center of town, and, thanks to a rapidly growing populace and Stanley's business acumen, it quickly became a thriving business.

Stanley yielded the reins at age ninety to his eldest son, Matthew, who in turn gave them over to his eldest, Elmer, the father of Nat. Nat was as shrewd as any of the Contremonds. She was also, by far, the smartest.

By the time she was fourteen, Nat realized that she had gotten from school all that it had to offer. As she said, she could read well enough to see the handwriting on the wall, and she was so good at math that she could do even the most complex calculations in her head. And what she could calculate best of all was the value of something. That value, when it came to learning about the doings of men long dead, or why an apple fell from the tree, she calculated at precisely nil.

So she left school and went to work for Gino Palucci at Palucci's Diner. Her salary was fifty cents a week. At first her duties were limited to washing dishes and cleaning up. But she was a quick study, and before long Gino was letting her help out with the cooking, then with taking orders, and finally with reckoning the bill, so that by the time she was sixteen she could have run the place on her own.

The year was 1930. The country was in the throes of the Depression, and Dumster, like so many small towns in America, was short on cash. The mills had shut down for want of customers, and there was no work—none that would pay ready money at any rate. People got by doing what they could for themselves and did without what they couldn't. So that a man was not going to throw away what little he had by paying someone to make him a cup of coffee or slice him a piece of pie when he could just as well do it for himself.

And so one day in April, Gino came into the diner and announced to Nat that he was selling out to a fella from downcountry and going back to his native Sicily—where he figured his savings would provide for a more liberal retirement than in America.

"How much?" asked Nat.

"Fifty dollars."

"I'll buy it," she said without hesitation, "for fifty-one."

"Where you gonna get that kind of money?" asked Gino not unkindly, for he had a soft spot for his hardworking girl who always opened up and closed the diner rain or shine, never shirked a duty, and now managed his books much better than he ever had. She was, in fact, more a partner than an employee, and it was in large part thanks to her efforts that the diner was worth anything at all.

"I'll git it," she said.

"Well," Gino said. "The fella is coming by Friday. If you can get the money by Thursday, the place is yours."

That was on Tuesday. Nat asked Gino if she could leave early to tend to business, and Gino said yes. She went straight home, took out her cash box with the twenty-four dollars and thirty-seven cents she had saved up, and walked down to Dumster Federal, where she asked to see Mr. Cabot, the bank manager.

"What would you like to see him about, Natalie?" asked Alice Foster, his assistant.

"A loan."

"A loan," repeated Alice, not quite suppressing a smile. "Well, that *is* important. Please have a seat, and I'll let him know that you are here."

After about half an hour she informed Nat that Mr. Cabot was available to see her and ushered her into his office.

The Cabot family was one of Dumster's oldest and most distinguished families. Whether they were actually descended from the great Cabots of Boston was not entirely clear, but it was definitely possible that they could have been, and it was beyond doubt that they behaved as if they did, so it was generally agreed that they might just as well have been. Gerald Cabot was a handsome man with a full head of white hair, clear blue eyes, and a trim figure. He looked every inch just what he was, a gentleman.

"Good morning, Miss Contremond," he said, addressing her with the same courtesy he would have accorded a member of the chamber of commerce. "Please have a seat. I understand from Mrs. Foster that you are interested in a loan."

"Yessir."

"Would the purpose of that loan be business or personal?"

"I'm gonna buy out Gino."

"That would be business. And how much were you expecting to borrow?"

"Twenty-six dollars and sixty-three cents."

"Mr. Palucci is willing to sell you the diner for twenty-six dollars and sixty-three cents?" he asked, not concealing his surprise. As a banker it was his job to know what each and every parcel and plot of land was worth, and he was well aware of the offer for fifty.

"He's selling it for fifty-one. I already got twenty-four thirty-seven." She pulled out her cash box. "It's right here if'n you wanta count it."

"That won't be necessary, Miss Contremond. If you say you have twenty-four dollars and thirty-seven cents, I am sure that is precisely the amount you have. So, twenty-six dollars and sixty-three cents. Well, this is—as I am sure you are aware—a very difficult time for the bank. And at present, our board of directors is *most* reluctant to issue any new loans. But seeing as how this is an established business, and you are a—er—*well-known* figure in our community, even if you are not an established customer, perhaps we could make an exception. But first, of course, I will need to examine the establishment and inventory the equipment."

Despite himself, Gerald Cabot sighed slightly at the end of his speech. He knew it was a good speech. It ought to be. He had polished and refined it many times over the past two years. But it was a lie.

"Gotta be tomorrow," said Nat.

"I think we can arrange for tomorrow," he replied. "Shall we say, nine o'clock?"

And so promptly at nine, Mr. Cabot and Mrs. Foster walked across the street from the bank to Palucci's Diner. First Mr. Cabot walked around the outside of the building to inspect the siding and the sills and the foundation. Then he went into the basement where he poked around at the wiring and the plumbing and the boiler. Upstairs he looked into the oven and the icebox. He even tested the grill. Mrs. Foster counted the plates and cups and silverware. And she looked into the cash register. When they were done, they had a very complete inventory of the establishment. Not that it was at all necessary. Except for Monday, which was Rotary, Mr. Cabot had been a patron of Palucci's Diner for lunch every workday for the past thirty years, and he could calculate both the contents and their value with his eyes closed. Furthermore, as the front window of his office looked right across at Palucci's entrance, he had a very good idea of the trade. With his banker's eye for profit and loss, he knew the worth of the business just about to the penny. It was more than twenty-six dollars. However, as few people knew, but many were about to discover, the bank was on the verge of collapse. It had not a penny to lend. But Mr. Cabot admired the courage of the youngster, and he felt he owed her the same courtesy he showed in turning down some of his oldest friends and best customers.

"I'm afraid we can't do it at present," he said. "It's just not the kind of investment the bank is looking for in its current portfolio. Perhaps, though, at a later date . . ."

Nat looked at him. Her face showed not the slightest surprise or dismay.

"You got a dollar, Mr. Cabot?" she asked quietly.

"Yes, of course," he said, "but I'm not really hungry right now, Miss Contremond, seeing as how I just . . ."

"Willya lend it to me?"

She didn't give up easily, he thought. "What good is a dollar going to do you, Nat? I'm afraid the bank isn't going to lend you twenty-five any more than they will twenty-six."

"An' sixty-three cents," she replied. "You gonna lend me the dollar?"

"Well—I—er—heck. Of course I'll loan you a dollar, Nat." If she was that hard up, it was the least he could do for the poor thing. She was so determined.

He pulled a dollar from his pocket and handed it to her. She took it. "An' write me up a note."

"That won't be necessary, Nat," he chuckled despite himself. "I know where you are."

"On bank paper."

So they all went back to the bank, and Mr. Cabot took out a piece of bank stationery and wrote out a promissory note for one dollar to be paid back in twelve months at the amount of one dollar, with five cents interest. Nat insisted on that. "So as to prove it's a proper loan," she said. "Just in case." Then he signed it, and Nat signed it, and Mrs. Foster witnessed it. Nat stuck out her hand, and they shook on the deal. Then she thanked him and left.

She took the note to her father and showed it to him. He agreed to loan her a dollar under the same conditions as those Mr. Cabot had agreed to. Armed with these two promissory notes, she went around to every Palucci customer in town, and from forty-five of them she managed to raise the remaining twenty-four dollars and sixty-three cents. Some paid as little as a quarter, others the full dollar. And each one got a promissory note from Nat payable at 5 percent interest in one year.

Thursday afternoon she gave Gino the fifty-one dollars, and the diner was hers.

Nat never bothered to change the sign, that being an unnecessary expense, but from that time to now it has been known as Nat's Lunch, and at age eighty-seven Nat is still in charge.

Secure in the knowledge that the good people of Dumster have simple tastes and a deep mistrust of anyone who charges to prepare their food, Nat provides the townspeople with the kind of food they are willing to eat at a price they are willing to pay.

The coffee is always fresh. She serves eggs or oatmeal for breakfast. For lunch you can get tuna or burgers or wieners with beans or slaw or fries. On toast or not. There is no daily special, and there are no free-range wasabi-crusted tuna in an apricot reduction sauce, or organic baby *haricots verts amandine* with a rosemary béarnaise.

Nat's food is adjective-free.

And so, as I was to discover, were the good people of Dumster. They were what they were, they lived the way they lived, and that was that. And they were a tolerant lot, willing to take their chances with the overtrained and underqualified doctor who had come to town. Just how unqualified I was, and how tolerant they would have to be, I learned rather quickly.

It started with Hiram Stedrock.

I Never Broke One Before Neither

··········

It was my first week at Emmeline Talbot Memorial Hospital. I got a call from the emergency room. It was Loree Ellis, the nurse in charge.

"Hiram Stedrock is here," she said. "It's his Madeline."

There was no more. Apparently Ms. Ellis considered this enough information.

"Madeline. She—uh . . ."

"She sat down."

"Ah. Sat down, did she?"

"Yes."

"Um—I'm don't quite . . ."

"Would you please come out?"

No amplification on the complaint apparently being forthcoming, I trotted out to the emergency room. There I was greeted by a man in a red-and-black-checked shirt, rubber coveralls, rubber boots, and a green baseball cap with AGWAY lettered on the front. Although he was clean-shaven, and his pants and boots looked recently scrubbed, there was a distinct odor of cow manure in the room. He sat quietly with one arm folded across the other.

"Hello, Mr. Stedrock," I said. "I'm Doctor Conger. I'm pleased to meet you."

"Stedrock," he said.

"How are you today, Mr. Stedrock?"

It's a common inquiry, and it has a common response, one that both the one who asks and the one who answers know full well never contains the smallest grain of truth.

Hiram paused to consider the question, and then answered slowly.

"Could be worse."

"Well, that's something at least," I said. "What seems to be the problem today?"

"That's what I came here to find out."

To some, this might seem like a rather silly reply, but as I was to learn, it was the standard Dumster response to this standard doctor question. The reason is quite simple. The people of Dumster were a considerate lot, and the last thing they wanted to do was put their doctor in a pickle by proposing a complaint that was beyond my grasp. They would rather put the diagnostic ball right in my court, thus permitting me any line of inquiry I felt inclined to pursue. If matters gastroenterological were my forte I could investigate the stomach, an organ never without some bit of grumbling. Or, if I felt inclined to delve into cardiac regions, careful inquiry as to a touch of chest pain now and then would invariably yield some result.

I told Hiram I would do my best. Then I inquired about the as-yet-unseen Madeline, upon whose behalf he was apparently now present.

"She's okay."

"I'm glad to hear it." Nor was I surprised. Something about the act of coming to an emergency room often removed the complaint that had prompted the visit. "Shall we take a look at her then?"

"Better not to," he said.

"No?"

"She's not here."

"Oh. Where is she then?"

"She's at home."

Asking questions was not bearing much fruit. So I remained silent.

"You see . . . ," he said awkwardly.

"Actually, I'm afraid I don't," I said. "Not at all. Madeline is—"

"—well, she looks Holstein, but she's got some Jersey in her from way back, so I guess you'd have to call her a mix."

"Madeline is a *cow?*"

Hiram nodded.

"A cow who sat down."

He nodded again.

Ignorant as I was about farm life, my bias about cows was that sitting down was pretty much in their line of work.

"I still don't understand," I said.

Hiram gave me a pained look. Exposition was not his best event.

Nonetheless, he made an effort, and after a few minutes we finally got to the crux of the matter, which turned out to be the right wrist of Hiram, said wrist having been underneath Madeline when she made her descent. He produced the appendage in question. It was swollen and discolored. I ordered an X-ray.

The wrist was broken. I knew it was broken because, even though as an urban internist the sum total of my orthopedic knowledge extended only slightly beyond the wrist bone being connected to the arm bone, while I was studying the X-ray in the vain hope of inspiration, the technician pointed to an obscure little black squiggle overlying a roundish white blob and said helpfully, "Looks like a Colles' fracture."

"Ye-ss. I would say so."

"Nondisplaced too."

"Quite."

Armed with this information, I reported our findings to the nurse, and asked her to get the orthopedic surgeon.

"That would be Doctor. Shoemaker," she said.

"Doctor Shoemaker it is then."

"He's in Springfield."

"All right. Let's give him a call."

"You want me to call Doctor Shoemaker about a broken wrist?"

"Please."

"A *nondisplaced* broken wrist."

"That would be the case."

"In Springfield?"

"If that's where he is."

As I was to learn, the Emmeline Talbot tree had an insufficient supply of broken limbs to provide Dr. Shoemaker a comfortable living. Accordingly, we were required to borrow his services from the hospital in Springfield, some thirty miles distant, and, as such, were at the mercy of their needs. With no attempt to disguise her reluctance, Nurse Ellis placed the call. As it turned out Dr. Shoemaker was in the operating room fixing a broken hip. He had two more cases after that. There was no way he was going to drive over to Dumster that day.

I explained to Mr. Stedrock that he would need to go to Springfield to have his wrist tended to.

"How?" he said.

"You won't have to drive," I said. "We'll get an ambulance."

He frowned. "An ambulance? That's another arm and a leg. Won't leave me much to work with."

"Don't worry. I'm sure your insurance will cover it."

"Insurance?"

"I'm afraid there isn't much choice, Mr. Stedrock. Unless you can find someone to drive you."

"Whyn't you fix it?"

"I've never fixed a broken wrist before."

"I never broke one before neither."

He allowed as how if I did the best I could that would be good enough for him, and so with the nurse supervising, I wrapped him with enough plaster to sink the *Titanic*. Hiram looked at the cast.

"Don't guess I'll blow away in the wind," he said.

"You'll take it off," Nurse Ellis said.

That was my introduction to the Dumster way. With a tolerance born of the knowledge that however hard one might try, and however successful one might appear, when it comes right down to it, we are all woefully inadequate to perform the tasks of life. All they ever expected of anyone was that he would do the best he could.

They also knew that in the interaction between the doctor and the patient, it was the patient's job to get better, and it was the doctor's job to get the credit. Because the patient didn't need the credit. And the doctor needed plenty.

Over the years Hiram Stedrock has taught me a lot—some about farming, quite a bit about farmers, and a lot about talking too much and listening too little. I've been a slow learner. Fortunately, Hiram Stedrock is a patient man.

Not Enough Misery

···········

That was a long time ago. I have since become very comfortable in Dumster. It is an easy town to be comfortable in. Neither a big town nor a small one, Dumster is pleasant looking, but not particularly scenic. People live in Dumster. They do not visit it. The downtown has a gas station, a post office, a bank, a general store, a Laundromat, and two dining establishments to serve the bodily needs of the town. For nourishment of the soul there is both a Congregational and a Methodist church, although Dumsterians, being ecumenical in their worship, know them by their architectural rather than denominational character, as the Brick Church and the White Church, respectively. At the corner of Main and Hill there is a traffic light. There is one tenement building known as The Block. There are no B&Bs. Dumster is just right for the kind of town that it is.

After thirty-five years I know Dumster, and the town knows me. I am their doctor, and the townspeople are my patients. So every now and then they come to see me in my office, where I fuss at them the way doctors do. But that is not very often. Most of the time they are regular people. As am I. They are people who fix my car, or teach my children, or sell me bread. Some are friends. We share the same place, and although each connection by itself does not run very deep, in total they create a tie that binds almost as strongly as family.

It makes for quite a nice place. Halcyon, some even have said. Not anyone who actually lives here, of course. On the contrary, there seems to be an inverse relationship between the halcyonity with which one views the Green Mountains, and the distance from which that view originates. So that people who have never actually been here, but who have a sense of what Vermont is like from the issues of *Vermont Life* that they have picked up while waiting in their dentist's office, can see halcyon much better than those of us for whom it is right in front of our noses. Take us, for example.

When Trine and I lived in Berkeley, we subscribed to *Vermont Life*. We read the magazine religiously during the year that we knew we were going to move here. And then pretty regularly for a year or so afterward, at which point, without us doing anything about it, the magazine just stopped coming, apparently of its own accord. As if both of us knew that there was no longer any point.

One gets the impression from *Vermont Life* that most of the year is autumn, and that most of the buildings are on farms, and that many modern conveniences, like Cumberland Farms and Walmart, have not yet arrived. And that there is no such thing as freezing rain or traffic. That is only as it should be. Because the purpose of *Vermont Life* is to point out our niceness to those who haven't experienced it, or who may have experienced it only briefly and need to have their memory refreshed. And for a time, it helps remind those of us who have just moved here and are developing tendencies not to remember just why it was we made the move.

Which, as tendencies often do, become habits the longer you have them. Take, for example, someone who has lived here, well, not all his life, because, as he would point out to you if you were to ask him, he hasn't lived anywhere that long, as yet. But whose ancestors would have. And who would have lived on a farm. A farm that would have been on a dirt road, with a stone fence along the side and fallen leaves in autumn, and along which he took the bus to school or walked to the white church in town on Sunday, or to the general store, where he got tenpenny nails and fishhooks and soda from a cooler. That kind of person, no matter how much you try to point it out, never notices our niceness at all. Except maybe the last two weeks in November. Which is hunting season.

I used to think the failure of these people to notice our niceness was because, never having lived anywhere else, they didn't know any better. But that is not the reason. Because they do go places. To places like Boston and New York. Even to Florida.

Last summer Margaret Stone, Maggie as she is usually called, went on holiday with her husband and two children. Maggie Stone is a nurse. Because she works with me, some would say she is *my* nurse. But this would not be correct. Maggie is my responsible adult. All doctors have a responsible adult. As the name implies, the duties of this person are manifold, consisting as they do of taking care of all those adult behaviors a doctor is too busy to pay attention to, like being on time, or doing what the doctor said she would do. And most importantly, of making sure that anything, no matter how well intentioned, that the doctor might interpret as criticism does not interfere with the doctor in the performance of her duties.

Maggie Stone's Vermont pedigree is as good as it gets. Her family moved up from Connecticut with the first wave of settlers in the early nineteenth century. They settled on land in Steddsville, where her brother and uncle still live. After Maggie married Bill Stone from West Dumster, they moved into town. She went to work at the hospital and he at Contremond's. Like most townspeople, their lives stayed pretty close to home. A big trip for them was going up to their camp on Little Averill Pond or over to the state fair in Rutland. Or maybe to the Manchester Mall for school clothes. But last year they went to Disney World. For the kids, she said. I asked Maggie how the trip was for her.

"It was very nice," she said.

For me, who comes from New York and has an aunt I visit in Florida, the idea that any of these places could be considered nice seems strange. But maybe that's just it. Nice is just someplace where you don't usually go.

Some people up here, newcomers mostly, think that what makes Vermont nice is that there aren't very many of them here—people that is. And they worry that, being so nice, people would start to move here and then keep on moving here until all the niceness was pretty much gone, like it is in some places. But they don't.

Because of November. For the ones who don't live here, November is the time of year that makes them realize that Vermont, like chocolate mousse or lying on a beach in the Caribbean, is best enjoyed in moderation. Those people don't live in places that have November. Not that their years are any shorter than ours. But for them, although they do have thirty days listed as November on their calendar, they are not actual November days. So that, for example, what is listed as November 17 in New York is actually October 48, or, in Baltimore, September 78.

In November, Vermont pretty much clears out of all those people who had thoughts that maybe it would be really nice to move up here permanently and open an inn, or telecommute, or live off their savings. In November those thoughts pretty much disappear. Vermont is not the only place that has November, of course. There are plenty of others. In some of them November starts in September. Places like Canada and Norway and Ulan Bator. But most people don't live there either.

On this particular November morning we had freezing rain. All night the snow had been falling, that heavy snow where each flake, with a weight rendering it both oblivious to the path of its fellow travelers and impervious to the diverting efforts of a blustering wind, drops, like a stone, plumb to the ground. In the driveway, the pines, bowed down by the snow and cemented in place by the ice, arched their backs in a futile attempt to release themselves from imprisonment. So embedded were they that it almost seemed as if the snow was reaching up from below to grab the branches and pull them to the earth. But whether they were stalactites or stalagmites, the end result, when viewed from the kitchen window, was the impression of descending into a cave, the exit from which seemed unlikely in the foreseeable future.

Not that I wanted to. Being nicely cocooned inside a warm house, with several feet of snow on an unplowed driveway, where one's major concern was whether there were sufficient provisions to obviate a trip to the woodshed, lent itself well to staying in place.

Dearly Beloved and I were savoring the precious opportunity that only the likes of freezing rain on snow can provide—a second cup of morning tea. She was reading the *Valley News*, and I was reflecting contentedly on the certainty that, after twenty-five years of practice, I had finally gotten the hang of things, and I could anticipate spending my remaining days stamping out pestilence and basking in the general adoration that a small town dispenses to its Kindly Old—not so much on the merits of his accomplishments, but simply on the grounds of his having endured. Because to do otherwise would reflect ill on both of us. Things, as I was just about to say, were *not too bad*.

I was forestalled.

"You know what it is?" exclaimed Dearly Beloved abruptly.

Thirty years with Dearly Beloved have taught me the fine distinction between a question asked and a question to be answered. The introduction just recorded indicating beyond doubt a case of the former, I fixed my most attentive gaze and took a considered sip of tea.

"There's not enough misery."

Another sip.

"Here."

I remained at full teacup.

"Hardly any, in fact. Unless you want to count The Block. Which," she declared pointedly, "I don't."

Of the many endearing features of Dearly Beloved, my favorite is her consideration. She knows that, for one who spends most of his waking hours reassuring the unreassurable and tracting the intractable, to expect active participation in ordinary interspousal communication would be quite beyond the pale. Accordingly she has taken it upon herself willingly, and even, I might say, at times eagerly, to maintain not only her end of our tête-à-tête, but mine as well. She asks only that I appear attentive while she is we. It is the least I can do.

Although Trine is Norwegian, born and raised, she has adapted so well to our language and customs that it is virtually impossible for someone who does not know otherwise to discern that she is not one of us. There are, however, times when the stamp of her native country shows through, such as when we get ready to trim the tree at Christmas, and the first decorations out are the elven *nisses* and the string of small Norwegian flags. Or when her need to alleviate the misery of those in our society who are less privileged makes her indignant at America's spirit of the freedom to be poor. And which is why she gave up a very successful law practice to pursue a career bettering the lives of those families with the least among us.

"You see," she said, looking at me fixedly, more of habit than necessity, for I had long since learned that *you see* was preface to the meat of our discussion, and the time had come for appearance to become reality.

"It's not really anyone's fault, I suppose. It's just there aren't enough people around here. Poor people that is. And as for the downtrodden and oppressed—well, when it comes to them—it just doesn't, if you know what I mean."

An acquiescent nod seeming judicious at this point, I obliged.

"Look!" She pointed out the window at the expanse of snow, which cast a forgiving blanket over everything within our view. "Not a spot of decay, not a speck of dilapidation. Not a bit of color. It's all so—so white!"

"Ye-ss." Although strictly speaking, a response was not called for, I have noticed that an occasional heartfelt acquiescence has a stimulatory effect on our discourse.

"I mean—" She held up the newspaper and jabbed her finger at it. "What are the big issues here? Road salt. School budgets. And those bloody concrete balls on the Ledyard Bridge. Which, in the grand scheme of things, are not exactly Big Whup."

Sensing, perhaps, the direction of our conversation, my teacup quivered slightly. And then it came. If not entirely out of the blue, at least rounding a corner at a substantially higher rate of speed than I had anticipated.

"It's time to move."

"To Burlington?"

The Queen City was not exactly a haven of despair, but it did have a small immigrant refugee community in the old North End. They came from places like Somalia and Bhutan, and Bosnia, and although they are well treated here, they have brought with them the scars of a subjugation more horrendous than I would think a person could bear. Besides, Burlington was where we had originally planned to settle upon emigrating from Berkeley, until we discovered that the Vermont Law School was located not at the university in Burlington but in South Royalton, a town just north of Dumster with a population of not quite five hundred.

"To Philadelphia."

"Philadelphia?"

Although its credentials in the field of urban decay were impeccable, we had never been to the City of Brotherly Love, nor to the best of my knowledge had we ever discussed it, other than in passing reference to the inferior quality of its mayoral offerings.

"Yes, Philadelphia."

"I see."

"I doubt it."

"Dimly, perhaps."

"Poorly. I'd say."

"But—"

"But if you did, you would see that it's the only place we can go. It can't be Boston, because Boston is too provincial, and it can't be New York, because New York is too—well, it's just too—New York. And Baltimore is too close to Washington, and Washington is just hopeless, and after that, it's the South. And we're not going to the South. Besides, I know the commissioner in Philadelphia, and she has promised me a job helping their abused and neglected children find permanent homes, if we come. So there you have it."

And there I did. For I had no choice but to agree. When we left Berkeley to come to Dumster, it was on the condition that if either of our careers ran aground, we would pull up anchor and set sail from the peaceful land in which we now lived. I knew it was bound to happen at some point. It was inevitable that Trine's passion to set things right would someday make her yearn for greater injustices to fight than the rather meager offerings of our beloved state.

I raised a set of feeble objections, all of which she dispensed with easily. The kids were all off on their own. We need not sell or rent our house in Dumster. It would serve very nicely as a Vermont vacation getaway. And with my experience, getting a job should certainly be easy indeed.

I wasn't worried about that part. I was confident I could weather the move. After all, before coming to Dumster, I had cut my professional teeth at Boston City Hospital, Grady Memorial Hospital, and San Francisco General Hospital. Admittedly, it had been a few years since I practiced urban medicine, but sick was still sick no matter where it was.

A doctor spends a lot of time in his place of practice. And although inside the exam room, what goes on between a doctor and a patient is pretty much the same everywhere, the world in which that exam room resides varies considerably. And if that world is one ill suited to your own particular needs and desires, it can make for a pretty miserable day. So before I made a decision about where in Philadelphia I was going to work, I did my homework. First I looked for practices that were advertising for a general internist. There were eleven of these. Then I made a list of all the hospitals in the city that had departments of internal medicine. There were nine. Finally, I checked with the city of Philadelphia to find out if they needed any doctors in their clinics. They needed four.

I wrote to all the places, and I visited each one, and I talked to the people who worked there—not just the doctors, but the nurses and the receptionists too. And I talked to the patients in the waiting rooms. I wanted to know if it was a place where the staff treated you like a person rather than a disease. I wanted to know: Was it a friendly place, the kind of place that I would want to be if I were a patient? That kind of knowledge you couldn't get by talking to the people behind the desks or wearing the uniforms or carrying the stethoscopes. Plus, the patients had a lot more time to talk to me. It took me a long time to do this with the twenty-four places, but it was worth it. When I made my final decision, I was sure it was the right one. I went to the place that offered me a job.

A Hallucination

....

Philadelphia would be considered a big city. There are a million and a half people in Philadelphia, and they live in a space not much larger than Dumster, West Dumster, and Steddsville combined. That's a lot of people in not very much space.

But the odd thing about Philadelphia is that it doesn't feel like a big city. I don't mean that Philadelphia isn't overcrowded or dirty or noisy, or that it doesn't have people living in cardboard boxes and roving the streets pushing shopping carts full of who knows what. Philadelphia has plenty of all that. When it comes to urban milieu, Philadelphia is second to none. Not even to the Big Apple.

Nonetheless, Philadelphia feels like a small town. Or, more properly, it feels like a thousand small towns all packed in cheek-to-jowl, each one living its own life and not very interested in, or sympathetic to, what's going on in the next. For example, if you ask someone from Philadelphia where he lives, he will never say, *Philadelphia*. First, he would tell you where he used to come from, not where he lives now, because wherever that place was, it isn't the same place it used to be and has changed always for the worse. Unless he came from the Main Line, in which case you probably wouldn't be talking to him—unless you came from there also, and then you wouldn't need to ask. Next he would tell you the name of his neighborhood, and finally his block. For all its size, Philadelphia turns out to be not much more than a big set of scattered blocks.

So in a way, it's not very different from Vermont. Of course, when people in Philadelphia asked me where I was from, I just said Vermont. Even that was a bit too much. They would look at me puzzled, and then they would say "Vuh-mont. What state izzat in?" Which felt a little odd at first. But eventually I got used to it.

I suppose it's no different than being from New Mexico. I've heard

New Mexicans can go places where the people they meet don't realize that New Mexico is not part of Mexico, which is divided into two parts—New Mexico and Old Mexico. And they probably have to explain about how, although it was once part of Mexico, in 1846 Colonel Stephen W. Kearney took his troops into Santa Fe and declared that it was now part of the United States. And he did so without firing a shot, because, just to make sure everything went okay, President Polk had paid off the Mexican governor ahead of time. Now that I think of it, this might actually be the kind of history that people living in New Mexico would just as soon not talk about, at least not to an outsider.

So I didn't tell them about the Green Mountain Boys. Or that Vermont was once a kingdom. And I didn't tell them that, not only did we have two hundred and fifty-one towns, we also had three gores and a grant. Warner's Grant. Which, if you wanted to go to it, say, on a bicycle, you would have to carry your bike up from Norton Pond, because the only road into it has turned into a bog. I know this, because it was the last place I had to go to complete my quest to bicycle to all the two hundred and fifty-five places in Vermont. It's a quest that you might say sounds pretty pointless, and I would agree. But then, if life won't let you do something pointless now and then, what's the point?

But I never mentioned any of this to anyone in Philadelphia, because I could tell by the look on their faces that by the time I'd said "Vermont is . . ." I had lost them. So I'd just say that we're near Canada. And then they'd say they'd heard it's pretty cold up there. And I'd allow as how it was, and we'd leave it at that. Near Canada was about all they wanted to know.

Except for Shirley Covington. Shirley worked at William Penn Hospital, which was where I doctored while I was in Philadelphia.

Emmeline Talbot Memorial Hospital was built on five acres of farm and woodland on a hill above town. It is an unobtrusive building that in summer is almost invisible from the road. There are no elevators at Emmeline Talbot. Nor are there any stairs; it's all on one floor.

There are stairs aplenty at William Penn Hospital, and those few who use them exclusively to move from floor to floor are a hardy bunch, like those who spend their spare time hiking the Appalachian Trail or trekking through Nepal. The land upon which the hospital was built was previously a vacant lot. I don't know about the acreage, because they don't have acres in Other Philadelphia, but that is the only respect in which William Penn is smaller than Emmeline Talbot. For William Penn is not unobtrusive. Towering formidably above the two- and three-story ramshackle buildings that surround it, William Penn is a pretty typical multistory big-city hospital. From an architectural point of view, the two hospitals couldn't be more different. Except in one respect.

Trees.

That Emmeline Talbot would have an abundance of trees gracing its grounds should come as no great surprise. You could hardly expect otherwise. That William Penn was similarly endowed was, I'll admit, a bit of a shocker. Along the front is a majestic canopy of old-growth oak, and along the sides are a profusion of birch, cypress, and beech. Japanese cherry line the North and South Entrances, dogwood the East and West. There is even a lush grove of royal palms on the southwest corner.

It is not just in the variety, however, that the trees of William Penn differ from Emmeline Talbot. While the trees at Emmeline Talbot began their lives as seeds in the ground, growing upward, first as seedlings and then as saplings, increasing in size and beauty at each succeeding stage, until they reached their full beauty after many years, those at William Penn are just the opposite. They started fully grown at the peak of their glory, and, with each succeeding year they became a little more faded and a little more decayed. And they grew, not up from the ground, but out from the walls, placed there not by the hands of a modern Johnny Appleseed, but by the brush of a modern Diego Rivera, courtesy of the Philadelphia Mural Arts Program.

Shirley Covington was a People Person. She told me this the first time we met, and no sooner had we been introduced than she wanted to know all about me and where I came from. She even wanted to hear about my bicycling around the state. "That must have been very interesting," she said. "I can tell you are a very interesting person."

I told her that was very nice of her to say, and that the trip was very interesting for me to do, but not so much to talk about.

"Tell me anyway. I bet it is," she said. And so I told her.

I won't say that she wanted to know more about my trips than I wanted to tell, but I will say she was about the most interested person I have ever met.

Shirley worked in the Department of Medicine. She was an administrative assistant. Since at Emmeline Talbot, we didn't have administrative assistants, I didn't know what they did. So I asked Shirley.

"Well," said Shirley, "my primary responsibility is to assist in administration. But I have Other and Assorted Responsibilities as well."

"That sounds like a lot," I said. "Especially with the Other and Assorted Responsibilities."

"It is. But it's not as bad as it sounds. With the Other and Assorted Responsibilities, I do get to delegate."

"To whom?"

"Myself mostly, but sometimes to Darlene. She works in cardiology, and when things get too busy we trade delegations."

"That must be a big help."

"Yes. But just now Darlene's having trouble with her daughter, Danika, who is fifteen going on twenty-two, or so she thinks. So does her boyfriend, Billy, who just dropped out of Simon Gratz and supposedly is working at KFC, but the money he's flashing isn't fried-chicken money—if you know what I mean. And her sister Jewel, the one who's married to Antoine in security, she's up on Seven East right now with a tumor on her lung. I heard from Betty over in CT surgery that Doctor Kazawa was not too optimistic. That's not a good sign. He's such a good surgeon. And he always sees the positive side of things. Even when it looks hopeless to everyone else. I don't think he ever met a tumor he couldn't take out. They did the biopsy today, so, needless to say, she's got a pretty full plate. I wonder if maybe she's worrying on Antoine too—he's a terrible flirt, and he's spending a lot of time over in Grant Hall chatting it up with that floozy receptionist Serena. While the cat's away, you know. Not that it's anybody's business."

But Shirley was one of those people who specialized in the business that was not anybody's.

Then Shirley asked me did I want a cup of coffee. I said no, thanks. I didn't want to put her to any inconvenience. Shirley explained that it was no trouble really, and besides, there was nothing like a cup of coffee for helping folks get acquainted. In that case, I said, I'd take a cup of tea.

"Oh," said Shirley. "Tea?"

"Or coffee. Coffee would be fine."

So Shirley fetched two cups of coffee, and we sat down at her desk to get acquainted. "I've been working in the department for ten years," she said. "Before that I was in banking. I was head teller in the Germantown office of Progressive Bank. That was a good job, and it was close to home. Well, when Progressive merged with Wells Fargo, they closed the Germantown office, and they said I would have to transfer to Roxborough, which would mean I had to take the Twenty-three down to Broad, then get the Broad Street line to Allegheny, take the Allegheny bus over to Ridge, and then all the way out Ridge on the Thirty-two. And I still would only be a teller. So I came here. But it's worked out for the best. Because I'm more of a People Person, don'cha know? Although I'm awfully good with numbers. I do have a small tax business on the side—not during work hours, of course, except just a little before April fifteenth. But then only on my lunchtime, and if I have to, I always stay to make sure everything is done. Let me know if you need any help with your taxes. It's tricky here with the state tax and the city tax separate. But I'm glad to do them. Unless you have capital gains. Capital gains are a major pain in the you-know-where. If you ask me, the whole stock market is nothing more than a pig in a poke anyway. I always say give me a good CD anytime. It's money you can bank on." She giggled.

I asked Shirley where she came from.

"I used to live in Germantown at Tulpehocken and Baynton, but the neighborhood changed, so we moved over to East Mount Airy at Cliveden and Clearfield."

I passed by these streets on the way to work, and I would have to say that, to an outsider, Tulpehocken and Baynton looked pretty similar to Cliveden and Clearfield. All were quiet streets with neatly kept row houses on both sides, neither one looking particularly more or less prosperous than the other, and they were situated no more than half a mile apart. But, as Shirley explained, they had become completely different. I asked her in what way.

"Well," she said, "my old block used to be nice. But then some people moved out, and some others moved in, and then our captain left, and it changed. Not so much at first, but then, well, it wasn't the same block. So we moved."

As I was to learn, the functioning community unit in Philadelphia is the block. On our block, for example, the ends are sealed with cars in the summer, and there is music and dancing and barbecue and spouting hydrants and the kids play in the street. In the winter the people on our block band together to clear the street of snow.

Every block has a block captain. The block captain makes sure that everyone keeps his yard neat and clean and reports to him promptly any undesirable activity. The block captain ensures that the municipal services are up to snuff. If we are dissatisfied with any of the services, we tell the block captain. So he can Take Care of Business. The block captain does a lot of taking care of business. He also lets us know which public officials will best take care of our business. And he makes sure that all the block's residents will come out on Election Day to cast their votes for those public officials.

That's the way it is in most of Philadelphia. But that's not the way it is in Other Philadelphia. In Other Philadelphia there are no block parties, and the fire hydrants are broken, and when the snow falls it sits there until it melts. In Other Philadelphia many of the houses don't even have people living in them—except the nomadic tribes that make their living purveying various natural herbs, which have been imported from South America and Asia. And most of the vehicles in the streets of Other Philadelphia never move. There is no city councilor or commissioner or judge to represent the best interests of Other Philadelphians, and although the mayor from time to time will make reference to them, usually referring to them as "our less privileged brethren" or some such euphemism, no one takes him seriously. Certainly not the Other Philadelphians. And there are no block captains in Other Philadelphia.

William Penn Hospital is located in Nicetown, which is pretty much Center City for Other Philadelphia. For someone who was raised in a town called Pleasantville, to work in Nicetown seemed only fitting. But Nicetown is not like Pleasantville. First, it isn't even really a town. It doesn't have the usual things you would find in a town, like a grocery store or a hardware store or a gas station or a wine store—although there are plenty of stores in Nicetown where you can buy wine, it's just they don't sell only wine, and the vintage of the wine they sell is by the month, not the year. Nicetown doesn't even have a Starbucks. Which, in all fairness, Pleasantville doesn't have either. Although you can get a pretty decent mocha cinnamon swirl latte there at the Dragonfly Café.

Of course Shirley wanted to know where I came from. I told her all about my hometown, Pleasantville, and that I had lived in Boston and Atlanta and Berkeley before moving to Vermont. Shirley wanted to know about my neighborhood in Dumster and my block too. And my house. So I told her about Dumster and about Maple Street and that we lived in the Partridge House.

Shirley was particularly interested in the Partridge House because it sounded so "historical." I explained that it wasn't perhaps quite as historical as she might think, the house itself having been built in 1953 by Walter Bugbee, who sold it to Tom and Mary Partridge about ten years later. Tom and Mary worked at the National Acme plant until it closed, and then, as they were both sixty-five, they retired. But after Tom died of a stroke, Mary sold it to us and went to live with her oldest daughter in Massachusetts. Since the Partridges had lived in it before us, it was called the Partridge House when we lived in it.

"But it was Mr. Bugbee who built the house?"

"Yes."

"So why isn't it called the Bugbee House?"

"It was back when the Partridges lived in it."

"So first it was the Bugbee House when Bugbee lived in it?"

"No, then it was the Talbot place."

"But if Mr. Bugbee owned it first?"

"Well, he didn't really own it first. He bought the land from John Talbot."

Shirley said she didn't understand, and I said that in Vermont the house you live in is never yours until you leave it. Shirley wondered why this was, and I told her I didn't know, and that when we moved to Vermont we asked the same question, and nobody else seemed to know either. "But don't you wonder?" she asked. I explained that I used to, but now I don't so much anymore. She thought that was very interesting too and wondered why that was. I allowed as how I couldn't be sure but it might have something to do with being Near Canada. This made sense to Shirley. From time to time after that Shirley would ask me questions about what Vermont was like and why it was that way, and I would tell her how it was and that I didn't know why. I think she liked asking a doctor questions he couldn't answer. And I liked being asked questions that I didn't have to answer.

In return I asked Shirley if she could help me learn the ropes at William Penn and, of course, she said it would be her pleasure and asked what did I have in mind.

"If you would be my Responsible Adult," I said, "that would be a big help."

She said sure she would, but could I tell her what her duties would be.

"I don't think we have any responsible adults here," she said. "I've never seen a job posting for one. And they have to post everything. So anyone can bid on them. Not that I'm dissatisfied with being an administrative assistant, mind you. It's a great job. But I just find it interesting to see what other things people might be doing. If you know what I mean."

I said I did, and then I told her about Maggie Stone back in Dumster, and about my being so busy saving lives that I didn't always have time to be both responsible and an adult, and sometimes not even just one of them alone. She said she had noticed that, and although Responsible Adult was not quite up to assisting in administration, it could certainly fall into the category of Other and Assorted, and therefore would be okay. Which was a big relief to me. For although having Shirley as a neighbor would, I expect, be a bit much, having her as a colleague— especially when you are the new kid on a very big block—well, that was another matter altogether.

After we had finished getting acquainted, Shirley told me that what I needed to do was go to Human Resources. She told me how to get to Human Resources and explained that they were really a lot nicer than they seemed. Especially after work. Then she said I would

meet the chairman of the department, who was not at all stuffy. "For
a chairman."

At Human Resources they gave me a pile of papers to fill out, which
I did, and when I was all done, and I had turned them in, they asked
me for my driver's license. I showed them my license. The Human
Resources person looked at it suspiciously.

"What's this?" she asked.

"It's my driver's license."

"Where's it from?"

"Vermont."

"Vuh-mont?"

"It's Near Canada."

"It's no good."

I told her I had been driving with it all over the place, and nobody
seemed to mind. They said maybe it was okay for Near Canada, but it
was no good for William Penn. The problem was the picture.

There wasn't one.

She said I couldn't work there if my license didn't have a picture.
Otherwise how would they know I was who I said I was? I conceded
it was a good point. They certainly didn't want just any Jack off the
Street coming in and pretending to be a doctor, so he could gratify
some perversion on their patients. She said right, and until I had a
picture ID, I would have to leave. Then she called security to escort
me from the hospital.

"Whazzamatta?" asked the guy from security as we walked out.

"I don't have a picture ID," I said.

"Whatchyado?"

"I'm a doctor."

"Whassyaname?"

"Beach Conger."

"Whakinnanamizzat?"

"It's a family name. My father got it from his father, and he gave it
to me."

"Sonofabich."

"Exactly."

"Commidme."

I followed him to a room with a chair in one corner and a camera mounted on a tripod facing it. He pointed to the chair.

"Siddovahdeh."

I sat down. He took my picture. After a minute out came a plastic card. The card had my picture on it and under the picture were the words:

BEACH CONGER, MD
WILLIAM PENN HOSPITAL

I took the card back to Human Resources and showed it to them. They told me okay, I could go to work.

Armed with my new ID, I went to meet my boss. The title on his office door said the occupant was the Dimitri Papadopoulos Chair of the Department of Medicine. The current Dimitri Papadopoulos's actual name was H. Jackson Fitzwallow. Later I asked Shirley if Dimitri Papadopoulos had been the department head before Dr. Fitzwallow, and was that why they named the chair after him? Was it like we do with houses in Vermont? Shirley said no, that wasn't the case. Before Dr. Fitzwallow it was Lawrence Postkauer. Dimitri Papadopolous was a guy who owned a lot of real estate in Other Philadelphia.

"Like Donald Trump," she said.

Even though he sat in a chair named after someone like Donald Trump, as Shirley had said, Dr. Fitzwallow was not all stuffy. He shook my hand vigorously and welcomed me to William Penn and said how glad he was to meet me. I said likewise. Then we talked for a while about where he came from before he came to William Penn Hospital and what kind of research he had done, and how many papers he had published. And he showed me pictures of his family and some awards he had won, and he gave me an autographed copy of a book he had written. And then he asked me about my publications. I looked at the book he had written. It was over six hundred pages long. It was about the molecular physiology of stem cell transplantation. I told him I had never written anything. He said that was okay, not everyone is cut out for critical analysis. Then he asked did I have any questions before we figured out what I was going to do. I asked him what the H stood for.

"Horatio," he said. "I don't use my first name."

"Me neither."

He said that was very interesting. Then he asked me what kind of doctor I was.

"Well," I said. "I'm a pretty good doctor—a little weak sometimes on ordering tests, but I stick with it, and pretty much I always get there eventually."

"I see," he said. "I was interested in what kind of patients you treat."

"Oh, all kinds," I said. "Whoever comes knocking, I guess you would say."

"Ah," he said. "A PCP."

When I lived in Berkeley, I worked at the Free Clinic, and we did some things there that would seem pretty weird by traditional medicine standards, like hugging our patients and calling each other by our first names, but that was the extent of it. We didn't mess with drugs that couldn't be prescribed.

"No sir!" I said. "I've never done PCP."

"That's okay," he said. "I'm sure you'll pick it up. Being a primary care practitioner is easy. A lot of them aren't even doctors."

"Ah," I said. "A *Primary Care Practitioner*."

"I'm sure it will suit you just fine."

"What exactly does a primary care practitioner do?"

"You are a gatekeeper."

"And as a gatekeeper—"

"—you keep the gate."

He explained to me that in order for patients to get into the system, they had to come in through the gate, of which I would be a keeper. Once I got them in, others made sure they didn't get out.

"How do I do that?"

"You sign referrals."

"That's it?"

"It's the whole bowl of wax."

"Sounds a bit drab."

"It's important. Your work feeds the whole department. Without PCPs the rest of us would starve." He smiled. "Proverbially speaking."

This was some consolation. And maybe easy and drab wasn't such a bad place to start, seeing as how I was in a very different world from where I had practiced the last twenty-five years.

I told Shirley that I was going to be a PCP.

"Oh," she said. "That will be interesting."

"Interesting. As a job, you mean?"

"Interesting."

So I became a PCP. I had an office, and I saw patients, and when I found out what their problems were, I decided what specialists they should see. It reminded me of my days in San Francisco. And as Dr. Fitzwallow had said, it was pretty easy. But it wasn't much fun.

Then one day they called me to the emergency room. They needed an emergency referral. So I hotfooted it on down.

Miguel Velasquez was seventy-nine years old. He came from Guadalajara, and he did not speak any English. He had fallen on his steps coming back from the store, and a neighbor had called 911 when they saw him lying there. He lived with his daughter, who usually translated for him, but she was at work.

After an X-ray showed a broken hip, the emergency doctor called orthopedics, and orthopedics called me. They wanted a referral to endocrinology and cardiology. Anesthesia had said his sugar and his blood pressure were both too high to operate. I had been studying Spanish, since we moved, and I was eager to try it out. I told Mr. Velasquez that my *nom* was Dr. Conger, that he had *diabetica*, and that his *precision de sangria* was *mucho alto*.

Miguel nodded.

Did he take any *medicina*, I asked. He nodded again.

"*¿Que typo?*" I asked.

"*Píldoras—muchas píldoras,*" he answered.

I asked did he know the *nom* of these *muchas píldoras*. Miguel shrugged. So I asked him who his doctor was. Miguel shook his head.

"*No hay doctor.*"

I asked him how he got his pills.

"*Hija mia.*" His daughter.

"*No es possible,*" I said. "*¿Solo un doctor prescribe su medicina?*"

Miguel shrugged again.

I asked him what he did when he was sick.

"*Vengo aquí,*" he said, looking at me as if I were a complete idiot. Then he erupted into a rapid string of Spanish that exceeded my comprehension. It had to do with *farmacia* and a *tarjeta plástica.* Fortunately HIPAA did not extend to the emergency room at William Penn Hospital. The man in the bed adjacent to Miguel had been following our conversation with interest and offered to help. He was bilingual.

A long conversation ensued between the two. It appeared to center on the *tarjeta plástica*, which, after some rummaging around, Miguel managed to produce. He handed the card over to our interpreter, and after further discussion, in which *la playa* was frequently mentioned, the interpreter turned to me.

"He says he gives this card to his daughter, and she calls the number on the card, and then she goes to the pharmacy and he gets the medicine. He never has to see a doctor."

I looked at the card. It read:

Keystone Mercy Managed Care
PCP group: William Penn Physicians
PCP: Beach Conger, MD

The next day I went to Dr. Fitzwallow and told him I didn't want to be a PCP anymore. He asked me why.

"It's just what I thought it was," I said.

"Which is what?" he asked.

"A hallucination."

"I see," he said.

I didn't say anything.

Well," he said, after a bit, "I suppose we could make you a hospital attending."

"That sounds better. I like taking care of sick patients."

"Oh, no. You won't be taking care of patients."

"Upon whom would I attend?"

"The residents."

"On second thought, maybe I'll stay where I am."

"Don't worry. They won't give you any trouble. They're a good bunch."

"That's not it. It's the teaching part. I've done a lot of doctoring, but—well, as a country doctor, you see, I don't actually have to know much. I just do what has to be done."

"Nonsense. You must know *something*."

"Oh, I do. I know a lot. It's just that I'm not sure how much of it is still true."

"That doesn't matter."

"Really?"

"They never listen anyway."

· 5 ·

Attending Physician

....

I told Shirley about my new job.

"Goody!" she said excitedly. "That makes you a hospitalist. And that means you are part of the Section of Hospital Medicine. Hospital Medicine is one of my responsibilities. So now you belong to me. Officially."

Even though I had no idea what the new job held in store, I was reassured by Shirley's declaration. It didn't seem possible that I could go too far astray under her supervision. I asked her who else was in the Section of Hospital Medicine.

"Well, there are the other hospitalists. Doctor Jean and Manny and Doctor Keith and Doctor Biz. Doctor Biz can be a sketch sometimes. But they're all very nice—and very good doctors too! And sometimes the officists are attendings, but they're not really part of the section. They're more like tourists—if you know what I mean."

I didn't quite. I had never heard of an officist or a hospitalist before, but I could tell from Shirley's tone that an officist was not the kind of person that one generally associated with if one were a hospitalist. And I was soon to learn, she was right. In the university caste system, officists were the Untouchables.

"What is an officist?" I asked.

"Well . . . ," she said slowly. "That's what you were before you became a hospitalist."

"Ah. So an officist—"

"—works in the office."

"And hospitalists work—"

"—in the hospital."

"What if you did both?"

"You mean worked in the hospital *and* in the office?"

"Yes. That's what I used to do."

"Oh no." She laughed. "Nobody does that now. You have to be one or the other. You see, the officists are mostly PCPs, although there are a couple from Infectious Disease. And then there's Sugar Scotty—that's Doctor Schulman. His first name is Saul, but everyone calls him Scotty because of his dog. He brings him in when he does rounds on the weekends. And Sugar because he is a diabetologist. He is awfully sweet, though."

"So he sees patients in the office and the hospital?"

"Oh yes! His patients wouldn't let anybody else touch them. But I don't count him, because he is as old as Moses. He's been here forever."

"He sounds like my kind of doctor."

"He's wonderful. Anyway, the reason that officists don't take care of their patients when they get sick is because they are too tied up in the office—filling out applications, and making referrals, and submitting Prior Authorizations. You remember what that was like."

"Unfortunately."

"Besides, they wouldn't be paid if they did—because of managed care. So they refer their patients to us when they need to come in to the hospital. We get paid for hospital work."

"So we take care of the medical patients."

"Surgical patients too. Some of them anyway."

Quite a few actually, as I was to discover. Especially for those doctors who preferred only to see patients when they were asleep. And who didn't want to worry about the little things that happen to patients after surgery, like pain or infections or blood clots or heart attacks. Neurosurgeons, for one. During the whole time I was at William Penn, I never talked to a neurosurgeon directly, even for something important—such as when the patient died, for example. I just passed the information on to the nurse, and the nurse told them. It was not like that with the orthopedic surgeons, though. I saw them a lot. They always said how glad they were to work with me because I did a much better job at managing the whole patient. That was nice to hear. Maybe that was why they said it. I didn't ask.

"Well," said Shirley. "Now that you're in Hospital Medicine, we'll have to get you a white coat. And then we need to get you a team."

I thanked Shirley but told her I didn't wear a white coat. Naturally she wanted to know why.

"On account of my post-traumatic stress disorder," I told her.

"PTSD! My goodness!" she said. "That *is* interesting. What happened to you?"

And so I told her about when I was a little boy, and my grandmother took me shopping with her, and we went to the butcher's, where the butcher took a chicken hanging from the wall and put it on the block and chopped his head off. And then wiped his bloody hands on his bloody coat, and ever since then, white coats made me a little sick to my stomach. Shirley allowed as how that was understandable, and wondered if that meant I didn't eat chicken either. And I said no, I could eat chicken okay. It was just the coat.

"That's good," said Shirley. "Because the hospital has really good fried chicken. Some say it's better even than KFC."

That a hospital could have anything really good in the way of food seemed pretty far-fetched to me, and I told Shirley so. Shirley conceded maybe she was exaggerating slightly, because her cousin Laverne worked in dietary and was in charge of the fried chicken, but it was certainly pretty darn good.

"Anyway," she said, "let's figure out who will be on your team. That's the most important thing. I'm going to make you a really good team."

She explained that my team would consist of me and three residents. Two of them would be junior residents, and they would belong solely to me. The third would be a senior resident whom I would share with another team. Then she pulled out a sheet of paper that had written on it the names of all the residents.

"Let's see," she said. "You want a really smart senior resident, because then you won't have to worry about what to do with your patients."

"Well," I said, "I like the idea of a smart senior resident, but I sort of like worrying about what to do with my patients."

Shirley frowned. "That's not such a good idea. You see, attending physicians don't really have much to do with patients. What with all the teaching and the supervising and the evaluations—that keeps you pretty busy. So when it comes to the actual patient, well, you don't usually get too involved."

"But if I am their attending physician, how can I not be involved? I mean, I am the physician of record, aren't I."

"Oh yes," she said quickly, "for billing. But when it comes to treating the patient—well, that's the team's job. Not that you can't make suggestions. You'll do that all the time. You just have to ask."

"I have to get permission to make suggestions?" I asked. It seemed incredible, but as I was learning quickly, the rules here were quite different from Emmeline Talbot.

"Oh no," she said quickly. "Not that kind of ask. Let me explain to you how it works. Let's say you have a patient with a fever. Maybe you know why the patient has a fever, and maybe you don't. It doesn't matter. You say to one of the junior residents, 'What do you think is causing the fever?' And the resident tells you what he thinks. Then you turn to the other junior resident, and you say, 'What else could be causing the fever?' And that resident tells you what she thinks. Lastly, you ask the senior resident. 'What do you think about all that?' And the senior resident will tell you. That's why it's important to have a smart senior resident. Sometimes, though, one of the junior residents is actually smarter than the senior resident, but that's okay. You just have to know who is the smartest, so you ask that person last."

"It almost sounds Socratic."

"Actually, they call it pimping."

It took a little getting used to, but eventually I got the hang of it. And both Shirley and Dr. Fitzwallow were right. I didn't have to do hardly anything at all. When I wrote to folks back at Emmeline Talbot, I told them about my job. I said I had found a new specialty. A Poison Ivy Doctor. I could look, but I better not touch. In fact, the whole time I was at William Penn, I didn't make a single diagnosis. Well, once I did. But that was an unusual case.

After a lot of discussion with herself, Shirley had picked my team. Vijay and Maria Elena would be my junior residents, and Abe my senior resident. "Abe knows everything," Shirley told me. "Vijay and Elena are smart too. And they're all very nice."

Shirley was right. Abe knew everything. Most of it, as far as I could tell, appeared to be true. Vijay and Maria Elena were no dummies either. And they were all very nice.

· 6 ·

Eastern Queen

....

M ost people agree that death is inevitable. If pressed, some even concede that their own particular death is an event similarly without recourse. But people prefer to consider death in general. Death in particular is not a pleasant thought, interfering, as it tends to do, with one's illusion of immortality.

Because so many people die in them, hospitals are especially sensitive to this issue. They understand that a patient who notices that his neighbors are dropping like flies is not a happy patient, and so they do their best to make sure this does not happen. And they have gotten much better at it.

When I started my medical career at Boston City Hospital, patients were housed in capacious rooms known as wards. A ward's complement of beds was thirty, fifteen on one side, fifteen on the other. I was nursed and weaned and took my first baby doctor steps in the Peabody Building, a structure as venerable as the family after which it was named, and equally as antiquated. The ceilings were high and arched, and from them hung a set of globes that emitted a feeble yellow glow. The long narrow windows, darkened by years of accumulated soot and grime, made no discernible contribution to visibility. All in all, the illumination was not quite adequate for performing any medicinal ablutions other than identifying that the form upon which one labored was most likely human. The floors were covered with linoleum whose original color could once have been any hue but were now an indeterminate gray. As for decorations, there were none save a large clock above the exit. It was a singularly unattractive place, resembling more a dilapidated railroad station than a house of healing, and its inhabitants, rather than patients, seemed like either those who had missed their trains and were waiting for morning in the hope that they then could depart, or those who had nowhere else to go.

There was no privacy in a ward. The desperately ill lay next to the hardly sick. The recovering were neighbors to the dying. When a patient left, it was in full sight of all, whether that departure was by choice or necessity, upright or recumbent. Death, when it occurred, was never out of sight.

The wards are all gone now, and hospitals are better able to satisfy their occupants by concealing the less propitious happenings behind closed doors. Should someone happen to take a turn for the worse, he is quietly dispatched to an intensive care unit, whereupon he is inflicted with such a profusion of tubes and wires and machines that go beep in the night that when the Grim Reaper finally comes, his appearance is just another blip on the monitor, hardly distinguishable from the myriad that preceded him.

William Penn Hospital was no exception to this model. It was well stocked with Units of Intensive Care. Which was good planning on its part. Because, although it is true that most people get sick before they die, I can safely say that in my forty or so years of stamping out disease, the people of Other Philadelphia got sick sooner, stayed sick longer, and when they were sick, were sicker than any people I have ever seen. They were that way when they came into the hospital. They were that way when they went out. And for many of them, the time out was not very long. They were in and out with such frequency that not infrequently upon their return, they were placed in the very same bed from which they had just departed, there having been too little time to fill it with another patron. In airline parlance they might have been called frequent fliers. At William Penn they were called "regulars."

Eastern Queen was a regular.

Although I frequently was his attending physician, Eastern Queen was never an actual patient of mine. This was because it was against policy at William Penn Hospital for doctors to have patients.

"You won't have any," Dr. Fitzwallow had explained to me when I had asked him who my patients would be. "It would be counterproductive to our mission. You see, if doctors had patients, then it wouldn't be long before patients would want doctors. And patients, being what they are, might pick Doctor B instead of Doctor A, when in fact Doctor A would be a better choice. Because it was Doctor A who had a special interest in their particular condition, whereas Doctor B might simply be, well, he might be . . ."

"Likable."

"Precisely. Well, you can imagine what would happen if patients went to doctors merely because they liked them."

"Hard to imagine—here."

"I would hope not. But you can't be too careful. Just think . . ." Dr. Fitzwallow shuddered slightly. "No—impossible. It would be a terrible blow to our teaching programs, and a disaster for our research."

"Like informed consent."

"Don't get me started on that," he exclaimed. "If I could put my hands on the fellow who invented informed consent, I'd wring his neck. What was his name? Miranda, wasn't it?"

"I think Miranda was actually a prisoner."

"Yes, perhaps he was. Anyway, you can see why it wouldn't do here, just wouldn't do at all, for doctors to have patients."

I allowed as how I did, and so I didn't. Although I would have to say that if I had had any, Eastern Queen would have been my number one.

"Mr. Queen is a thirty-seven-year-old African American male who comes in with a chief complaint of chest pain," said Vijay in his clipped British accent as we stood outside the room, while he began what is known as The Presentation, an ancient and respected ritual whereby the junior doctor recites to the senior every fact of the case that could be of no possible value in helping the latter comprehend what is going on with the patient, thereby assuring the impossibility that the latter will interfere with the plans of the former.

"He has a history of HIV, ESRD, CHF, CVA, PVD with bilateral AKA, and ED." He recited it all in the same indifferent monotone, as if the significance of the man's impotence were neither more nor less than the fact that his immune system was ravaged, his kidneys had stopped working, his heart was shot, the right side of his body was useless, and he had not a leg to stand on.

It was not that Vijay was a callous person. On the contrary, when we discussed the plight of our patients, he was sympathetic and deeply disturbed about the miserable lives of the people we cared for. Vijay was a sensitive caring doctor. But like any good soldier, once on the battlefield he adopted that obdurate insensitivity to the lives of others that is necessary if one is to avoid the despair of doing futile battle, with woefully inadequate weapons, against an all-powerful enemy.

"On examination he is a thin black male looking older than his stated age. The blood pressure is ninety-two over sixty, pulse one hundred and twenty-eight, oxygen saturation eighty-eight percent on room air . . . ," he continued, reciting the litany of findings in a manner not entirely dissimilar to a weather report. Which, in a sense, it was. A low-pressure system, accompanied by a high pulse and reduced oxygen aloft, all predicted storm warnings for the organs ahead.

"The cardiac enzymes were negative, and the EKG showed no acute changes. The chest X-ray showed pulmonary edema and a widened mediastinum. The urine drug screen was positive for cocaine. Lactate levels were normal. It is a most interesting case," he continued, his animation suddenly returning as he left the story of the patient and began the plan of the doctor. "The differential is extensive and includes . . ."

Interesting cases were the *spécialité de la maison* at William Penn Hospital. And I might add, in the event that anyone reading this might find himself in a large teaching hospital, an interesting case is something you never want to be.

I raised my hand in protest.

"Stop," I said, having heard more than I could possibly digest at one sitting about this body, the occupant of which was as yet totally unknown to me. "Let's go meet him."

We went into his room. Despite being the owner of as ravaged a body as I had ever beheld, he had a complacent manner that was almost cheerful. He nodded toward me, cocked his finger at me, and shot.

"Looks like we got us a new leader of the pack today."

"Good morning, Mr. Queen," I said. "I'm Doctor Conger. How are you today?"

"You tell me," he said. Then he smiled and pointed to my name tag. "Funny name you got there, Doc."

"Talk about the pot calling the kettle black."

"Turnabout's fair play," he said. "I'll tell you how I got mine if you tell me how you got yours."

"Deal," I said.

"Our turn first," said Vijay and Maria Elena simultaneously.

"Ah," I said. "The pot and the kettle."

It had started with a patient we saw the first week we were working together. She was an elderly woman, small and thin. But quite spry.

No sooner had I entered the room than she wagged her finger at me fiercely.

"That last medicine you gave me was a doozy! Made me sick as a dog!"

I allowed as how my memory was not what it used to be, but unless she had been up Near Canada recently, it was unlikely that I was the culprit.

She looked at me closely. "Well," she said. "It was one just like you, anyway."

"I suspect it was."

"Yes. It must have been some other *elderly* doctor."

"Did you say *elderly*?" I said. "I think you just better wash your mouth out with soap."

She laughed. Then she said she just meant that I looked more *experienced* than the others.

"That's different from elderly," I said.

"Yes," she said. "Of course it is. I didn't mean any disrespect, Doctor, especially to someone of your—"

"That's okay," I said. "I'm sure you didn't."

Afterward, in the hall, as we were reviewing her case, Vijay asked what it was about American dogs that made them so sick, and what was a "doozy," and what was it about her throat that made me suggest she wash it with soap?

Vijay had come to William Penn Hospital from India via England, where he had attended medical school at Cambridge. He had only been in the United States for a year. Maria Elena had gone to William Penn Medical School and had lived in Philadelphia for several years before that, but her world was the close-knit Nicaraguan community in South Philadelphia, and her exposure to what might pass for American slang culture was limited.

I explained the idioms. Vijay wrote them down in the notebook he always carried with him, and Maria Elena asked would I please teach them more of the American expressions.

There not being much other knowledge I had to impart to these smart young doctors, I was only too glad to comply. But as Eastern Queen had said, turnabout was fair play, and for each American expression I explained, they needed to find a match from their world. As always, they were eager to oblige.

"In such an instance," said Vijay first, "we would say it is the sieve that tells the needle it has a hole."

"And what we would say is this: The pan tells the kettle, 'Move away. You blacken me,'" said Maria Elena.

"Which you probably got from the English," I said.

"It comes from *Don Quixote*," she said.

"Which was written a long time ago."

"Sixteen oh five."

"Well then, as we say, maybe I got it *bass ackward*."

I didn't have to explain the idiom.

"So, Mr. Doctah—sir!" said Eastern with mock deference. "Now that we're done with Show and Tell, if I might answer your question."

"Please."

"Well, this here kettle was born on Easter, so my mother named me in honor of the occasion. My father was not consulted, owing to the fact that he was not around. So I started out as Easter Queen. But when I entered school, *Easter* became *Eastern*. It was all on account of Sister Mary Arabello, my first-grade teacher. She told me it was a sacrilege for a child to be named after the holiest of days, particularly a kid of *my kind*. And, having a higher sense of duty to her God than to the Philadelphia Board of Health, she made the correction. The only thing I know for sure," said Eastern, "is that nobody gave a damn what I thought."

"Except you."

"Except me."

"And so . . ."

"When they called me Eastern, I didn't answer. So most of the teachers just stopped calling on me. Which was fine by me. But then I got older and started getting in trouble. And when the teacher would holler, 'Eastern, get away from the window,' or 'Eastern, get your head off the desk,' and I paid her no mind, they would send me to the principal's office. The principal asked me what I had to say for myself. I told him how I figured it couldn't be me they were talking to, as my name wasn't Eastern. He didn't give a damn either, but he was smart enough to see that I would be more trouble as Eastern than Easter, so he changed it back."

"But now you're Eastern again."

"I am."

"Who changed it?"

"I did."

"Why?"

"Simon Gratz."

"Who is Simon Gratz?"

"Dead white guy."

"How did a dead white man—"

"He got a school named after him. Simon Gratz High. It's a big school. And I was a little kid—not as little as I am now, but then I had both my legs. And I'd be walking down the hall minding my own business and a couple of senior boys would come by, and one would say to the other, 'Ooooooh! Lookee! It's the Easter Queen. But she's lost her bonnet.' And they'd grab a wastebasket and shove it over my head and make me sing the Easter Bonnet song."

"And that was the end of Easter Queen."

"Yup."

"I understand," I said.

"Sure," said Eastern. "You a Doctah. You always understand."

"In fact, I do. You see, when I was born they called me Chip. I was supposed to be a chip off the old block. I wasn't, but they didn't find that out until much later. Then, when I went off to high school, my mother said I was too old to be Chip and I should use my real name, which was Seymour Beach Conger the Fourth. With a name like that it sounds like I should be rich. But I'm not. Back in the 1850s there was a circuit-riding minister in Huron County, Ohio, by the name of Enoch Conger. One of his stops was in the town of Fitchville. Among the congregation of Fitchville Presbyterian were two elders, John Beach and John Seymour. Precisely what it was about his relationship with these two men, or what for that matter what went on in this church, is not addressed in the family archives, but whatever it was, it was enough that when Enoch had a son, he named him after the other two. May just be happenstance, but none of the descendants of the other two have anyone with *Conger* in their names.

"Anyway, when I went off to high school, my mother said now that I was going to high school she thought it was time to take my proper name. Well, I was pretty shrimpy then too, and pretty soon the word got out that there was this little freshman kid with a big name. Like any high school, we had a lot of exceptionally mature senior boys, and if a pair of them happened to be walking down the hall at the same time as I, one would nudge the other and with a wink and a nod point to me and say, 'Do you?' and the other would reply, 'Do I what?' and the first would say, 'See more beach.' And then he'd grab me and pull up my shirt and squeeze my nipples until I yelled 'Titty.' So I became Chip again real quick."

"But now you're Beach again."

"Since I became a doctor."

"Helped being a doctor."

"Yes."

"And white."

"That too. But—"

"Yeah. Always a 'but.' And you know, where you put your 'but'— that's what counts."

"Doctor covers color."

"You *sure* got that right, Doc. Black in white *is* white."

I don't know how many of Eastern Queen's days were spent at William Penn, but it was enough so that when he went home we always kept his bed vacant for the next day, just in case. Not infre- quently, he justified our precaution. One resident wag suggested that if Papadopolous had a chair named after him for his contributions to the William Penn coffers, there should be a bed named Eastern Queen, in honor of his. And the truth of the matter was that Eastern Queen most likely contributed more to medical education at William Penn Hospital than all the distinguished professors and named chairs combined. For what he lacked in education and money, he more than made up for in the riches of disease. Diabetes. High blood pressure. Heart failure. Kidney failure. Stroke. Hepatitis C. Peripheral vascular disease. AIDS. And, of course, ED. The student who had mastered Eastern Queen was ready to face the world.

Fluent in the terminology of his medical history, Eastern took particular pleasure when, after some poor medical student, preferably female, had finally finished taking his exhaustive medical history and was about to leave, he would remind her, as was invariably the case, that she had neglected to address the problem that bothered him the most.

"My e-rectile dysfunction," he would say to the discomfited student. "Whatcha gonna do about that, Mizz Doctah?"

Usually Eastern Queen came in because the Paratransit that was supposed to take him to his dialysis center on the other side of the city didn't show up, and he got short of breath from too much fluid. But sometimes it was because the ulcers on his backside got infected. And once a month it was because of the chest pain he got whenever he used cocaine.

Erythroxylum coca. Averse to cold, fussy about soil, and always thirsty, it is not a particularly hardy plant. But what it lacks in blessings from nature is more than made up for by its blessing from man, who is so taken with this delicate shrub that he will literally move mountains to ensure its prosperity.

For most of its natural history, coca's caretakers were Incas. A wad between cheek and gum enabled them to get through an ordinary working day without need for food or rest. Which, when the day was sixteen hours and you were high up in the mountains, was a big help. It wasn't until 1860 that an enterprising Corsican named Angelo Mariani figured out that if you dissolved the leaves in alcohol, you could dispense with the chewing. *Vin Mariani* was a big hit in the medical profession. Particularly with a brilliant young psychiatrist, who figured it was just the thing to cure depression. Particularly his own.

I am procuring some myself, he wrote. *Perhaps nothing will come of it, but I shall certainly try it.*

Then to his fiancé: *Woe to you, my princess, when I come. I will kiss you quite red and feed you till you are plump. And if you are forward, you shall see who is stronger, a little girl who doesn't eat enough, or a big strong man with cocaine in his body. In my last serious depression I took cocaine again and a small dose lifted me to the heights in a wonderful fashion. I am just now collecting the literature for a song of praise to this magical substance.*

And so, with the ringing endorsement of Sigmund Freud, cocaine took the medical profession by storm—promoted as a cure for everything from brain fag to opium addiction, with respect to which it did rather a creditable job.

Prior to Philadelphia I had not had much exposure to cocaine. Both at Boston City Hospital and in Dumster, alcohol was the poison of choice. And in San Francisco it was heroin.

Now, I would never admit this, except in the privacy of a book, but I am exceedingly fond of doughnuts. Jellied, glazed, sugared, chocolate, or plain, I love them all. Under pressure from more gastronomically correct members of the family, I have publicly switched to bagels. But my heart isn't in it. Too much chewing for too little taste.

We lived in Chestnut Hill, about six miles from William Penn Hospital. A drive to work, under usual conditions, took thirty minutes. Parking was ten minutes from the hospital and cost one hundred and twenty dollars a month. I could also take the metro. It was a mile walk from my house to the train station, and another mile from the train station to William Penn, and it cost one hundred dollars a month. The train, which ran most of the time, on a good day took forty minutes. So I rode my bike. It was just twenty-five minutes, door-to-door. On the corner of Germantown and Broad Street, right on my way to work, was a Dunkin' Donuts. So the trip to work was faster, cheaper, and tastier.

My second week at work, when I got to Germantown and Broad, there was a guy directing traffic at the intersection. I could tell right away he was not one of Philadelphia's finest—because of his uniform. It consisted of a green wig topped by a rhinestone tiara, a purple halter top, basketball shorts, and pink flip-flops. His baton was a yellow plastic bat, and his traffic gestures were mixed with a liberal sprinkling of orchestra conducting, bullfighting, middle-finger gesticulations, and a movement that was unambiguously suggestive of what a man in need might do without a woman. He wobbled unsteadily about the intersection, although somehow he managed to avoid being struck by any of the oncoming traffic, which paid him absolutely no heed. *A staggering drunk*, I said to myself, as I propped my bike against the side of the Dunkin' Donuts and went inside.

While I waited my turn, I watched him as he made an elegant three-hundred-and-sixty-degree pirouette, and then, in slightly less time than it took me to leave my place in line, rush out the door, and make a futile grab, he had hopped on my bicycle and was furiously pedaling down the street at a pace I had no chance of matching.

"Stop!" I yelled pointlessly.

The manager came to the door. "He took it," I said. "That drunk stole my bicycle."

"Crackhead," said the manager.

It was my first experience with the powers of crack cocaine. After that, I always brought my bike into the store when I went for doughnuts. It crowded things a bit, but the manager didn't mind, because I was a regular customer, and besides, it gave him the opportunity to tell the story of the Flying Pink Flip-Flop Bicycle Thief.

Unfortunately, when applied to a failing heart, the stimulatory effects of cocaine are less salubrious. As Eastern Queen proved only too often, raising the blood pressure while constricting the coronaries tends to make one's myocardium less than fully gruntled. And the fact of the matter is, when it comes to affairs of the heart, the descendants of opium are a kinder, gentler addiction. They lower the pressure and dilate the vessels. Even today, in the treatment of a heart attack, morphine is a first-line drug.

I brought up this issue with Eastern.

"You want me to what!"

"It's called the Halsted plan."

"Uh-huh."

So I told him about William Halsted. Halsted was the first chief of surgery at Johns Hopkins University. A brilliant surgeon and teacher, he is today best known as one of the pioneers of modern surgical technique. Less recognized is his work in the field of addiction medicine.

Like many of his colleagues, Halsted had followed Freud's recommendations, and for years it appeared to afford him considerable benefit. Tireless in his devotion to his patients and unrivaled in his skill with a scalpel, he was easily the most admired surgeon of his day. Unfortunately, his addiction eventually got the best of him. He became erratic, irritable, and error-prone. Because he was impervious to all suggestions that he needed to kick his habit, his colleagues in desperation abducted him one day from the hospital and loaded him on a sailing vessel that carried him off to the Caribbean. There he spent several months on a quiet island, removed from all temptation. He came back a changed man. Exactly how changed was not to be discovered for almost one hundred years. By prior agreement that it not be released until sixty years after the death of its author, William Henry Osler's *Secret History of John Hopkins University* was published in 1959. Only then was it learned that Halsted had cured his cocaine addiction by switching to opium.

Eastern wasn't interested.

"The devil you know, Doc."

"You know it's likely to kill you someday."

"Instead of what?"

He had a point. There was a lot we could still do *to* Eastern at this point, but not an awful lot *for* him.

"On my disability, I can manage three nickel bags a month. Used to only need one, but ghetto produce isn't exactly gourmet quality. You might say it ain't what it's cracked up to be, if you know what I mean. I use all three together, and I feel almost good."

"For how long?"

"Half hour."

"Half an hour, once a month—doesn't seem like much to me."

"It's enough."

"Really?"

"Yup. It's the thinking about that half hour that gets me through the rest of the month."

· 7 ·

The Optimist

··········

"**I** don't feel so good, Doc."
 I see a lot of people who tell me they don't feel so good. Most of them, actually, look pretty good to me, more or less. Or at least not too bad. And more often than not, after the usual fussing and scurrying about, it turns out that they are, if not quite up to good, at least, given the circumstances—and especially as they might have been if things had been otherwise—better than expected. And usually I can convince them that *better*, even if it is not quite as good as *good*, is at least good enough.

It's an odd language, Medicine, full of linguistic phenomena that seem more designed to obfuscate than elucidate and to convey a meaning precisely the opposite of its apparent intent. Such as the fact that when it comes to *good* and *better*, the comparative form, rather than being superior to the adjective, is actually inferior to it. Or take, for example, the word *probably*, which, in ordinary English, implies that a particular event is sufficiently likely enough that one could almost count on it. In everyday life, *probably* is an encouraging word. But not in Medicine. Take for example *probably nothing*. You have just seen your beloved healer because of a nagging ache, which, despite being ignored, just won't go away, and is now beginning to feel as if it might be Something Serious. You have had the usual inspections and detections, and at the end the doctor says, "Well, there is a small spot on your lung. But it's *probably nothing*." Does this offering constitute the kind of reassurance that you were looking for to convince yourself that you were just a worrywart? Not exactly.

But perhaps the most interesting word of all is *interesting* itself. Shakespeare's English would imply that the adjective refers to a consummation that, if not devoutly to be wished, should at the very least one not be turned down when offered. Well, I can tell you that if there is one thing in Medicine that you do not want to be, it is *interesting*. There is nothing more indicative of trouble on the horizon than to be lying in scantily clad apprehension in a hospital bed and to see before you a herd of white-coated whippersnappers, from among which some sagacious-looking omniscient proclaims, after hearing their review of your situation, "Yes, an interesting case indeed."

There were, however, no *probably*s or *interesting*s in the case of Clarence Purnell's ship of state. And *better*, if it was anywhere on the horizon, was not currently visible to me, and, even if it were, given the turbulence of the waters, navigation in its direction was likely to be problematic indeed.

For when I looked at him, Clarence Purnell did not look good—and *not looking good*, when your doctor notes it, tends to put a bit of a damper on the possibility of an error in the feeling department. Because how you look to a doctor—excepting dermatologists and plastic surgeons, who don't have much in the way of insight—is not that Who-Is-the-Fairest-of-Them-All look you might get from your Mirror, Mirror on the Wall. It doesn't come from the color of your hair or the shape of your nose or even the size of your cellulite. It is a No-Frills and Stripped-to-the-Bone look. It is not a flattering one.

In all fairness to Clarence, I should point out that Not Looking Good was pretty much his usual appearance. To continue the nautical analogy, his bilge pump was on its last legs, the hold was rapidly taking in water, and the clouds above were drenching the sails in sheets of water. In short, the good ship Purnell was struggling to keep afloat. The Clarence I beheld, however, was not a dramatically different Clarence from the ordinarily cheerful soul who came cruising into my office in his Big Boy wheelchair full of his latest schemes and dreams.

Clarence Purnell was an optimist.

"You gotta have hope, Doc," he said to me once. "Otherwise, what's the point? And being in the service industry as I am—they'll see it right off, you know—if you don't have hope. And then the game's over, the jig's up, and it's time to pack up and move on. That deal is dead. I've seen some who try to pretend, but it's no use. You can't fake hope. Either you got it or you don't. And if you don't—well, if you don't, then I guess I'd have to say there's no hope for you. If you know what

I mean? Which you would, I'd guess, us being more or less in the same line of work."

I did. Notwithstanding the question of whether our work was more or was less in the same line, he had a point. A positive outlook on things, as long as it was not so excessive as to lead to a patient becoming overconfident about his prognosis, was most certainly as beneficial to my business as it was to Clarence's.

Clarence Purnell was a hustler. In his earlier days he was more of a general practitioner. Horses, dice, women, drugs, he went wherever the money was. But in his declining years, which for Clarence began as most of us are just hitting our stride, he found his calling. Ticket scalping. And in Philadelphia's world of scalpers, he was the undisputed king. It was Clarence Purnell who managed to clear eight grand when the Sixers got into the play-offs. It was Clarence Purnell who could get double the admission price for tickets to Duck Boat rides. And it was Clarence Purnell who, year after year, could even make a profit off the Philadelphia Flower Show.

And when I asked him once, Clarence Purnell got me tickets to the Wing Bowl, right on the fifty-yard line.

Philadelphia is a city proud of its sporting tradition. Be it football, baseball, basketball, hockey, or boxing, whatever you pick, the fans are plentiful, loyal, and fiercely devoted. Especially to the crème de la proverbial crème of the city's sporting events. The Wing Bowl.

It is a fitting tribute to the land of cheesesteaks and fried dough that year after year this spectacle draws more press, more crowds, and more passion than any other. Fitting indeed therefore, that it has spawned a champion whose competitive accomplishments, like the mythical Rocky himself, stand as testimony to the determination of one man to succeed against all odds.

El Wingador.

(Those of you whose diet consists of foods designed for grazing animals, or who believe it is preposterous that gluttony should be idolized, may want to skip this next section. It is not for the faint of stomach. But for the rest—voyeurs, closet bingers, or simply folks who like a good contest regardless of the sport—read on.)

El Wingador came into Wing Bowl Twelve as three-time champion and the odds-on favorite to win his fourth crown. He was well on his way to victory when an errant belch in the final seconds caused him to suffer an upset defeat at the hands of his most despised opponent, the Black Widow.

For the benefit of those not familiar with the world of competitive eating, the Black Widow is a ninety-eight-pound slip of a woman who, like her namesake, devours her male opponents. Despite her diminutive stature, the Black Widow has held, at one point, virtually every major eating record. The list includes, in addition to the one hundred and sixty-one chicken wings in Wing Bowl Twelve, the following: Crab cakes: forty-six in ten minutes; Oysters: five hundred and fifty-two in ten minutes; Hard-Boiled Eggs: sixty-five in six minutes and forty seconds; Cheesecake: eleven pounds in nine minutes. She is the only person ever to break the pound-a-minute barrier. In her prime, she was unbeatable—save, of course when it came to hot dogs. (That honor belongs to the immortal Kobayashi. A six-time winner of the Nathan's hot dog competition, his record of fifty-three and three-quarters dogs in fifteen minutes has never been seriously challenged.)

The Black Widow's secret, as with all great athletes, is in her training. In season her sole diet, five times a day, consists of two pounds of cabbage and one gallon of water, all of which she consumes in thirty seconds or less.

Dispirited, El Wingador announced he was withdrawing from competition. He was neither seen nor heard from for almost a year. But just a month before Wing Bowl Thirteen, El Wingador announced he was staging a comeback. A shadow of his former self, he looked thin and out of shape. Except to his die-hard Philadelphia fans, he was all but written off by the eating public.

Attending the match primarily out of curiosity, I was quickly captivated by the enthusiasm of the crowd and the tension of the competition. Falling behind during the early competition, in the final period El Wingador found his inner strength and came storming back from a ten-wing deficit to tie Black Widow at the bell. The stunned Widow was never able to recover, and El Wingador went on to win by three wings in overtime. There were those, including the Black Widow, who cried foul, pointing out that, although he did consume more wings, by the rules of the International Federation of Competitive Eating the prize should have gone to the competitor who consumed the greater weight in wings, in which case she would have been the victor. But this was Philadelphia, where rules are made to be ignored.

I must admit that it bothers me, this competitive eating stuff. Not so much what it implies about our society, its values, and the future health of Americans. For despite all our exhortations to the contrary, doctors know that gluttony, sloth, and a life of excess in general are rather good for business. One of the subjects that we never discuss when musing upon the state of our country's health is what would happen if everyone were to live healthy lives. The mere thought boggles. Oncologists for one, and endocrinologists for another, would be hard-put to make a living, and cardiologists most likely would be out on the dole. And what we would be left with is the one disease that remains when you have prevented every other. The worst one of all. The disease that takes away the person who once was and replaces him with—well, I'll just say *something else* and leave it at that.

No, rather it is the fact that I can remember these morsels of gastronomic trivia that terrifies me. Like squirrels wintering in the eaves, they have managed to insinuate themselves into the attic of my ever-feebling brain, one that is now shedding its memory faster than a collie's coat in springtime. And they must, I am certain, be displacing far more important stuff. At times I can almost feel them nibbling away at the old gray matter, gobbling up data that is essential for one's daily operations, such as which end of the stethoscope goes on the patient, or what Trine told me to pick up at the store before I come home.

Clarence, however, had no such concerns. His problems were on a larger scale, the one located down in Shipping and Receiving, to be precise.

"You gotta fix me up, Doc," he gasped hoarsely. "The Super Bowl is in two weeks, and they got a double-wide going down to Jacksonville." (For non-Philadelphians, I should note that in Philadelphia, the term *double-wide* refers not to mobile homes but to the special seating found on public conveyances. It is reserved for the greatest of the great. At five hundred and forty pounds, Clarence qualified easily.)

I tapped on his waterlogged lungs, I pressed upon his sodden ankles, and I listened to his palpitating heart, struggling valiantly to maintain the circulation in a body thrice the size for which it was designed. I told him that the poor pump was just about worn out, and that it was now time to consider bariatric surgery to get his weight down to a more human size before it gave out altogether.

"No dice, Doc," he said. "I'll be okay. Just get me down to the weight I was at when I was feeling good."

"That may not be easy," I answered. "What poundage exactly are you shooting for?"

"Five hundred would be good."

Five hundred I could do. So I wrung him dry with diuretics, and in just two weeks he had shed almost twenty quarts of water and was down to a svelte four ninety-eight. Just in time for the bus.

Clarence Purnell was not an ignorant man. Nor was he unconcerned about his health. It was hard for me to understand his aversion to losing weight.

"Why?" I asked him as he prepared to leave.

"Look at me, Doc," he replied, stretching is arms to expose his full expanse. "I'm black, I'm uneducated, and I'm poor. In the eyes of the world, I'm nothing. If I looked like you—no disrespect intended, but you ain't all that much to look at—I'd be just another Invisible Man. People wouldn't pay me no mind. But when I walk down the street, they notice. And when I step on the bus, they make way. And when I set up my spot in front of the stadium, nobody tries to move me. I mean nobody. Not even the cops. They don't want to try to get me in their paddy wagon. I'll admit, it's a heavy price I pay, but it makes me somebody. And everybody's got the right to be somebody."

I couldn't argue with him. It is not easy to be somebody, when you come from Other Philadelphia.

Differential Diagnosis

....

Doctors are an odd lot. Take, for example, today's crop. With all due respect (none in my opinion) to those who harp about medical errors and unnecessary deaths and excessive costs, what doctors have accomplished since the not-too-distant days when castor oil and leeches were the mainstay of medical therapy, and the primary diagnostic tool was the taking of the pulse, is pretty darn impressive. What we have learned to do for, and to, our patients in just the forty-some years since I started plying the trade is nothing short of phenomenal. Joint replacements, bypass surgery, transplantation, and a whole host of medicines that can get rid of all kinds of troubles we don't care for and provide us with a plethora of happinesses that we dearly desire. And all that at only a fraction of the gross national product. So you would think we would be pretty pleased with ourselves.

But if you did, you would be dead wrong.

It doesn't matter what the brand. From the lowliest cardiac surgeon to the highest family practitioner, almost no one I talk to has anything good to say about life as a doctor. Whenever I ask a colleague how things are going, all I get is grumble, sputter, and mutter. In short, whining. Whining about malpractice, whining about work hours, whining about paperwork, and whining especially about lack of appreciation. In droves, I see colleagues either taking early retirement or turning to some other line of work. I know one fellow who, at the age of forty-eight, decided he was burned out and went to New Zealand to take up sheep farming. And another, well, here's a story you may find hard to believe, but it's true. He gave up a perfectly good practice in partnership with his wife—I certainly don't mean to imply that that had anything to do with it—to become, of all things, a governor.

"It used to be fun being a doctor," they all say. "It isn't anymore."

I suppose each of us has to figure out for ourselves what is fun and what isn't. And I have no problem with the doctor who no longer considers her job fun. Doctoring guarantees employment, and it pays awfully well. I don't know if it has to be fun. However, one thing I do know. You have only two choices in life. You can be either a health care provider or a health care receiver. And no matter how bad things get for the former, it will always be much worse for the latter.

I except in this pandemic of professional malaise the medical residents at William Penn Hospital. Most of them were in awe of what they could do, and joyful when they could do it. Maybe it is because they were young, or maybe because, often foreign-born and -educated, they were less well endowed with the assumption of entitlement that permeates the native of the species. They had a devout reverence for the privilege of being able to practice a profession that they recognized as second to none. No matter how difficult it was for them to do their job, and at William Penn that was pretty difficult, they never complained.

My team especially. They remained eternally cheerful—despite the daily reminders of the futility of ever accomplishing even a fraction of what they were trying to do. Maria Elena, Vijay, and Abe were kind to their patients, considerate with the staff, and respectful in the extreme to me. Whether this was due to a sense that I was old and wise, or merely old, I was never entirely sure, and I never tried to find out.

I was quite fond of each of them individually, but as a team they presented me with an awkward problem. Whereas my role was, in theory, somewhat akin to that of an orchestra conductor with a well-trained set of musicians—modestly useful and accorded an excessive credit for the performance—with these three I was not so much the man in front of the orchestra as the chap standing in the wings, the one whose sole function was to signify the beginning and the end of each performance by pulling the curtain open and shut. I was an accessory after the fact. It wasn't so much that they knew a lot, although they did. But rather whatever they didn't know they always found out. And they found it out before they presented their cases to me. Which left me with almost nothing to do except nod my head from time to time and occasionally clear my throat to remind them I was still there. I can't honestly say I ever did anything useful.

Except maybe once. Even then, it wasn't so much useful in the sense that I did anything of any value in treating the patient, but I did, much to the surprise of all, make a diagnosis.

Chantel Williamson had been admitted the previous evening with shortness of breath. Her blood pressure was two sixty over one forty, and she had water up to her eyeballs. The working diagnosis was pulmonary edema due to a dilated cardiomyopathy, a fancy way of saying that her heart had given out.

Chantel was what the residents jokingly referred to as an Advanced Placement patient. While Advanced Placement generally gives the rider just a bit of a push to help him up the steep part of the hill on the Tour de Life, for Other Philadelphians it was more than a bit of a push. It was a shove—one great enough to propel a body up to the summit, over the top, and down the other side so rapidly that it reached the finish line at a time when the rest of the pack was just hitting its stride.

Because she had come in around midnight, Chantel's initial workup and treatment were done by a Doctor of the Night, so none of us had as yet actually seen her. But we had a detailed description of the nocturnal fussings, and how she had responded to them. A morning report given to Maria Elena, whose patient she now was, declared that she was presently in no acute distress.

When we arrived at her bedside, Chantel was sitting comfortably in her bed, enjoying her breakfast, and chatting amiably with the nurse. One might be tempted to say that under the circumstances, she was looking pretty darn good.

Although *one* might well, *we* would not. In medicine, tip-top and the apple of one's eye are not selections available on the menu of How One Is. The best our meager fare can offer is, as Maria Elena correctly stated, No Acute Distress. This, as the term implies, still leaves manifold opportunities for distress aplenty—as long as it has been around for a while and has no intention of departing in the near future.

Although Chantel did appear devoid of any distress of the acute variety, she was sweating profusely, a phenomenon that had not been mentioned in the morning report, either because it had only recently appeared or, which is more likely, because it had escaped the notice of the night float, in whose eyes a little extra water loss would most likely have been no big deal. But the beads of sweat on her forehead and the soppy wet johnny were impressive. I had no idea as to the cause.

"She is sweating," I opined judiciously.

Abe, Maria Elena, and Vijay all concurred that she was, in fact, diaphoretic, and they marveled at my powers of observation.

"She is sweating *a lot*," I thought it safe to add.

This point was also conceded as well taken, at which point an animated discussion commenced as to whether the magnitude of diaphoresis was of any diagnostic or prognostic significance, general opinion holding that it was probably not.

"Why is she sweating?" I asked.

I was puzzled, and I fear my tone betrayed it. I should have been more careful. Although it is quite commonplace that an attending physician fails to grasp exactly what is going on, doubt is the one thing he should never display. The accepted etiquette in this situation is to adopt a Socratic pose and query the residents in the manner of a teacher quizzing his students. Thus, the proper expression in this situation would be, "Doctor Velasco, what would be the differential diagnosis of diaphoresis in this case?"

If Maria Elena recognized my puzzlement, she gave no sign of it. She nodded deferentially and fell silent for a minute as she collected her thoughts before replying.

"The record says she has a history of drug abuse. With her acute cardiac decompensation, I'd be concerned about sepsis. Staphylococcal bacteremia and bacterial endocarditis would be my first considerations, although if she has HIV/AIDS, for which she is high risk, I'd also consider Bartonella and *Mycobacterium avium* complex. Perhaps we should get HIV antibodies, blood cultures, and an echocardiogram."

It was a well-reasoned plan, and it made perfect sense to me. Loath to commit myself, however, before hearing what the rest of the gang had to say, I gave only a noncommittal nod.

I turned to Vijay. "Doctor Gupta, can you think of an alternative to the sepsis hypothesis?"

"Sepsis is certainly a possibility," he said tactfully. "But it wouldn't be my first choice. She does not have a fever, and her white blood count is not elevated, although, of course, this could be falsely normal if she has AIDS. Still, I would consider drug withdrawal more likely."

Here was another perfectly logical explanation. Unable to choose between the two diagnoses, I turned to Abe to resolve the issue.

"Sepsis and drug withdrawal are certainly definite considerations," I said in my best professorial tone. "Winston, tell us, please, how you would determine which is the correct diagnosis?"

Abe smiled slightly. It was the kind of smile that a benevolent parent would bestow upon a child who had satisfactorily completed his lessons. Although his gaze was directed at the residents, I had the unsettling feeling that it included me.

"The diaphoresis presents an interesting differential. I agree that infection is unlikely, but the urine drug screen reveals only cocaine, which would make narcotic or benzodiazepine withdrawal unlikely. Cocaine being an adrenergic stimulant, withdrawal symptoms tend to produce more lethargy than sympathetic activation. And the normal gamma-glutamyl transpeptidase would seem effectively to rule out alcohol as a consideration.

"But for the lack of tachycardia, inappropriate sinus tachycardia would be my first choice. Familial dysautonomia, although theoretically possible, can be ruled out by her age and stature alone. Under the circumstances, I would favor a pheochromocytoma, although Hodgkin's lymphoma should also be considered. In a series of two hundred cases of unexplained diaphoresis at the Mayo Clinic, reported in the March nineteen ninety-eight issue of *The Journal of Infectious Diseases*, British Edition, the former accounted for twenty-eight percent of cases of unexplained diaphoresis, and the latter fourteen percent. A normal urine for VMA and metanephrines should rule out the latter, and a CT of the chest, abdomen, and pelvis would identify either lymphadenopathy or a mass on the adrenal gland, in the latter which case a metaiodobenzylguanidine uptake scan should confirm the diagnosis. Although not as sensitive, it has a much higher degree of specificity than the CT for a pheo."

I was in a pickle. In general, as Abe was a lot smarter than me, I always deferred to his opinion. But I had never actually seen a case of pheochromocytoma, and I had always harbored the suspicion that it fell into the category of those conditions that were invented by cogno-scenti in large academic centers solely in order to befuddle poor souls like me.

For want of anything better to do, I looked again at the patient. She was quietly studying us, a faint look of amusement on her face.

"Might I ask the patient a question?" I said.

Unusual as the request was, they agreed readily, for we had been through this before. The first time I addressed a patient directly there was an awkward silence, as my team was torn between loyalty to their senior, and the knowledge that this was something attending physicians just did not do, it being more or less akin to the queen of England doing her own laundry. With great deference, they explained this to me, the reason being, they said, that the patient might begin to think that the attending was actually their doctor, and that could lead to no end of difficulties. I admitted I could see their point, and promised I would try not to do it again, but having doctored to patients in my former life, the temptation was a strong one, and one I was afraid I might not always be able to resist. They agreed that under such circumstances, an excep-tion could be made, but requested only that I would always ask first, so they wouldn't be taken by surprise. It was a request I strictly honored.

"Ms. Williamson, when was your last period?"

"It's Chantel, Doc. And it's been a while."

"And when you get these sweats—do you ever get hot flashes?"

"Oo-o-wee! Baby, don't you *know* it! Like an oven on broil."

"And all this all started up exactly when?

"When I stopped taking my pills."

"Which pills were those?"

"My hormone pills."

"Why did you stop?"

"Couldn't afford them."

"I'm sorry to hear that."

"Me too."

"How old are you, Chantel?"

"Be thirty-nine next month."

"Quite young."

"Mebbe to you, but sure don't feel like it to me."

"Young for the change, I meant."

"Oh that."

"Yes, that."

"Well." She raised her hand to her chin and rubbed it a couple of times. "I had some work done."

"What kind of work was that?"

"Down there." She pointed to her nether regions.

"I see. And was this work—would you say it was just what you might call a basic oil and lube job? Or was it more of a—uh—general overhaul?"

"More in the line of general overhaul."

"With maybe an engine rebuild as well?"

"That too."

"And that's when you started the hormones?"

"Yep."

"To keep everything in good running order."

She smiled broadly. "You got that right."

"Chantel, do you mind if I ask you a personal question?"

"You're the doctor."

"About before you had the surgery?"

"Fire away."

"What was your name then?"

"Same as it is now. Williamson."

"I was thinking more of your first name."

"Ah. That was different."

"And it was . . . ?"

"Charles."

"So if I were to examine you now, *down there*, that is."

Chantel put her hands protectively over her crotch. "Please, Doc. Not now."

"Still some more work to do on the rebuild?"

"When I get the dough."

"Of course," I said. "Well, good luck, Chantel. I hope everything comes out all right."

"Thanks, Doc. So far so good."

In the hall, my team all told me how impressed they were with my diagnosis. Even Abe.

"How did you know she was—?" he asked. "I mean wasn't—that is, how did you deduce that her actual gender was other than it appeared?"

"Elementary, my dear Winston. She stroked her chin."

· 9 ·

An Encounter

···········

When George Washington crossed the Delaware in 1776, the conditions were perilous. There were raging currents and ice jams and torrential rain. It was a most difficult crossing, requiring many boats and much bravery. It was a big deal. They even made a painting of the event, which resides in the Metropolitan Museum of Art. Although the artist who painted it was born forty years after the crossing, I have been assured by all the authorities on the subject that the painting is accurate down to the last detail.

When he crossed the Schuylkill River a year later at Swede's Ford, Washington did so by taking his wagons and placing them one next to the other, thereby making a bridge of them. It was no big deal.

Eventually the Schuylkill works its way down to Philadelphia, where it enters the Delaware. Even there it is not very big, remaining, as it does throughout its one hundred and thirty miles, a modest and well-behaved river. But Philadelphians are quite proud of the Schuylkill, and I have to admit they show a far greater respect for their river than do the residents of my home city for the Hudson. Along both sides of the river is a wide swath of green space where people play, picnic, and stroll. On the side of the river where we lived, there is a bike path. In Manayunk the bike path crosses Kelly Drive at a traffic light and continues along Wissahickon Creek into Wissahickon Park, a broad expanse of forest in the midst of which one can actually forget that one is in a city. In the middle of the park a trail leads up from the valley floor into Chestnut Hill, just a mile from our house. As did I, Trine bicycled regularly to her work downtown. At the end of the day, we would meet at Fairmount Park and cycle home together. It is a pretty route along the river.

The traffic on Kelly Drive at that hour is so heavy that it moves at a glacial pace, and we easily outdistanced the commuters on their way home to the suburbs. We enjoyed the view and the exercise and the fact that we were saving the environment, but in the end we did the trip for that most basic of human reasons. To feel superior to the people around us.

One day, as we were crossing Kelly Drive at the light, we encountered a taxi. Ordinarily, an encounter with a taxi in the city would not be worthy of comment, but this was not an ordinary encounter. The driver of this particular taxi might have been thinking of the green light he had seen the last time he was at that intersection, or perhaps he was just thinking how much nicer it would be if the light actually *were* green—or even orange if that was the best it could do. But more likely he was not really thinking about the particular color of the light at all, considering, as did most Philadelphians, that a traffic light, like the Liberty Bell or the bronze Ben Franklin, was yet one other piece of local statuary that had been set out solely for his visual appreciation. And because it was time to get home to his evening meal of scraps on a bun, by the time we entered the intersection he had already dispensed with his appreciation of said light. At which point he neatly swept us right off our bikes and very nearly into the Schuylkill River.

After which Trine, having picked herself up off the pavement, looked at her banged-up legs and my shredded shirt, then announced in a tone brooking no dissent,

"We can go home now."

Going Back

....

A lthough I enjoyed my time in Philadelphia, the prospect of finishing out my professional years in the community I knew so well and with people who knew me in like manner was sufficiently appealing that the idea of moving back gave me no pause. There was also the small matter that each passing year was now less likely to produce additions of Experience on the credit side of my ledger than it was to compile Behind the Times in the debit column. And I knew that the good people of Dumster did not concern themselves as to whether I was up to snuff on the latest advances, as long as they could escape from their visit to me without serious bodily harm. They would be a more tolerant and forgiving lot than those who dwelt in the dog-eat-dog atmosphere of the city.

There is a character in *David Copperfield* by the name of Wilkins Micawber. Utterly irresponsible in his domestic finances, he is forever hopelessly in debt. Nonetheless, Mr. Micawber remains eternally optimistic about what he calls his "prospects." These prospects, always *just round the next corner*, are, of course, purely illusory, but they are no more so than his ability to adhere to that principle he claims as his guide in matters economical, namely:

> Annual income twenty pounds, annual expenditure nineteen pounds nineteen pence, result happiness. Annual income twenty pounds, annual expenditure twenty pounds one pence, result, misery.

Although more honored in the breach than the practice by more than Mr. Micawber, the homily is nonetheless sound. And not just in matters financial.

To illustrate this point, I turn again to Dickens. In his novel *Great Expectations*, the hero is a chap by the name of Philip Pirrip, Pip for short. Raised the son of a humble blacksmith, Pip unexpectedly acquires a mysterious benefactor who provides him with capital and, with it, the promise of Great Expectations. In his pursuit of those expectations, the once poor-but-happy Pip becomes a restless and miserable soul, displeased with himself and distrustful of the world.

I have a son and two daughters. As those of you who have sons and daughters—or who have ever been sons or daughters yourself—know full well, sons and daughters are different. Both of my daughters are teachers, one high school, the other university. Both have happy and healthy families of their own. Both are financially secure. Both, like their mother, have a strong sense of fairness. And both, like their mother, spend much of the time that is not devoted to their family or their students solving the problems of poverty, injustice, and why people are not nice to each other. In order not to interfere with their busy day, they usually do this between two and four in the morning.

My son, on a busy day, is laid-back. He believes in Live and Let Live. As content as Ferdinand the Bull, he sleeps like a baby.

By traditional measures my daughters would be considered successful. But no matter how much my daughters accomplish, they expect to accomplish more. And no matter how little my son does, he expects to do less. In short, my son's accomplishments exceed his expectations, and my daughters' do not. For my son, the result is happiness. For my daughters, it is misery.

Which is the long way around to saying that the key to life is low expectations.

Whether it was born to them by Nature, or taught to them by nurture, the people of Dumster have learned this lesson well. And they are blessed with the contentment that can come only to those who appreciate the value of never expecting too much—even from their doctor.

So no sooner had we arrived home from our bicycle misadventure, and a brief query had satisfied me that Beloved Spouse's Declaration of Independence was not a sign of traumatic brain injury, than I sat down and wrote a letter to Herbert Shiftley, the CEO at Emmeline Talbot Memorial Hospital. The letter was a particularly clever one. It made allegorical reference to the Boston Red Sox, to which, like many

Dumsterians, he had a passionate devotion. It might seem like an odd choice for people from a small town in Vermont to root for a team in Boston. But it isn't.

Like most of us, the people of Dumster are proud of where they come from, even if they are no longer there. So that a former Dumster resident who moved to, say, San Diego, and who has no intention of ever returning, even for Old Home Day, still claims a passionate love of his native town. Or Trine, who, if you asked her where she is from, would say Oslo, and then go on to extol at length the virtues of life in Norway as compared with her current country of internment. But if you were to ask her would she ever want to go back there, she would look at you as if you were off your deep rocker.

But Vermont doesn't have a professional baseball team of its own, unless you count the Monsters, which I don't, because I can't be sure by the time this book comes out they will still be here. So if you are a baseball fan, it's Red Sox or nothing.

Playing on this sentiment, in the letter I wrote, I asked Shiftley to imagine that he was general manager of the Sox, and that he had received a call from Roger Clemens—before, I emphasized, the revelation that he suffered from hormonal imbalance—announcing that he wanted to return to the team where he had started his career. I outlined the predicament of what to do with an aging star who was popular with the fans and bound to be a big draw at the box office, but who had an uncertain shoulder and whose place on the roster would most likely mean having to send back to the minors a promising young left-hander. I thought it summarized the situation nicely.

For a hospital administrator, Shiftley is not a bad sort of fellow. Most would even concede that he is *not half bad*. Excepting the rare individual who might rise to okay, *not half bad* is the highest accolade Dumsterians ever afford to their town officials.

This high opinion of Shiftley is held by all but one of the trustees, Wilbur Cox. In all fairness to Shiftley, I should point out that Mr. Cox always makes a point of dissenting from favorable opinions, particularly when they are widely held. Cox is the town tree surgeon, and something about a life spent primarily in the company of trees has made him pessimistic about human behavior.

In his eyes, not only is Shiftley not worth a hill of beans, but the position he holds is itself utterly useless and a complete waste of money. He is particularly fond of reminding the other trustees that there was one year when the hospital had no administrator at all, and it appeared to do just fine.

Shiftley's predecessor had died unexpectedly, and the hospital trustees set about finding a replacement at their usual methodical pace. As always, they were more concerned that something new was likely to be, if not necessarily worse, at the very least different, which in their eyes amounted to pretty much the same thing. So that by the time they had finishing recounting all of the town managers and police chiefs and school superintendents who had been inferior in every possible manner to those whom they succeeded, omitting to consider (as they were philosophically averse to doing) that this same predecessor had been a similarly unsuccessful successor, it was well over a year before they settled on Shiftley, the only candidate who had been willing to wait them out.

I would see Shiftley once or twice a year on our return to Dumster at holiday time, and he was always most gracious in telling me how much he missed my services and that an office was always waiting— all I had to do was call, and it would be mine. Nonetheless, I knew that the news of my return would come as quite a shock, not perhaps as great as it was for the family Lazarus, but at least rivaling that of the parents of the Prodigal Son, inapplicable though the latter analogy may be.

Thus, I did not expect an immediate call from Shiftley. He would need time to let the news sink in. But after more than a week had passed without any communication, I became a bit concerned. He might be merely on vacation, but what if something had happened to him? I decided to call.

"Emmeline Talbot Memorial Hospital, Member of University Medical Alliance, Office of the CEO," answered a familiar voice. It was Kathy Ducharme. Kathy's official title was executive administrative assistant to the CEO. Kathy knew everything that needed to be known about everyone in the hospital. She knew the names of all the members of their family, what their kids were up to, their likes, their dislikes, whom they got along with and whom they couldn't stand, and how Mr. Shiftley regarded them. Kathy ran the hospital.

"After that speech, you probably need a rest."

There was a brief pause on the other end of the line. "Beach!" she exclaimed. "It's good to hear your voice."

"Good to hear yours also. How are things doing up there on the homestead?"

"You know, same old same old. Of course it's just not the same old without you. How long before you're coming back? You promised, you know."

It was her standing line for me. I gave her my standing response. "Not too long."

She asked me about Trine and the kids and my job, and did I know that they were going to pave the county road, and that Dr. Cracker was a grandfather, and a few more things just to make sure I caught up, and then she asked did I want to speak to Mr. Shiftley.

"Please."

"He'll be glad to talk to you. Can I tell him what it's about?"

"A job."

The line was quiet briefly. "Here?"

"That was the idea."

"Oh! That's gre—" There was another pause, this time longer. "I'll put you through."

"Thanks."

Shiftley came on the line right away. "Beach," he said with a jollity I had not heard before. "How are you, old man?"

"Not so old, I'd say. And I'm fine. Expecting, actually, to be even better."

"Great! Glad to hear it. What's up?"

"You got my letter?"

"Sure did. Most amusing. And of course, very good news. Excellent news actually—that you *might* be coming back. At *some* point. I'm thrilled. Absolutely delighted. At the *idea* of it."

"And then there is the actual *it* of it."

"Which '*it*' would that be?"

"*It* is time."

"Time? For what?"

"Leaving Philadelphia."

There was a long silence on the other end.

"You mean?"

"I mean now. We're packing up as we speak."

"But—er—I thought you were planning to stay—longer—that Trine needed to finish what she set out to do, and you had your teaching."

"We were, but no more. The pace is too hectic. Time to come home and relax a bit. Declining years and all that, you know."

"Yes—well—interesting. The letter also—especially that Roger Clemens bit."

"Perhaps not the best analogy."

"But apt."

"Perhaps. Anyway, we'll be leaving Philadelphia at the end of June. I was thinking of taking the month off. August would be good for me to start."

"August?"

"Yes. I was thinking of the seventh. If that works out at your end."

"August the seventh."

"Of course I could start earlier."

"Oh no," he said. "No need for that. In fact . . ."

It was a peculiar habit when speaking for Herbert to use *in fact* rather than the more customary *but*. Something to do, I suppose, with his being an administrator. In any event, the meaning was the same, putting the listener on notice that everything he had said up to that point should be disregarded.

"Our situation up here has changed, you see."

"As situations are prone to do."

"Doctor-wise, we're pretty well set. Just hired a crackerjack young internist from Boston. She'll be starting in August. So at this particular time, we don't actually need another doctor. Of course if anyone leaves, you'd be first on my list."

"Herb."

"Yes?"

"I am not exactly *another* doctor!"

"Heavens no! Of course not. I didn't mean—that is—still, there is the issue of what we would *do* with both of you."

"The words of Chairman Mao come to mind."

"I beg your pardon?"

"Grow more patients."

"An appealing thought, but perhaps not very practical. Dumster is not exactly expanding by leaps and bounds these days."

"Then we'll share. I'm willing to give up some of my patients, those that agree anyway."

"Very generous of you. Naturally, many of the patients will prefer to see you."

"Naturally."

"The older ones anyway."

"The devil you know."

"Which puts a bit of a damper on the prospects for the new doctor developing a practice. It does create a bit of a sticky wicket, you see. Tell me, how long do you think you will—er—before that is—well, none of us is getting any younger, if you know what I mean."

It was a fair question, and I knew it would be coming. Nonetheless, it irritated me. Whether professional or personal, no one is ever overly pleased to be reminded of one's inevitable mortality.

"I hadn't given it much thought," I lied. "Let's just say I think I can outlast you."

"Ah," he said. "Well then, I guess that pretty much takes care of that."

"My sentiments exactly."

"So that only leaves the practical matter of where we would—and with whom you could—and how we might—it's all rather complicated, you see. Especially with so many—unless. Unless . . . I know it's a bit silly to ask, but I don't suppose there's any chance you could work on Friday?"

"Friday's a problem?"

"It seems that Friday has become a part of the weekend—for the doctors that is."

"I can do Friday."

"The whole day?"

"Sunup to sundown."

"Seriously?"

As a rule, I never answer this question. It tends to put a bit of a damper on one's options. But in this case I was willing to make an exception.

"Cross my heart."

"Then it's settled," he said. "August seventh it is. Unless, perhaps, you wanted to start earlier. Say, first week in July or so?"

And so we sold our house in Philadelphia, and, with a quick stop in New York at Patricia's of Greenwich Village, where I selected an outfit appropriate for the Old Home Day parade, we headed for home.

The Farmer and the Preacher

....

"**D**iarrhea."

He was sitting in the room when I entered, his hands folded upon his lap, clean-shaven, wearing freshly pressed overalls and a clean checked shirt. He had a faint but distinctive aroma, a mixture of sour milk, dried hay, and fresh manure. He looked at me with that open face of his, behind which lay an intelligence easy to underestimate.

He didn't say *Hello* or *Good to see you again*. He didn't even nod. He didn't need to. Because he knew, not only that I knew he was glad to see me, but that I knew that he knew without his telling me. He just sat and said the one word that told me all he figured I needed to know, at least for now.

It was almost as if, not only had I never left Dumster, but that the two of us had never even left this room. But not quite. Because there was something different. It was so quick I might have missed it if it weren't for the fact that I had never seen it in the thirty-some years we'd known each other. A twitch. No, not quite a twitch. Just a slight drawing back at his lips. And then it was gone. As if he were going to smile, but then his face decided that even that wasn't necessary.

It was good to see him again after my years of wandering in the urban wilderness. And it was comforting—a comfort born out of a life shared, not just here in the examining room, but outside as well. He was the man from whom I bought manure for my garden. I was the father of the girl who had been his daughter's classmate. And both of us were folks who sat in Comstock Hall once a year and listened to debates over winter salt and bus routes and reserved balances at Dumster's town meeting. It was a comfort, superficial though it may have been, that gave us a sense of a shared existence. Not on a par with a married couple certainly, but more than passengers on a bus. Deep enough, at least, that we knew each other's talk. So that although the greeting from someone who had not seen his doctor in five years may have seemed a bit abrupt, it was no more than I expected—or wanted.

As had been the many generations of Stedrocks before him, this last remaining member of the stock that settled Steddsville some three hundred years ago was as thrifty a man in word as he was in deed. *Waste not, want not*, he might have said if asked to explain his taciturnity—except that he never would, because to say what was obvious without being said would have been another waste of words. And words, to Hiram, were like hard-earned capital—great in value and finite in quantity. As such, they should not be spent recklessly—on the possibility, however remote, that at some point in his advancing years, he would find himself in dire straits, only to discover that after saying "I need—" he had used up his entire stock and was now verbally bankrupt.

Accordingly, it was his custom upon entering the office to state his complaint immediately, thereby forestalling the need for unnecessary introductions and salutations.

I did likewise.

"How long has this diarrhea been going on?"

"A long time."

The importance of being able to measure precisely the passage of time dates back thousands of years. The ancients used sundials, water clocks, and hourglasses to keep track of exactly when you last didn't get something done, how long it would have taken not to do it, and when you would have to not get it done again. Now we have much more precise instruments for this purpose. But regardless of the timepiece, they all rely on the same principle: that time is a finite measurable object, and it can be divided up into discrete units of equal value: seconds, hours, years, and the like. So a minute, for example, would be of the same duration regardless of the situation in which it occurred. It is a convenient concept. And it is patently absurd. The idea that *Just a Minute*, and a *Doctor's Minute*, and the *Final Minute* of a football game are of identical length defies common sense.

Back in the time of the Greeks, when philosophy was invented as a way of reducing unemployment among the overeducated, this whole business of the nature of time was a popular subject for debate. Those who held to the belief that time was a particular thing that progressed in linear and predictable fashion were called realists. Those who held, to the contrary, that time was more of a concept, and it depended on—well, they said, that's a tough one to answer, because it depends on the point from which you view it. These people were called transcendentalists. The transcendentalists were the laughingstock of the philosophy community. At least they were until a couple of thousand years later when Einstein came along and proved them right after all. Einstein got a lot of credit for figuring this out, and everyone makes him out to be quite the genius. Which may well be the case. I have no reason to doubt them. But as with most discoveries, the person who got the credit didn't actually make it. He just had a better marketing strategy.

Einstein named it the Theory of Relativity. Everybody congratulated him on his brilliant discovery. He even got a prize for it. That was not so long ago. Around Dumster folks have known the theory for, well, for a long time. If they were to have given it a name, which, not being inclined to make a fuss about something so obvious, they didn't, it most likely would have been called the Theory of the Farmer and the Preacher, in accordance with one of the numerous parables of these two that constitute the *principia* of the Dumster way of life. The parable goes like this:

> *Preacher to Farmer: How's your wife?*
> *Farmer to Preacher: Relative to what?*

Accordingly, for Hiram Stedrock time exists in only two states, "a long time" and "not so long." Which of the two it might be at any one time is, of course, relative. Fifty years of ice melting from the Hubbard Glacier is but a proverbial drop in the bucket, and a two-week vacation can disappear in a flash. But five minutes waiting to get your morning coffee when the person in front of you orders a double soy cinnamon frappuccino no whip light can be an eternity.

And then there's how long it takes a watched pot to boil.

12

The Flux

....

"Diarrhea?" I repeated.

Hiram nodded.

Hiram would never come to see me because he had diarrhea. He was as considerate as he was thrifty, and he would not waste my time or his money with such a trivial complaint. No. It was not Hiram. There was only one possible explanation for his visit.

"One of the girls?"

Hiram nodded. Stoic as he was about his own health, he was a veritable mother hen when it came to his family.

"Diarrhea. In a cow?" I said, thinking it was only to myself.

Hiram looked pained. *Cow* was not a word he used.

"If I remember correctly," I said, hurriedly correcting my indiscretion. "Most of the family has left the farm now."

He nodded again. Age and the cost of farming had forced him to reduce the size of his once large and extended family to only a few.

"Well, let me see. Who would still be at home?" I ticked off those I could remember. "There's Annabelle and Betty, Clara and Dorothy, Esther, and Francine. That would make six."

Hiram raised a finger.

"Seven?"

It was seven.

Who would it be . . . "G-gertrude?"

Not Gertrude.

"Gloria?"

It was Gloria.

To some, veterinary medicine might seem rather out of my line of work, but not to Hiram Stedrock. When I came to Dumster, Doc Butterfield was the vet in town. He had been there for a long time. Those who remember his arrival say he was still in his cavalry uniform when he came to Dumster just after the war in 1946. He bought one of the six old brick federals on North Main Street, a set of stately buildings that were reminders of a time when Dumster, with its tool-and-die factories, was the economic center of the Connecticut River Valley. He set up an office in the back of the house and converted the barn to an examining area for large animals. In front of the house was a signpost, but it was unreadable. There was no need for a sign. Everyone knew who was there.

Doc Butterfield was a hefty man, with a great shock of white hair, a broad open forehead, and a set of full lips that always had a smile. It was a smile that inspired trust and the confidence that, however bleak the situation seemed, all would now be okay. His most remarkable feature, however, was not his face, but his hands. Huge almost to the point of acromegaly, they could, with equal ease, pull a reluctant calf out of the womb or sew the ear back on a kitten who had tried to play tag with a neighboring dog. There was not a soul in town who wouldn't be willing to put his beloved pet's fate in those hands. Or, should the need arise, their own. On more than a few occasions, when I was out of town, Doc Butterfield capably filled in. I, in turn, on the rare occasion when he took a day off, would dip my toes in the more shallow waters of the veterinary seas. This medical miscegenation seemed only natural to Dumsterians, for whom a plumber could, in a pinch, repair the wiring, and the history teacher, if need be, could teach biology. As always, they expected only that one would do one's best.

One year, at the tender age of eighty-five, Doc Butterfield decided to retire. He sold the house and the practice to a young veterinarian couple from Pennsylvania. Then he packed up his belongings and headed south in the camper with his wife up front and their two horses in the trailer behind. "Someplace I won't have to wear wool," he said when I asked him where he was going. Last November I got a card from him postmarked Ocracoke, North Carolina. On the front was a picture of wild horses grazing on grassy dunes with the ocean in the background. On the back he had written two words.

Don't retire.

The young couple spent six months fixing up Doc's place before they moved in. To do the work, they hired a firm from Salem,

Massachusetts, that specialized in historic restoration. When they were done with gutting the interior, sandblasting the exterior, and landscaping the grounds, there was hardly a brick or a beam or a bush that they hadn't restored. Around the property they built a stone wall. As far as anyone knew, it was the first stone wall within town limits. On the front lawn they put a well. The siding for the well was from an old barn in Pomfret, and the cedar shingles for the roof were handmade in Ferrisburg. It had a crank with a rope, at the end of which was attached a historically correct eighteenth-century oak water bucket that they found on eBay. It came from Santa Monica, California. Thanks to an underground pump connected to the house, you could actually draw water from it. There were a few grumbles about Flatlanders, and Old Sturbridge Village, and who did they think they were anyway. These were mostly from their North Main neighbors, whose property had suddenly acquired a rather tired and dingy look. But even the least gruntled had to admit they had done a nice job.

They put new lettering on the sign. It read:

ABENAKI ARK
HOLISTIC VETERINARY SERVICES

I took our dog, Bonger, to see them shortly after they opened. He was due for his rabies shot, but mainly I wanted to see what they were like. The office was as changed as the rest of the place. The old bare walls had been Sheetrocked over and painted in two shades of orange. The fold-up chairs had been replaced by expensive-looking upholstered couches. In each corner was a collection of brightly colored beanbag-type chairs, one set slightly larger than the other. Over the larger was a sign that read CANINE QUARTERS, and over the smaller CALICO CORNER. The walls were decorated with pictures of happy-looking dogs and cats. There was a large sign advertising a special price on organic vegetarian animal food and a poster showing a smiling dog and cat with their mouths wide open to display a full set of gleaming teeth. Under the picture was a caption that read, DENTAL HYGIENE ISN'T JUST FOR PEOPLE. ASK US ABOUT OUR DENTAL CLEANING AND GUM MASSAGE. Behind the counter were two sets of diplomas documenting the qualifications of Paul and Melinda Barker-Purris. Both had graduated summa cum laude from the University of Pennsylvania School of Veterinary Medicine, and both had completed with distinction a residency in small-animal medicine from Cornell. In addition, Paul had a fellowship in animal behavior, and Melinda in comprehensive dentistry.

They both came in to see Bonger. "We practice as a team," they explained. They were friendly and cheerful and certainly seemed to know their business. They looked in his ears, and listened to his heart, and prodded around his stomach. They took his blood pressure and stuck his paw for blood sugar. I think they may even have checked his prostate, but I didn't ask what they were doing with that part of the examination. They were very thorough. And when they were done, they gave me a three-page printed sheet on their findings, the sum and substance of which was that it was remarkable Bonger had survived as long as he had, given our utter neglect of his well-being. There were blood tests to be done, and vaccines to be given, and drops for his ears and pills for his bones. They even gave me a prescription for his blood pressure. I was impressed.

I still bring Bonger in occasionally, although not as regularly as they recommend. They are always very friendly, but every time I leave, it is with the vaguely uncomfortable feeling that I have been a bad owner.

I don't think Hiram has ever been to see them.

Doc Butterfield used to say, on the occasions of our mutual consultations, "The way I see it, Beach, you can divide animal and human troubles into two types: those that cross over and those that can't." And he was right. If somebody called him up with, say, a pain in his chest or told me that he had a horse gone lame, we would each have to say, "Gee, that's too bad." And leave it at that. But a boil, on the other hand, is a boil.

Diarrhea is at least enough of a crossover trouble that I was willing to take a shot at it.

Doctor or vet or plumber, when a customer presents with a problem, before one starts merrily down one's path, what one has to do first is answer a single important question. Is it *A Big Deal*, or is it *No Big Deal*? If the answer is *A Big Deal*, like a belly that's about to burst, or a foot of water in the kitchen, then right off the bat you know you have to take the situation very seriously. If, on the other hand, the determination is *No Big Deal*, say a drippy nose or a drippy faucet, you can be pretty sure things will turn out fine no matter what you do. The problem arises when you find yourself faced with a problem that by itself is no big deal, but that may be a sign of a very much bigger deal somewhere else. Diarrhea is like that.

Except in the very young or the very old, diarrhea is one of those things best left alone, being sure always, naturally, to recommend some innocuous intervention so that when it does finally disappear of its own accord, you can get the credit. Not always, though. Some diarrheas can poison your bloodstream, infect your heart, and shut down your kidneys. But that is pretty uncommon. The big-deal question is where the diarrhea is coming from.

Until 1854, nobody thought much about this question. The flux, as they called it, was spread by miasma, which, as any good physician knew, wasn't something you could do much about, except maybe a little judicious bloodletting and a dollop of castor oil to flush it out. That year, however, saw the outbreak of a horrific cholera epidemic in the Soho district of London. The rest of the city, except for an isolated case occurring randomly here and there, was pretty much spared.

"Divine intervention," declared the Reverend Henry Whitehead, a leading vicar in the area. He said it was the Lord's retribution for the evil and slothful ways of the parishioners of that notorious district. Whitehead's view was not surprising. He generally attributed all natural disasters, even the unnatural ones—Jack the Ripper for one—as part of the Almighty's plan for sin control. Of course, that was a long time ago.

There was a surgeon in Soho named John Snow. Dr. Snow was as God-fearing a soul as any man, but he was skeptical that the Almighty would go to so much trouble for such a small spot of sin. He suspected that the cause was more likely in the here and now rather than the hereafter. So he started asking around. He went around from door to door, stopping at each house to find out if anyone inside had gotten the flux. Then he made a map of where all the victims lived. He discovered that almost everyone who got cholera lived within a few blocks of the corner of Broad and Cambridge Streets. On this corner was located a well from which the neighborhood drew its water. Water for bathing and washing—and for drinking. He speculated that maybe the water was the source of the cholera. Everybody, from the board of health to the Vauxhall Water Company, laughed at him for such an absurd idea. The Reverend Whitehead declared it heretical.

Dr. Snow was undeterred by the ridicule. He decided to find out for himself if what he suspected was true. So he went to the intersection and removed the handle from the Broad Street pump, thereby forcing people to get their water elsewhere. At first there was a lot of complaining about the nuisance of having to travel to get water, but when nobody else got sick, that stopped as quickly as the diarrhea.

"It was the water," said Dr. Snow.

"It was the hand of God," said the Reverend Whitehead.

"I'm honored," said Dr. Snow.

Nowadays we know how important it is to have safe water to drink, and around here at least, water is clean and pure. Well, there was that business of the tritium in the wells down in Pownal, but nobody paid much attention to that except the politicians. At any rate, the likelihood of picking up an infection from what we drink is pretty slim. What we eat, however, is another matter altogether.

When it comes to ingestible infections, we now have a wider selection than ever. Most are imported. Depending on one's inclination one can find at one's local market New Zealand *Campylobacter* Chicken, Guatemala *Cyclospora* Raspberries, Mexican *Salmonella* Jalapeños, or, for those with more expensive tastes, the French *E. Coli* Camembert. But if you prefer to buy American, there is still plenty to choose from. Tomatoes from Florida, spinach from California, and peanut butter from Georgia are among the most popular brands this year. From time to time there are more exotic offerings.

During the time I was an epidemiologist at the CDC, we had an outbreak of more than one hundred cases of a strain of salmonella called *Salmonella eastbourne*. Most years this bug would cause only two or three cases. Ten would be a lot. The cases came from all over the country: Maine, Florida, California, even one in Vermont. At that time foodborne illnesses were usually local, because that's where people got their food from. Unless they happened to acquire it from an airline meal. Although the cases were not clustered geographically, they were in time, and all of them occurred just after Christmas. We had a devil of a time trying to find out where it came from. By the time we received the reports in Atlanta, the cases were several weeks old, so it was hard to pin down the culprit. Imagine someone calls you up and asks you what you had to eat two weeks ago. We were stumped. Then we found out they were having the same problem in Canada, especially the Eastern Provinces. So we called back again. Did you eat anything you bought from Canada? we asked. This time we hit the jackpot. Turned out there was a candy factory in Quebec that was importing the bacteria on cocoa beans from Ghana. They used the beans to make a chocolate syrup, which they then poured over cherries. After cooling, the whole toxic bundle was wrapped up in bright red and green foil for an extra-special Christmas treat. It just goes to show. You never can tell with food.

None of this, of course, was of any concern to Hiram. But as we both knew full well, should one of his cows have something that could be transmitted to the others, or to the dozen or so families in Steddsville who relied on Hiram for their raw milk, that would be a disaster. Therefore, Gloria's diarrhea might be *A Big Deal*, or it might not. I had to know. Fortunately, the answers to a few simple questions would tell me which it was. As I would with any anxious parent, I approached the subject cautiously:

"Anyone else in the family sick?"

He shook his head.

That was a good sign.

"Just Gloria?"

Hiram nodded.

"For how long—er—never mind. Would you say she has been sick— let's say, at least a week?"

He would.

"Two perhaps?"

Two was a possibility.

"As long as a month?"

Not, apparently, that long.

"And there's no blood in her stool?"

None.

"Nor any fever?"

Another negative.

"Is she milking okay?"

She was.

"And she's not off her feed?"

Hiram shook his head vigorously. Cows or people, that was a good sign. I was encouraged that things might be better than I had feared. The cow was not really sick, and as there were no secondary cases after two weeks of illness, there was no evidence the illness was transmissible. I wanted to say that it was most likely Just One of Those Things. But diarrhea has to come from something. Hiram's herd was all grass-fed in one pasture, and being the last farm in Steddsville didn't have much opportunity for bovine socialization. Only one cow. It just didn't make sense. Unless—

"Gloria is your youngest, I believe?"

She was.

It had been a very wet summer, and the first haying was yet to occur. So hay stores were pretty low. Hiram would be supplementing the hay with more grain than usual.

"Feeding them mostly corn these days, I'd venture?"

He was.

"With some soybeans thrown in to complete the protein?"

Some.

"I'm not a vet, of course."

Hiram shrugged.

"But I can tell you this much. With two weeks of diarrhea and only one of them sick, it's not contagious. And without a fever or blood in the stool or being off her feed, it doesn't involve any damage to her bowels. In a person, particularly a child, that would mean a food allergy. If it were one of my kids, I wouldn't worry about it. But I would take her off the soybeans and let her feed on her mother's milk until she can pasture. It's something to do at least. And it might even take care of the problem."

Hiram nodded. He rose to go.

"Of course," I added as he got to the door. "She could be lactose-intolerant."

Hiram smiled. "Thanks, Doc," he said.

"My pleasure," I said. And it was. Whether they meant it or not, most everybody thanked me when they left. Coming from Hiram, however, those two words were quite a compliment. Those two *unnecessary* words.

13

It Must Be Stratospherical by Now

....

The day after Memorial Day was a glorious morning. The trees were in full leaf. The sun was finally over Mount Abenaki. And on the way to work, I saw Elsie Perkins out planting her tomatoes. Spring finally had the place all to itself.

Spring had actually arrived in town a couple of months ago, and had promptly set to work making itself at home. It melted the snow. It set out the daffodils. It put the blossoms on the apple trees. But Spring couldn't really settle in and get comfortable until Winter left. If it were a proper season, upon seeing Spring at its doorstep, Winter would have taken the hint, packed up its bags, and headed down to Tierra del Fuego until December. But around here Winter is company that just doesn't know when to leave. You yawn, you stretch, you make repeated references to how early you have to get to work. Eventually, you change into your pajamas and brush your teeth. Yet there it sits, warming itself beside the fire, with its feet up on the hamper and a cup of hot cider in its mitts, jabbering about nothing in particular, as if there were no tomorrow. And so it goes. March into April, April into May, and still no sign of lions turning into lambs. For every bid by Spring at trotting out a day of tolerable weather here and there, Winter sees it and raises it one: a week of clouds, a blustering wind, and a rain so cold that the best you can hope for is that it will get just a little colder and turn to snow. This is the time of maple syrup and mud. It is not a pleasant time. Old Vermonters spend their days collecting sap and their nights huddled around the woodstove. Everyone else that can goes south.

Having just come back from two weeks of practicing my tropical yoga, I was nursing a cup of tea and trying, without a great deal of success, to get myself in the mood for saving a few lives when the phone rang.

It was my direct line. It bypasses the One If By Land, Two If By Sea menu that was set up by the latest in a series of productivity consultants who make their living devising ways of preventing patients from talking to their doctors, since, as they love to remind you, talk is cheap. Instinctively my hand went to my pocket. At this hour of the morning it would most likely be Trine, letting me know that I had either forgotten my lunch or taken her car keys. The former was no big deal, but the latter meant I was in Big Trouble. Reassured by my empty pockets, I picked up the phone.

"It's killing me, Doc!" gasped a voice at the other end.

"Good morning, Fusswood," I answered. "Good to hear from you. What's up?"

"My CRP."

"Your CRP?"

"Yeah, it must be stratospherical by now!"

"But Fusswood, I have never . . ."

"I just heard about it on the radio. It causes heart attacks, they said. I can feel it, Doc. Piling up in my coronaries. Like cement. We gotta do something fast. Before they plug up completely."

"Certainly, I'll have Maggie set you up for an appointment at say—"

"I'll be there in ten minutes."

"Ten minutes it is."

"You don't think it'll be too late, do you, Doc?"

"It's never too late, Fusswood."

"I figured maybe, just to be on the safe side, you should call me in some of those toothpaste pills. I can pick them up on my way in."

"No, Fusswood. Crestor won't be necessary. Besides, I don't want anything to delay your visit."

"Good thinking, Doc."

"That's my job."

"See you in ten."

He rang off.

It may seem odd in this day and age that a patient would be able actually to talk directly with his doctor, but much as it violates our principles, under certain circumstances we do allow it.

One example is when you are a doctor for people who have money.

Now, when I say *money*, I'm not talking about the ordinary kind of money, the kind you get if you go to work and your boss gives it to you. And I'm not talking either about the kind you get if your aunt dies and leaves it to you in her will. I'm talking about a completely different kind of money. I'm talking about the kind of money that, if you are a person who has only ordinary money, you can't even imagine. It's the kind of money that people like Bill Gates and Warren Buffett and Martha Stewart have. It's the kind of money that nobody should have. This kind of money can buy you a special kind of doctor. The special kind of doctor is called a Concierge Doctor.

I know it sounds like an odd name for a doctor, seeing as how a concierge is a person who lives in the hotel where you stay, and is the person who takes care of all the things that you don't have time for, like laundry and bills and getting opera tickets and looking after your children. But it fits.

If you have a Concierge Doctor, you have that doctor's personal phone, and you can call him up at any time, for anything whatsoever. And I mean *anything*. Even if you just want to know whether it's raining outside. Or suppose some Saturday afternoon you have an emergency situation. You can call him up and say,

"Oh Beach, dear"—one of the benefits of having a Concierge Doctor is that you get to call you doctor by his first name—"it's Bill. Martha and I would be ever so if you could pop over this afternoon. Say, at four-ish. There's such a horrid tingle in my tummy. With company coming, it's such a bore. And Martha has an absolutely *ghastly* hangnail. What with the pedicurist at five and the ambassador at six, we're in a bit of a stew. And if you could be a dear and bring along some of those lovely green pills of yours. I'm so so fond of them, and I do so hate to run out. Tah tah."

To those who preach its virtues, Concierge Medicine is the cat's meow of primary care—perfect for both the practitioner and the practiced upon. No interminable insurance papers for the doctor. No waiting for appointments for the patient. It is, they say, medicine at its finest. But if you are an ordinary person or an ordinary doctor, and it all sounds too good to be true, take heart. It is.

Concierge Medicine is, quite simply, a return to the past, reviving the ancient and hallowed tradition of earlier centuries, when a doctor was a luxury available only to the wealthy, and to whom he was really no more than a servant—highly valued if he was good at his trade, but no more so than an excellent cook, a fine gardener, or a skilled keeper of the hounds. Although such a relationship may now be difficult to comprehend, it was commonplace formerly for the wealthy to condescend to a physician on the simple grounds that the physician had to work for a living. And it was not uncommon, in order to ensure answering the beck and call of his masters, for that physician to actually live on the premises of those to whom he tended. So to any of my colleagues who are considering the life of a Concierge Doctor, I have a word of advice.

Don't.

You need not take my word for it, however. Should you need proof of what I say, I commend to you *Doctor Thorne*, by Anthony Trollope. It is an excellent chronicle of the life of Dr. George Thorne and his relationship to his patroness, Lady Arabella de Courcy. Then you can decide for yourself whether the rose bed upon which the doctor chose to lay himself down was that of its flower or its thorn.

Be that as it may, the preceding has nothing to do with the relationship between Fusswood and me. I am not a Concierge Doctor, and Fusswood is not wealthy. The reason that lies behind his unusual access to me is founded not on his needs, but on mine.

Until a series of events that started with a urine sample many years ago, Fusswood was a hardworking and thrifty man who managed what ailed him the same way he managed his ten-year-old pickup. Minor things like oil changes and spark plugs he would tend to himself. And a rattle here, or a shimmy there, as long as it didn't take him off the road, he generally ignored. Only when his vehicle suffered from a serious malfunction did he turn to his mechanic. Accordingly, he sought the services of his doctor rather less than I would have liked and rather more than he would have preferred. But one day he had to come in for an insurance physical. The examination included a urine test.

The urine in question showed a bit of blood. It wasn't very much blood. But it was enough. One test led to another, and eventually an uncertain something was found in his right kidney. The something, when removed along with said kidney, turned out to be a perfectly harmless piece of fat. Not surprisingly, after all was said and done, the offending blood cells were still there. Fusswood was naturally relieved to learn that he did not have cancer, and was exceedingly grateful that I had been so thorough. The loss of his kidney occasioned but a brief period of mourning. The loss of his confidence, however, was permanent. No longer was he able to trust his sense of well-being. The ordeal had convinced him that good health was illusory, that the absence of symptoms only meant that the danger was well hidden, and the slightest of hiccups was like an iceberg for his good ship *Titanic*. It was perfectly understandable. Fit as a button one might feel, but if a simple cup of pee could give the lie to this feeling, who knew what evils lurked in the depths unplumbed.

And so it was that Fusswood came to view his body in a light more favorable to my needs: a precision machine, which, in order to be kept in good running order, required regular tune-ups, and for which the slightest tremor could be the harbinger of something seriously amiss. Those who don't know better would call Fusswood a hypochondriac. But *hypochondriac* is a sobriquet we never use. Fusswood was a good customer. And as a good customer, he was ever on the alert for the latest news that might be of importance to either one of us. Fusswood was, in fact, the best of my lookouts. As such he had a special place in my practice.

Back in the middle of the nineteenth century, there lived in the town of Nottinghamshire, England, in the pit village of Market Worksop, a fellow by the name of Bill One-Hand. Although he had of necessity a mother and a father and thus presumably at some point a surname, to the best of anyone's recollection he had always been Bill One-Hand. Bill was a giant of a man, standing well over six feet tall and weighing close to three hundred pounds. So strong was he that it was said he could drive a wedge into a coal seam with one hand. Improbable as this was, the story persisted, and for the miners Bill One-Hand was a folk hero, greater for them than his better-publicized predecessor in the neighboring woods of Sherwood Forest.

But it was not for his prodigious strength that Bill One-Hand became a legend beyond his own time. Although he had no family and no friends, he did have one companion, his faithful canary Lily. Wherever Bill went, there was Lily, perched on one shoulder or the other, chirping away to her heart's content. A more unlikely pair you had never seen. She never left his side, and he was as attentive to her as a young lover to his lass. She ate with him, she slept with him, and when he went down in the mine, she accompanied him. If it had been anyone else, there would have been a spate of jokes about Bill and Lily. But no one joked about them, not to Bill's face anyway. Sure, there were always a few wags who entertained themselves behind his back with witty observations about birdbrains and being for the birds. Once, when asked by a newcomer to the pit what he was doing with "that yaller bird" on his shoulder, Bill simply replied, "I look after her, and she looks after me."

One day, when Bill was working a seam deep in the Fornsby pit, Lily stopped singing. She showed no signs of ill health, and to anyone else she would have looked just as she always did. But not to Bill. Lily always sang, especially when Bill was driving a wedge. Something about the sound of steel on coal struck her musical fancy and set her chirping away at the top of her little lungs. Bill set down his wedge and put down his bucket, and he started walking out of the mine. "Lily's not right," he said as he passed his fellow miners on the way up. Although no one said a word, more than a few smiled to themselves at the sight of a grown man giving way to the whims of a little bird. It was to be their last smile.

Methane is a colorless and odorless gas that is generated when coal is heated by compression. Because of its great depth, methane is omnipresent in deep-seam coal mines like Fornsby. When extracted and transported by pipelines as natural gas, it is an efficient and cheap source of energy. But in the mine, it is a deadly poison. It can kill you slowly by replacing the oxygen in the air, or it can finish you off in a flash, when ignited by a spark.

Which is what happened in the Fornsby Mine Disaster of 1853. Forty-seven miners lost their lives when the pit exploded. The only survivors were Bill One-Hand and Lily. Nobody ever joked again about a canary in the coal mine. And from that time on, every mine had a canary.

Eventually canaries were replaced by lamps, and then by more sophisticated devices for measuring methane levels. But the principle had been established, and some hundred years later a bright epidemiologist got the idea of using birds in a similar manner to warn people about encephalitis. Encephalitis is a serious and deadly infection of the brain, caused by a virus transmitted from the bite of a mosquito. It comes in many forms: Eastern Equine, Western Equine, Japanese, West Nile. Birds are particularly susceptible to the virus, and thus, the epidemiologist figured, by putting caged birds in strategic locations, where they would be bitten by the mosquito, and then checking their blood for evidence of the virus, health authorities would be warned as soon as the disease was in the neighborhood and would be able to take appropriate preventive measures to protect humans. The bird so employed is a chicken, perhaps because it is so readily available, and also because the chicken has a long history of sacrificing itself for the well-being of humans. The chickens so selected are called Sentinel Chickens in honor of their role as lookout for intruders who would wreak havoc on their masters.

Fusswood serves the same role for me. He is my Sentinel Patient.

14

It's Probably Nothing

···········

The evolutionary road along which physicians have traveled has been a long and tortuous one, full of quagmires, pitfalls, and all the usual obstacles of a great pilgrimage.

Historians have long debated who it was that started the journey. On historical grounds, the First Doctor was an Egyptian by the name of Imhotep. Most, however, would disqualify him for two reasons. First, doctoring was for him only a hobby, a diversion from his day job as high priest to Ra, the Sun God. Second, after he died, it turned out that he was also a god, which would give him an unfair advantage.

Most, therefore, give the nod to Hippocrates, not only because of his prolific writings, but also because he was the first person to recognize that a doctor could not live by potions alone. Just as the employer cannot exist without a worker, the teacher without a student, or the jailor without a prisoner, so did Hippocrates recognize that one could not relieve suffering unless there was a sufferer in need of relief. (The word for "suffer" in ancient Greek was *patiens*.)

I suspect, like most remarkable discoveries, this one was largely fortuitous, and I have often wondered about the circumstances that occasioned it. So I ask the reader to permit me to take a minor liberty with history and engage in a bit of fancy. I ask this indulgence on the grounds that, if not strictly factual, it will make the point much better than strict facts could ever do, having, as facts are inclined to do, a tendency completely to miss the point. I promise to be brief.

Imagine a midsummer's afternoon in Athens. The sun is high in the sky, the air is hot and dry. It is not a time to be bustling about the work of creating civilization. It is a time for rest and contemplation. Hippocrates and his friend Plato are sitting quietly under the shade of a large oak tree, just below the Acropolis.

Plato turns to Hippocrates and says, "My dear Hippocrates, I have been thinking."

"As is your wont," says Hippocrates.

"I have been thinking upon my stomach."

"In this heat, upon your back might be better."

"Ah yes," says Plato. "The meaning of words is an interesting subject in itself. It was upon the *nature* of my stomach I was thinking."

"And what have you concluded from this thinking of yours?"

"I have concluded that the stomach may not be quite itself."

"Hmmm," says Hippocrates.

Plato considers this response. Then he says, "That may well be true, my friend, but it begs the question of what is the *itself* of a stomach that it might not quite be."

"Hmmm," says Hippocrates.

"Yes," says Plato, the question apparently resolved to his satisfaction. "My stomach is definitely not as it should be."

Hippocrates raises his eyebrows, but he says nothing.

Plato raises his toga and places his index finger on a spot just below his navel. "Here," he says.

Why he does what he does next, Hippocrates does not know himself, but at the sight of the exposed abdomen, he reaches out and lays his hands precisely upon the spot indicated by Plato.

"Yes," says Plato. "There."

"Hmmm," says Hippocrates. He lets his hand linger on the spot a few moments before gently withdrawing it.

"Ah," says Plato. "My stomach, I believe, is restored to itself. And as to belief—"

"It's probably nothing," says Hippocrates.

Plato's brow furrows. "Probably. Which is more than possibly. But less than certainly. It does make one wonder."

"Hmmm," says Hippocrates.

And in that simple act, Hippocrates created, out of an old friendship, a new relationship. And with it the two principles that have stood medicine in good stead ever since.

First, *do something*. (Later on, he created a version in which *something* was replaced by *no harm*, but that was solely for public relations and was not intended to have any bearing on professional behavior.)

Second, *create doubt*.

Although it may not seem like much, at the time it was as much as he could do. Not having the faintest clue what went on in the body, or how to set it right when things went awry, the only other option was to admit our ignorance, and that was a choice that would not do at all. Imagine that you came to your doctor, and after listening attentively to your story and looking you all over, she said, "Well, whatever you got, it sure beats me. It might get better eventually. Then again, it might not. Time will tell." Needless to say, such a policy would hardly be salutary either to your faith in the doctor or the health of her practice.

Absent any science to complicate matters, the principles of treatment back then were simple. The four humors—blood, phlegm, black bile, yellow bile—controlled everything, and the goal of treatment was to maintain their proper balance by removal of whichever among them was determined to be in excess. Ordinary illness could be satisfactorily managed by bloodletting, laxative, or emetics. For the more serious cases there was strychnine and arsenic. In all instances one took special care to avoid fresh air or bathing. The general premise was that treatment was most effective when the patient felt improved by its cessation.

The most amazing thing is not that we came up with such nonsense. The most amazing thing is that we got away with it for so long. Until 1910 to be precise.

By the beginning of the twentieth century, thanks to Harvey, we knew that blood circulated, and thanks to Pasteur that germs caused infections, and thanks to Lister that sterile technique would prevent them. Furthermore, surgeons had the ability to put a patient to sleep before sawing away, and medical doctors had a few drugs that actually did some good. So the time was ripe to give it a go at shaping up. Which was a good thing. Because in 1908 the Council on Medical Education of the AMA asked the Carnegie Foundation to evaluate the quality of medical education in America. The job was given to a professor at the Rockefeller Institute by the name of Abraham Flexner. Flexner did an in-depth study of the one hundred and fifty-five medical schools and two years later published a book-length report, which said, in essence, "You gotta be kidding."

As a result, the worst of the medical schools were shut down, and the best set about making medicine legitimate. And by and large we have succeeded. But it's hard to abandon a hallowed tradition. So you can still find here and there traces of the old humbuggery—like irritable bowel syndrome for one. And fibromyalgia for another.

And CRP.

Every year the drug companies, Big Pharma as they are known, get together to congratulate themselves on what a good job they have done helping people and to figure out how they can help them even more. Everybody comes, presidents, vice presidents, executive assistants, scientists, marketers, lawyers, salespeople, and doctors. The doctors who work for Big Pharma are not the kind you might go to if you had a pain in your chest or a defective knee. These doctors are much smarter than those doctors. These doctors have graduated at the top of their class in medical school, and they have been the top residents in their training programs. They have had long distinguished careers in research at the best medical centers. They work for the drug companies because they want to do even more to help people than they have already done. And to make an obscene amount of money.

One year recently the meeting focused on a set of drugs known as statins. These drugs lower cholesterol, and they do such a good job at it that people who take them can eat whatever they want and still have less risk of a heart attack than someone who lives on bean sprouts and celery sticks. They are good drugs, and Big Pharma is rightly proud of them. But they have their limits. Unlike a really blockbuster drug, like Prozac or Valium, doctors only prescribe these drugs for people who actually need them. If you don't have high cholesterol, you don't get the drug. Now, the cardiologists, who are well represented in Big Pharma, have done their part each year, by making it harder and harder not to have high cholesterol, but there are still millions of people for whom statins are just not on the menu.

"It doesn't seem right," said someone at the meeting. "I mean, these drugs are so good. Shouldn't everybody be taking them?" And everyone agreed that they should. So the conversation turned to the question of "How do we get them to do it?"

Someone suggested that maybe the cardiologists could lower the standards for cholesterol again, making them so low as to guarantee that no one would pass. The cardiologists said they weren't at liberty to release their new cholesterol rules just yet, but they hinted that if everyone were just a little patient, they might see their goal reached eventually. But someone in marketing pointed out that the problem with waiting is that by the time they got to zero cholesterol tolerance, the patents would have expired, and then what would be the point.

A woman from advertising had a bright idea. "Forget about cholesterol," she said. "Tell people it will make them more attractive."

The scientists pointed out that although with enough time they could whip up some evidence to suggest that the pills might do that, they didn't have any at present.

"But neither does beer," said the woman from advertising.

Then the lawyers explained that the Truth in Advertising rules for prescription drugs were a lot stricter than they were for alcohol.

There were a few more harebrained suggestions, but none of them got anywhere, until one of the doctors spoke up and said, "What about CRP?"

"CRP?" they all said. "Never heard of it."

"My point precisely."

And he went on to explain the story of CRP.

Back in 1930, two researchers at the Rockefeller Institute, William S. Tillett and Thomas Francis Jr., were studying people with pneumonia. They were looking for something they could write a paper on, since papers were what kept your paycheck coming at their institute. They had already found two unusual blood proteins and they had written several papers about them, but that well was getting pretty dry. They weren't having much luck, and were about to give up on pneumonia proteins, when one day another one turned up. Since it wasn't either the first protein, which they had called A, or the second protein, known as B, they decided, with the kind of imagination only a scientist can have, to call it the C protein. The full name was C-reactive protein, CRP for short. They wrote a paper describing CRP. And pretty soon CRP became the talk of the town for scientists who needed to write papers.

In no time flat scientists everywhere were writing papers about CRP. They wrote about CRP in patients who had syphilis. They wrote about CRP in patients who had cancer. They wrote about CRP in patients who had heart attacks. They even wrote about CRP in patients who had rheumatism. It seemed anyone who was sick had CRP. After they were done with all the sick people they could think of, they started checking healthy ones. Most of them didn't have CRP. But some did. Nobody knew quite what to make of CRP in a healthy person, but that wasn't a problem for scientists. They could write a paper about that too.

(I order a CRP sometimes. I'm not proud of it. It violates the basic rule about testing, namely if you don't know what you are going to do with the results of the test, you shouldn't order it. Of course, included in knowing-what-to-do-with-it is the option "pocket the money"—if you happen to own the test. But we all do silly things when we are desperate, and so, if I am particularly stumped by a complaint, I order a CRP. If the CRP is normal, I tell the patient, "Maybe you're not that sick after all." If it's high, I'll tell them we have to get more tests. It doesn't really tell me much, but it does buy me some time. I never tell the patient about the CRP itself, on the outside chance that she might say, "What's a CRP?" That would put me in the unfortunate situation of having to tell the patient that I don't know.)

The Big Pharma doctor knew full well that a high CRP doesn't really tell you anything. But he also knew that it didn't matter. He reasoned, correctly it turned out, that if you gave a statin to someone who had a completely normal cholesterol but a high CRP, you would reduce their chances of having a heart attack. Not because you were treating the CRP, but because anytime you give a statin, you lower the risk of a heart attack, *regardless of what the cholesterol is to begin with*. Nobody is exactly sure why this is so, but it is.

So he did a study. He gave statins to people with normal cholesterols and high CRPs, and, as he expected, the people who got the pill had fewer heart attacks than those who didn't.

Naturally, he told the press about it right off the bat. *Good Morning America*, CNN, and *The New York Times* all picked it up. *Too Much Considered* was on it like a dog on a bone.

I try to keep up with the latest in medicine. I read my journals regularly, and I suffer through medical meetings in the heat of Palm

Beach or Cancun. But I have to work for a living. And I can't spend the whole day with my ear glued to the radio or the TV. So in order not to appear a complete nitwit to my patients, I rely on my Sentinel Patient. I know that whenever there is some late-breaking medical news, he will be on the phone before anyone else. He gives me the time I need to scurry about and find out what is going on before the other calls start pouring in.

By the time Fusswood had arrived, I had read the article and was ready for him. The study in question involved two thousand healthy people. One thousand took a statin. One thousand took a placebo. Four of those who took the statin had a heart attack; eight who took the placebo had one. Which meant, the study was pleased to point out, that the statin reduced the number of heart attacks by 50 percent. "Cut them in half," the press proclaimed with much hoop-de-do. Being newspeople, they naturally are more interested in making news than in discovering truth. And if the press wasn't going to ask, the drug companies certainly weren't going to tell them. About *The Catch*. It goes by the statistical name of Number Needed to Treat, although I prefer to call it by its street name, Some Other Lucky Dude.

"So, Doc," Fusswood said anxiously. "Where's my pills?"

"All in due time, Fusswood. All in due time. First I have a couple of questions."

"Fire away, Doc."

"Would you consider yourself a generous person?"

"Well—er—I would like to think so. I mean, it all depends, doesn't it, on what you mean by generous?"

"Do you do unto others as you would have them do unto you?"

"I try."

"Do you believe that to each according to his needs, and from each according to his abilities?"

"Sure, within limits. I mean, I'm not a communist."

"Of course not. And would you say it is better to give than to receive?"

"I would."

"In that case, you're the perfect candidate for the pills."

I started to write out his prescription.

"Wait," said Fusswood.

"Yes?"

"What was all that about?"

"All what?"

"All that stuff about being generous."

"I had to know before I could write your prescription."

"What does generous have to do with my taking a pill so I don't get a heart attack?"

"It's about SOLD."

"Sold to who?"

"Not sold *to* anyone, Fusswood. S-O-L-D. It's an acronym. The pills you take won't help you. They will be for the benefit of *Some Other Lucky Dude*."

"I don't get it."

"It's simple. Although the study is correct that the risk of a heart attack was cut in half, that risk is a *relative* risk. Have I ever told you the story about the—"

"Yeah, yeah, I know," interrupted Fusswood. "The Farmer and the Preacher. Only about a hundred times. What does that have to do with the price of beans in Poughkeepsie?"

"Here's what it has to do with you. The people taking placebo had eight heart attacks. The people taking the statin had four. Half of eight is four. That is a fifty percent reduction, as claimed. But that's a *relative* reduction. The total *number* of heart attacks it prevented was four: eight minus four is four. Which means that out of the thousand people who took the statin, it only prevented four heart attacks. So the true rate of reduction of heart attacks was four in a thousand, or one in two hundred and fifty."

"Which means what?"

"Which means that two hundred and forty-nine people had to take the pill in order for Some Other Lucky Dude not to have a heart attack."

"You're saying most of the people would be taking the pill for some-one else?"

"Precisely."

"The side effects, does that go for them too?"

"No. You get full rights to side effects."

"Like the muscle damage."

"And the liver. Don't forget that."

"Well," he said slowly. "On second thought, Doc, maybe I'll wait on this. If you think it's okay, that is."

"Your wish is my command, Fusswood."

15

First Man

....

Adam Fairbrother is a troublemaker.

It isn't intentional. On the contrary, ask anybody in town, and that person will agree that when it comes to being thoughtful and considerate, Adam Fairbrother is as good as they get. And he doesn't make trouble for most people. Only for me, his doctor.

Adam Fairbrother was born and raised in Dumster. His grandfather owned Fairbrother's Feed and Grain, and when his grandfather retired, his father took it over. It was generally expected that as an only child, Adam would follow in his father's footsteps. It was with that intent that he went off to the university in Burlington after graduating from Dumster High. But in his first semester he was seduced by a course in introductory animal sciences, and he transferred to the College of Arts and Sciences to become a biology major. Four years later he left Burlington and returned to Dumster. In his possession were a bachelor of science degree, summa cum laude, a high school biology teaching certificate, and a history major by the name of Merriam Starkweather. That was thirty-five years ago and, except for some brief interruptions on Merriam's part for her three children, they both have been teaching at Dumster High ever since.

Every other year the Best Teacher Award given by the graduating class goes to Mr. Fairbrother. The alternate years belong to Mrs. Fairbrother. Should you ask any Dumster High graduate what they thought of him, even the most devout academiphobe would agree that he was a great teacher. What he actually taught them, they couldn't quite say, but that didn't signify. In the words of Albert Nutting, who, before he left school at the age of sixteen to work on the family garbage truck, had taken Mr. Fairbrother's freshman biology three times and could, therefore, fairly be considered an authority on the subject: "Can't rightly say as I got any bology in me, but if'n I did, it'd be Mr. Fairbrother's."

The most respected citizen in any Vermont town is not the richest. Nor is it the most powerful. Neither is it a doctor, minister, or the chair of the board of selectmen. That privilege is reserved for the person who holds the position that represents the greatest honor a town can bestow on a citizen. It is the position of town moderator. For as long as anyone can remember, that position has been held by Adam Fairbrother. It is no coincidence, the townspeople say, that his name is Adam. He is Dumster's First Man.

Fair but firm, and always respectful of an opinion, no matter how outrageous, he has a way of defusing the most contentious of arguments and terminating the fiercest of harangues in a manner that leaves all parties convinced he has seen the merits of their case. "I wish never to give offense to any person," he said once in ending a long and particularly acrimonious debate between the Sanders and the Salters on the winter maintenance of Clay Hill Road. "But especially, I do not wish to give offense to the truth."

Which is why he causes me trouble. For although it is certainly true that, in most life situations, being thoughtful and considerate is a distinct advantage, when it comes to the situation of the doctor and the patient, it can become a bit of a sticky wicket. It's not that I mind if my patients are thinking. I just prefer that they think like me. And Adam tries. It's just that sometimes—well, take for example when he came to see me recently for his regular checkup.

"Good morning, Doctor Conger."

"Good morning, Adam."

"How is the good doctor today?"

Since when Adam Fairbrother asks, it is because he actually wants to know, I told him.

"Not too bad, considering," I said. "But my hip is reminding me that I'm not as young as I used to be. And it seems to take a little longer now to get to the end of the day."

"I'm sorry to hear that. Is it perhaps time for you to start slowing down?"

"Oh, I'm already slowing down. It is perhaps time for me to start recognizing it."

"Funny, isn't it? That the age at which you can't do what you used to, and the age at which you know that you can't, don't always match up."

"No, they don't, do they?"

"These days I find that I prefer to look at it from the point of view that although I am older than I once was, right now I'm as young as I'll ever be."

"An admirable philosophy."

"Usually. Shall we see if it survives your inspection."

· "Indeed we shall," I said. "Which brings us to the question of how Mr. Fairbrother is doing."

"Well," he said. "I enjoy my students. Merriam and the girls are in excellent health. And a lovely day like this still makes me feel that it is a privilege to be alive. As to how I am doing, however, that is up to you to determine."

I ran through the litany of a doctor's how-are-yous. The eyes were seeing. The ears were hearing. And the nose smelled as well as could be hoped. The lungs were able to perform adequately what they had to do, and there was no attendant complaint from the heart. The bowels moved satisfactorily, the bladder perhaps just a bit less so, and the moving parts got through an ordinary day without either giving out when needed most, or complaining during the hours of sleep.

All in all, he did quite well on this part of his examination. But passing the Review of Systems is generally a relatively easy task for most patients, and it is made even easier by the tendency, among those not as scrupulous as Adam Fairbrother, not so much to lie outright as to minimize or, should need arise, overlook altogether an occasional malfunction of the mechanism.

But the quest for Good Health, like that of Jason for his Golden Fleece, consists of three trials, each one successively harder than that which precedes it. They are: the Review of Systems, the Physical Examination, and the Tests. Few indeed are those fortunate enough to pass all three. And at the risk of mixing my mythological metaphors, the Three Trials could fairly be considered Sisyphean, for even if one succeeds in rolling the rock up to the top of the Health Maintenance Mountain, it is to no avail. For each year he will find that same rock before him back at the bottom, waiting to be pushed up again. And so it will be year after year, until finally the rock is too heavy for his aging limbs, and it rolls back on him and bowls him over.

"Let's see how your blood pressure is doing," I said, commencing the Examination.

Two years ago, Adam Fairbrother's systolic blood pressure had been in the middle one thirties. Once it reached one hundred and forty. Without urging, he had eschewed salt, taken up the habit of walking the two miles to and from school each day, and lost twenty pounds. His blood pressure improved commensurately. Today it was one hundred and twenty-nine over eighty.

"I must be doing something right," he said. "That's better than last year."

"I'm afraid it's worse."

"I don't understand. I looked at my records before coming in today. The reading last year was one hundred and thirty-two over eighty-two."

"Indeed it was."

"And this year it is one hundred and twenty-nine over eighty."

"It is."

"Which by my reckoning would be lower on each front."

"By yours, it would."

"And by yours?"

"A bit high."

"So-o," he said, slowly. "What you are telling me is that my lower is your higher."

"I am."

He was silent for a moment. Then he said, "There would seem to be two possible explanations. As to the first, that the laws of arithmetic have been overturned in this examination room—to the best of my knowledge—has not occurred. That would leave only the second."

"The Farmer's Wife."

"Ah," he said, "you remember."

"It's hard not to."

"I suppose it is my favorite. Although I'm also partial to Farmer God."

"As are many in town."

At the start of each town meeting, it is Adam Fairbrother's custom to relate one of the parables of the Farmer and the Preacher. It helps to lend a lighter note to the proceedings, and it serves to remind all present that the moderator favors plain speaking over preaching, the practical over the pompous. In my thirty-some town meetings, I must have heard the parable of the Farmer's Wife at least a dozen times and almost as often the parable of Farmer God. The farmers were particularly fond of the latter. It goes like this.

> The preacher stops by to visit the farmer. He looks over the sleek cows, the well-tended fields, and the tall stalks of ripening corn.
>
> Preacher: It's a wonderful thing what Man can do when he and God are working together.
>
> Farmer: You should have seen the place when God was working it by himself.

"And so my blood pressure today, Doctor Conger, is elevated *relative to what?*"

"One hundred and twenty over seventy."

"That is a tough standard to meet."

"Very."

"It appears that the standard is getting tougher each year."

"It does."

"If you don't mind my asking, Doctor Conger, exactly how does the profession arrive at these standards?"

"It's up to the cardiologists. Every year they all get together in some quiet place. And the first thing they do is to count up all the cardiologists. Then they count up the number of patients belonging to the cardiologists. And if it appears that there is an imbalance between the two, they adjust the desirable blood pressure and cholesterol levels in order to restore that balance."

"Not by decreasing the number of cardiologists, I'd guess."

"No."

"By increasing the number of patients."

"Correct. Cardiology is a very popular career choice these days, and they've had to ratchet down quite a bit on both fronts. Future standards are a closely guarded secret, but I have seen a draft of their five-year plan. Without giving you any details, I can pretty much promise you that eventually it will be impossible for anyone to pass."

"Are you serious, Doctor Conger?"

I raised my eyebrows but said nothing.

"Excuse me, Doctor Conger," he apologized. "I never should have asked."

"That's okay," I said. "It still happens sometimes. Even among people who know me."

"It is understandable, you know. After all, you *are* a doctor."

"Yes," I admitted. "That does complicate matters."

"At any rate, you can at least tell me what this blood pressure means."

"It means you have essential hypertension."

"Essential?"

"Yes."

"Is that as in essential for *you*, or essential for me?"

"A good question."

I always compliment my patients on the quality of their questions. It is reassuring to them and salutary to the give-and-take of our relationship. And because years of experience have taught me *how* to answer every question even if I don't know *what* the answer is, it carries no risk.

"It would be the latter. The term comes from the days when we believed that whatever the blood pressure was, it was essential to guarantee adequate blood flow to the brain and, as such, was something that under no circumstances should be tampered with."

"That must have been a long time ago."

"That's all relative."

"Of course. What year would that have been?"

"As recently as the nineteen fifties."

"Not very long, then."

"No. But at that time being a doctor wasn't nearly so popular, what with being up at the bedside all night and no health insurance to guarantee a steady source of income. So that the few doctors there were kept themselves pretty busy taking care of the sick. We didn't have much time for the not-yet-sick."

"Not perhaps the wisest policy."

"It wasn't. And it killed one of our presidents. FDR died of a brain hemorrhage that could easily have been prevented. 'It came out of a clear blue sky,' his doctor said. But the morning of his death he had a terrible headache. His blood pressure was two hundred and fifty over one hundred and forty."

"Goodness gracious!"

He fell silent for several moments. When he spoke next, it was with some hesitation.

"Do you mind if I ask you a personal question, Doctor Conger?"

"Not at all." This question comes up from time to time, and I have a strict policy always to allow it. To do otherwise would be a violation of the basic trust that forms the basis of the doctor–patient relationship. It's not really a problem. As is invariably the case in any instance where my telling the truth as it actually is would tend to put a strain on our relationship, I tell rather the truth as it ought to be.

"What is *your* blood pressure?"

"Mine?"

"Yes. I believe we are about the same age. And I would assume you take your blood pressure on a regular basis."

"Well, uh, of course I do," I stammered. And I did. Although not as regularly as I used to. Of late, the readings had been not particularly rewarding.

"And, if I might pursue this a bit farther, is yours running in the one twenty over seventy range?"

Maybe it was a sign of weakness in my old age. Maybe it was because it was Adam Fairbrother. Whatever the reason, I told him.

"Not quite."

"Even though you exercise regularly?"

"I always have."

"And you stay away from salt?"

"Avoid it like the plague."

"So I would assume that you are taking something for your blood pressure?"

"Actually, yes. In fact, I just started."

"On what, if I might ask?"

"Well, of course, my case is a little different from yours."

"So I would assume, Doctor Conger. You have always impressed me with the importance of the individuality of each case, and the need to tailor treatment accordingly. My question was in your particular individual case, what it is you are taking for your blood pressure."

"Ah. Well, understand then, with that caveat—"

"Understood."

"And that it doesn't necessarily follow that this treatment would apply to anyone else."

"Naturally."

"I am taking chocolate."

"Chocolate?"

"Yes. Two ounces of dark chocolate every day."

Adam raised his eyebrows. "Two ounces of chocolate. That's all you do for your blood pressure?"

"Dark chocolate."

"Excuse me, dark chocolate. But that's all?"

"Heavens no. That wouldn't be nearly enough."

"What else, then?"

"I also have one cup of cocoa every morning, and one cup before I go to bed."

"I see. Well, that *is* different."

"As I said, each case . . ."

"Yes, but why chocolate?"

"I like chocolate."

"I mean, why chocolate for your blood pressure?"

"Because it is the treatment recommended by Jeanne Louise Calment."

"Who is a researcher on the medicinal value of chocolate in the treatment of hypertension?'

"In a sense."

"In what sense."

"If you would allow me to tell you a story."

"Please do."

16

Sometimes in Life You Make Bad Decisions

···········

"Once upon a time."
"Ah, that kind of story."

There lived in the South of France, in Provence, in the town of Arles, a woman by the name of Jeanne Louise Calment. She lived by herself in a pretty little cottage on a quiet street on the outskirts of town. It was not far from the home of the most famous citizen of Arles, Vincent van Gogh. Although not an artist herself, Madame Calment was on friendly terms with the painter, and rumor had it that it was even *very* friendly terms. This, by itself, would have made her an interesting person. But it is not the reason that she has become famous. That she has done in her own right.

Madame Calment lived in one of those picturesque eighteenth-century stone houses so common in the South of France. It had a moss-covered tiled roof, thick oak shutters, and a balcony on the second floor that looked out over the street. Hanging over the balcony was a row of window boxes filled with geraniums. There was a cobblestone path leading up to the front door bordered with wisteria. In the back was a stone patio and a formal garden. It was one of those places that people who were passing through Arles, though they had neither the time nor the inclination to learn anything about the town, went to take a picture of so they could show it to people back home and tell them what a delightful place Arles was.

Madame Calment was quite proud of her home. There was hardly a day when she couldn't be seen outside, puttering about happily among the flowers and the bushes. Everyone in town agreed that her home was a very nice home. Especially a lawyer by the name of André-François Raffrey. One day attorney Raffrey asked Jeanne Louise if she would be interested in selling her house.

"But Monsieur François," she told him. "I am living in it myself."

"Yes," he said, or rather, being French, "*Oui. Je comprends.* And I would not wish you to leave your lovely home. But I am so fond of it. If you are interested, I will make you a deal."

Jeanne Louise was not the kind of a woman to refuse a deal, if it was a sound one.

"I am interested," she said. "Tell me."

"*D'accord*," said Monsieur Raffray. "You will continue to stay in your lovely home for as long as you live. I will pay you twenty-five hundred francs a month, starting today. When you die, I will become the owner of the house."

Madame Calment thought this over. She had no children, and her nearest relative was a cousin in Paris who had no interest in ever living in the country. She thought to herself, *Why not?* And not being able to come up with a good reason to refuse twenty-five hundred francs a month, starting that day, she agreed.

Lawyer Raffrey was a pretty shrewd fellow. He figured it was a good deal for him too. At the time, Jeanne Louise Calment was eighty years old. If she lived another ten or even fifteen years, it would cost him only four hundred fifty thousand francs for the house. Back in 1955, this was a pretty good price for such a nice home. Lawyer Raffrey was only forty years old, and he hoped to live into his eighties, as had most of his relatives. In which case, he would have the house to enjoy for many years before he died.

Lawyer Raffrey was pretty close to right. He lived forty-two years, and he died at the ripe old age of eighty-two.

Madame Calment also lived a long time. She lived forty-two and one-half years to the extremely ripe old age of one hundred and twenty-two years and five months. She was, when she died, the oldest person ever, and it would appear that she is in no immediate danger of relinquishing that record, as her nearest current competitor, Besse Cooper, cannot surpass her until February 17, 2019.

After lawyer Raffrey died, they asked Madame Calment about the deal. "Well," she said. "Sometimes in life, you make bad decisions."

As the oldest living human, Madame Calment was the subject of considerable attention. People wanted to know the secret to her longevity. They were particularly interested in what she ate, and what she drank, and how she lived her days. As you would expect, Madame Calment did all those things one would want to hear in exhorting others to live a lifestyle conducive to a long and healthy life. She went for a walk every day regardless of the weather. She ate fish every Monday, Wednesday, and Saturday—when it came in fresh from Marseilles. Of course she cooked only with olive oil. And she had a glass of red wine with every meal, sometimes two. And, she told them, she didn't smoke.

"Never?" they asked, because they knew how much the French liked their Gauloises.

"Well, I used to, but I gave it up."

"Ah," they said. "When was that?"

She paused. "It was a long time ago."

"A long time?" said one of the reporters. (She was not from Vermont.) "But how old were you?"

"About one hundred, *je pense*. My arthritis." She showed them her gnarled hands. "I could not hold them anymore."

This was pretty disappointing news. The walking every day and the olive oil and the fish and red wine were all okay, although they weren't anything that special. But the bit about smoking was definitely a downer. It was not at all the kind of thing one could put in an article in *Good Housekeeping* under a title like "Jeanne Calment's Ten Secrets to Living Forever," number seven: smoke until one hundred. So the reporters asked her wasn't there anything else. Some personal philosophy, for example, that she could give to all those people who were trying so hard to live forever.

Jeanne Louise thought for a moment. "I am not a philosopher," she said. "Better you should ask Camus."

"But he is dead," they said.

"Well then, ask Sartre."

"He is dead too."

"Both of them?" she said. "*Voilà*. It just goes to show."

"To show what?"

"Ahhh, never mind."

"Please," they said. "There must be something you can tell us to write down for all the people who want to know the secret to your extraordinarily long life."

Jeanne Louise thought for a moment. "Well," she said. "*Peut-être,* there are two things."

And they all got their pencils ready.

"First, I never worry about anything I can't change."

And they all wrote down: *never worries.*

"Second, I eat two pieces of chocolate every night."

And they all wrote down: *eats chocolate.*

Then off they went to their papers and their magazines and their radio stations and their TV networks and told the world the secrets of Jeanne Louise Calment.

"Which is how I found out about the chocolate," I explained.

"That's it? Just because of one person's story, you are treating your blood pressure with chocolate? Forgive me, Doctor Conger, but that kind of evidence hardly seems your style."

"You're right," I said. "There's a bit more to it than that. The longer I have practiced, the more I have realized that this whole business of taking healthy people and giving them pills that make them miserable, in order to treat conditions that never bothered them, may not always be the best policy."

"Getting, perhaps, a little close to home at this point?" said Adam.

"I have also noticed," I continued, choosing to consider the question rhetorical, "as a result of this approach, many of my patients are now relying more on these so-called natural remedies."

"And less on your prescriptions?"

"It made me think that I should look into the subject."

"On the premise that if you can't lick 'em, join 'em."

"So I started reading about pomegranate juice and blueberries and green tea, and all those polyphenol-antioxidants of which the naturalists are so fond. I discovered that the food with the highest concentration of them all is chocolate. I like chocolate, so that was an appealing finding. But if I was actually going to recommend it to anyone . . ."

"You needed more than the testimonial of an old lady."

"Right. Fortunately, there is quite a bit of research on the subject. Especially in Dutchmen."

"Why Dutchmen?"

"They drink cocoa. The researchers have discovered that the more cocoa a Dutchman drinks, the less likely he is to have a heart attack."

"That's something."

"That's not all. He will also have a lower blood pressure."

"Which is why you recommend chocolate."

"That, and the fact that it tastes better than pomegranates."

"Even if we're not Dutchmen."

"The way I figure it, you can never be sure. Take me for example. My ancestors go back to sixteen twenty-five, when a Conger named John married a Sarah Cawood in Woodbridge, New Jersey. There is no record of any Congers anywhere in the country before that. It was as if Congers suddenly materialized out of thin air. There was, however, a fellow by the name of John Belconger from Boston who had the same birth date as John Conger. This Belconger had emigrated from Great Yarmouth, England, with his wife, Mary, in sixteen twenty-four. And then a year later he disappeared, never to be heard from again. Assuming that Belconger did a runner to Conger, I traced the Belcongers back. They were eel catchers, and they came across the channel from the mainland as Belkongers sometime in the fourteenth century."

"From Holland?"

"Seems likely. So, you never know. You could even be a little in Dutch yourself."

"Clever. But tell me, how are the chocolate and cocoa working on your blood pressure?"

"It's too early to tell. I just started."

We talked about it a little more, and Adam agreed to try my regimen. He would return in two weeks, and we would compare notes.

Two weeks later he came back. He had dutifully been eating his chocolate every evening, and found it a most satisfactory treatment. I took his blood pressure. Just to be sure, I waited ten minutes and took it again.

"It's exactly the same, one twenty-nine over eighty."

Fairbrother looked discouraged. "How about you, Doctor Conger?" he asked.

"Same for me," I admitted.

"Oh dear," said Adam. "Maybe we need more chocolate."

I didn't say anything.

"Or maybe we need to add pomegranate juice."

Just the thought made my mouth pucker. "There is one alternative." I took out my prescription pad.

Adam Fairbrother looked disappointed.

"I was hoping to avoid pills."

I wrote out two prescriptions and handed him one. I put the other in my pocket. He looked at his and smiled. "Ah," he said. "Calment Number One."

Don't worry about it, the prescription read.

17

It's Not a Tumor

···········

Sunrise Holbode looked a fright. Her normally rosy cheeks were the color of three-week-old snow. Her hair looked like burdock gone wild. She had deep lines in her forehead I had never seen before, and she appeared to have lost considerable weight. Despite the fact that it was a warm summer day, she was huddled up in her winter fleece, which hung upon her like a shroud. As I entered the room, she shivered at the slight draft created by the opening of the door. Looking old and sick, she bore no resemblance to the young woman who was the picture of health when I first met her.

Admittedly, that was over thirty years ago, but until today she had seemed not to have aged a day. It was standard between us, whenever we met, to compliment each other on how well we had retained our appearances—a polite fiction on her part, but true enough on mine—attributing it jokingly to the years we had each spent in Berkeley. Although we had been there at the same time and had frequented many of the same haunts, we had not met until we each made our emigration to Vermont, I to stamp out pestilence as a country doctor and she to live off the land she inherited from her grandfather, a camp with twenty acres just off the end of Steddsville Road. Sunrise had converted the camp into a sheep barn, and she had erected next to it a large yurt, in which she lived simply but comfortably with her two dogs, Ying and Yang. Despite her isolation, she did not want for company. There was a never-ending assortment of hangers-on who would appear from time to time in various states of decrepitude. They would stay at the homestead until, having been restored by the nutritious offerings of Sunrise's table, they became restive at the work involved in putting it there and moved on to their next way station in life.

She needs to see a doctor, I thought. And then I realized that was exactly what she was doing.

"Hello, Sunrise," I said, unable to bring myself to add our customary, *You're-looking-younger-than-ever* greeting and reluctant to ask *How are you?*

Sunrise looked at me listlessly.

"Hello, Beach," she said.

It may seem that for Sunrise to address me by my first name is not quite according to Hoyle, but I assure you that it was okay. Although it is true that Sunrise was not one of that class of people who are so wealthy that they have always been on a first-name basis with everyone, including not only their doctor but also, I would guess, although I have never had the opportunity to observe such in person, their teachers, their lawyers, their ministers, and, should the occasion arise, their presidents and popes. But because we were both alumni of the Berkeley Free Clinic, where not only were doctors and patients on a first-name basis, but the latter were accorded reciprocal examination privilege upon the former, she was accorded the privilege on my part without hesitation or misgiving.

After an awkward silence, I asked the question to which I already knew the answer.

"How do you feel?"

"Awful."

"What's the matter?"

"Everything."

I have learned after many a mistaken interrogation that sometimes it is best not to ask too much. A patient who comes in is a patient who wants to tell her story. And usually it is best just to wait and let her do that. With Sunrise, I didn't have to wait long.

"I just don't feel . . . right. I ache all over, but that's not the problem. I always ache—all day, every day. I know that's just my fibromyalgia, and I can live with that. I know if I just pace myself, I can get through the day okay. I just have to remember to rest, you know."

I did. However, I have to say, with all due respect to fibromyalgia, which is certainly no shy maiden when it comes to disability, Sunrise's pacing herself consisted of a day that started around five in the morning and ended long after dark, and included milking her goats, feeding her sheep, tending her garden, weaving her cloth, making her cheese, and the usual lugging and trudging and scurrying about that comes of having a farm with a farmhand of one. And at least up to this point, I had seen no evidence that her condition had in any way slowed her down.

"But this is different," she said. "It all started this spring, when I was sugaring. I dropped a sap bucket, just out of the blue. Well, that happens sometimes. You slip in the snow, or the bucket is too heavy. But then it happened again the next day, and I hadn't slipped, and the bucket was hardly half full. After that my right foot would go numb sometimes, and I started to feel a little dizzy in the morning, and sometimes my eyes were blurry. And at night my legs would twitch, for no reason at all. Just like I was a puppet, and someone had jerked the strings. And then I started getting these funny headaches that would start behind my right ear and shoot over to my left eye. And things go all wobbly from time to time."

"Wobbly?"

"Yes, you know, when you're trying hard to focus on something, like threading a needle, and then all of a sudden everything starts to . . . wobble."

"Ah. That kind of wobbly."

"But that isn't the worst of it. Two weeks ago, it was time for the dogs to come in for supper. One came right away, but the other was still out. I could see him plain as day. And I called to him, 'Ying, come in here.' And he just stared at me, funny like."

"Because it was Yang?"

"It was. And they don't look at all alike, you know. And then I started having these weird dreams at night, and then I'd wake up and hear this awful noise. *Grnnch, grnnch, grnnch,* it went. Like some giant machine grinding its gears. And then last night I woke up and saw this bird. It was a giant bird, black, like a vulture, and it was just hovering up there looking down at me, as if . . . Well, you know what vultures look for. I got up and turned on the light, and of course, there was nothing there. But I wasn't dreaming. I know I wasn't," she said in a frightened voice. "I'm losing my mind, Beach." And she burst into tears.

Customarily at this point I would ask a series of pointed questions designed further to elucidate her symptoms, perform a physical examination to uncover any abnormalities, and then discuss the possible diagnoses. But not with Sunrise.

"What is it this time, Sunrise?" I asked.

"Well," she said slowly. "With a negative test last week, I don't think it could be Lyme disease."

"Or AIDS." I said.

"Don't be silly," said Sunrise. "I couldn't have AIDS."

"No, of course you couldn't," I said. "I forgot for a minute that I wasn't in Philadelphia anymore."

When presented with symptoms that are sufficiently protean in their nature that they fail to point the way to an afflicted organ, one item that physicians will always consider from among their diagnostic repertoire is an infection of the smoldering and surreptitious variety.

For centuries past, and also, to a lesser degree, when I was in Boston and San Francisco, that infection was tuberculosis. There is no tuberculosis in Dumster. Here the lurking culprit is Lyme disease, an infection transmitted from deer to man by the bite of a tick. If recognized, it can easily be cured by brief treatment with a single antibiotic.

There were no deer in Other Philadelphia, and the predominant form of insect life was the cockroach, which, although repulsive to look at, does not transmit disease. At William Penn, the disease that one considered in these situations did not come from the bite of a tick. It came from the stick of a needle. And it didn't really matter how quickly one made the diagnosis, because the best that could be hoped for was that, with a perpetual menagerie of ever-changing antibiotics, it would progress only slowly.

The odd thing is that when patients who had AIDS were admitted to William Penn, it was always *with* the disease rather than *because of* it. For them AIDS was just another of the vicissitudes of life, unpleasant enough, but not really any worse than the poverty or the violence, or the general air of hopelessness that permeated the air they breathed. So they came into the hospital with the same ordinary afflictions that keep all hospitals afloat: heart trouble, emphysema, diabetes, strokes, kidney failure. Only they came in more often and much earlier than at Emmeline Talbot. At Emmeline Talbot most hospitalized patients are well into their seventies, and many are much older. At William Penn, fifty was old.

"And I doubt that it's multiple sclerosis," said Sunrise.

"Not that either."

"Although maybe we should check again. Just to make sure."

"I'd rather not," I said.

Along with her tests for Lyme disease, Sunrise had undergone several MRIs of her brain in the past few years. Although she was tested more frequently than most, her story was not at all unusual. Not Lyme Disease and Not Multiple Sclerosis were common conditions these days. Especially among the health-conscious.

"It could be a brain tumor."

"Sunrise!"

"Yes?"

"*It's not a tumor.*"

"Very funny," she said, unsmiling. "But it could be."

"No, it couldn't."

"How can you be sure?" she said indignantly. "You could be wrong, you know?"

It wouldn't be fair to say that the how-can-you-be-sures have been the bane of my existence, because they certainly have been a boon to business. But they certainly make my work harder. It used to be that if someone came to the office with a headache, I would listen to their story, and I would examine them, and then I would say they didn't have a brain tumor, and they would say thank goodness and go home. But that was before the Age of Expectations. Which, I would remind the president's minions, on the off chance that any of them might be reading this, is why all this talk of reducing costs by eliminating unnecessary tests is just so much carwash. These days I hardly ever see a patient who doesn't want to have a test to rule out the possibility of a condition that he doesn't have.

"Yes, I could be wrong. But I'm not. Consider this. Suppose you are out walking in the woods some night in the middle of winter, and you hear an animal up in the trees calling something that sounds like *who-cooks-for-you, who-cooks-for-you*. What would you say?"

"I would say it's the big barred owl that lives in the old dead oak tree just behind the barn, and it's the start of breeding season."

"But couldn't it be a robin?"

"Don't be silly."

"How can you be sure?"

"Well, in the first place, it doesn't sound anything like a robin, and in the second, you would never hear a . . . Oh," she said quietly. "So, I suppose you wouldn't want to order an MRI."

"To compare with the one you had in April?"

"I guess not. I didn't really think it was a brain tumor anyway."

"Your heart didn't seem in it."

"I just think it's important to consider all the possibilities."

"Good point."

"Besides, I think it's more serious than that," she said.

"More serious than a brain tumor?"

"Well, a brain tumor might be benign, like a meningioma, or a low-grade astrocytoma or oligodendroglioma. They have a pretty good prognosis if treated early enough. But even if it's a glioblastoma, there's always palliation, and I wouldn't expect to suffer for too long."

"You've done your homework, I see."

"I always like to be prepared for a visit with you."

"I appreciate that. But you were saying your current concern is more serious."

"You promise you won't laugh at me?"

"You know I never laugh at you."

"Not even behind my back—or when you write?"

"Sunrise!"

"I'm sorry. It's just—" She hesitated.

I waited.

"I think I may have scrapie."

"Scrapie?!"

"You said you wouldn't laugh."

"No, I won't. But you know that you can't have scrapie, Sunrise."

"I knew you'd say that," she said sullenly.

"And you know why?"

"Because scrapie is a disease of sheep. It's like mad cow disease, only it's in sheep, especially the older ones. Lucretia, she's my oldest, has been rubbing up against the fence posts all spring. It's one of the signs, you know, scraping themselves. It's why they call it scrapie."

"I didn't know that. But I do know that humans can't get scrapie."

"How can you be so sure?"

"Excuse me. To the best of my knowledge, transmission of scrapie from sheep to humans has never been documented."

"That's what they said at the NIH."

"You talked to the NIH about this?"

"I always check with them before I come in. I told you I like to be prepared."

"So I remember. Just out of curiosity, the NIH is a big place; where did you check?"

"The Office of Rare Diseases."

"Of course. So it wouldn't seem that you have scrapie."

"Maybe not."

"Maybe?"

"Well, they always say that although your symptoms don't fit any known condition, it's always possible that you have some condition that isn't discovered yet. Which I know is pretty rare, but still . . ."

"Actually, I wouldn't say undiscovered conditions are all that rare. I see at least one every couple of weeks."

"That's not fair!" she said. "I'm worried sick about this and you're not taking me seriously."

"I'm trying, Sunrise. But you're not making it easy."

"I know. But I've got to find out. And you've got to help me. I mean, that's what doctors are for isn't it? To help people."

"Yes, it is. And I will. Give me a couple of days. I need to consult someone."

"A neurologist?"

"Not exactly."

"What kind of doctor is he?"

"He is just the kind of doctor for this case."

"Is he smart?"

"He's the smartest doctor I know. If anyone will know the answer to your question, it is he."

"What his specialty?"

"He's a murinologist."

"A mu-ri-nologist?" she repeated slowly. "You mean he treats—"

"Mice. Although he doesn't treat diseases in mice. He creates them."

"I don't understand."

"He's a researcher. We were classmates in medical school. About halfway through, he decided that treating diseases in people wasn't very challenging. He recognized that in order to be a clinician, you didn't actually have to know what was going on with your patients. All you needed to know was that if the patient might have condition A, you looked up condition A in the book and did the tests that they told you to do, and if they were positive you gave them the pills that they said to give. Similarly for condition B. And if you couldn't decide between A and B, it didn't matter, because you could always call in a specialist. So he went off to the Karolinska Institute in Sweden, where he started doing research on diseases that we didn't understand, trying to figure out what caused them. First it was leukemia, and then AIDS, and now it is Creutzfeldt-Jakob disease."

"Which is like scrapie."

"They are called prion diseases, because they are caused by proteins called prions. If there is anybody who can help us figure out if you might have scrapie, it will be he."

"What his name?"

"Bruce Sherlock."

"That's a fitting name."

"Very. You can look him up. I think you'll be impressed."

"Oh, I will. Thank you, Beach. I knew I could count on you."

"My pleasure. It may take a while for me to get an answer."

"A long time?"

"Not that long."

"I'll come back next week."

That evening I placed a call to Dr. Sherlock. His offices are at the National Institutes of Health, which should not surprise anyone, since NIH is the premier government medical research facility in the country. What might surprise you, however, is that his office is not located in Bethesda, Maryland. It is at the Rocky Mountain Laboratories in Hamilton, Montana. Hamilton has about the same population as Dumster, a little more than three thousand people.

Hamilton, Montana, is probably not the first place you would think of calling if you want the world's expert on an exotic disease like Creutzfeldt-Jakob, but it just goes to show how resourceful our government is, especially when it comes to keeping something going, even after there is no longer any need for it.

Take, for example, my old stomping grounds, the CDC. Back in 1946 there was an outbreak of malaria in the southeastern part of the country. After a thorough assessment of the biology of malaria and a careful review of the most effective ways of bringing it under control, the government decided the best approach was to kill off all the mosquitoes, and thus rid the land of the insect that carried the malaria parasite—the female of the *Anopheles* species. To this end, they established the Malaria Eradication Program, and they put its headquarters in Atlanta. Armed with the motto No Home Left Alone, they unleashed a flotilla of spray trucks that spread DDT upon every swamp, pond, ditch, and pothole in which the pesky lady might be lurking. And to be sure they could prove what a good job they had done, they hired a doctor named Alex Langmuir to track their progress. Dr. Langmuir was an epidemiologist. Like all epidemiologists, he wasn't much of a clinician. He was a stickler for actually knowing what it was you were doing before you did it.

"Okay," said Dr. Langmuir, "I'll do it. But first we need to set some rules."

The first rule he set was that in order to report a case as malaria, you had to verify that the person actually had the disease. This is pretty easy to do because, just by looking at someone's blood under a microscope, you can see the malaria bugs easy as pie. Confirming a diagnosis may seem like pretty basic medicine, but back in those days if someone came to the doctor with chills and a fever, and the doctor didn't have the foggiest, he would call it *malaria* because that way (a) it would seem as if he knew what was up and (b) he had a pill that he could give, so that when (c) the fever and the chills went away on their own accord, he could get the credit.

Dr. Langmuir's second rule was that for each confirmed case of malaria, it had to be determined whether it was domestic or imported, meaning did the person acquire the malaria in this country or did he pick it up abroad and bring it back home with him. This was especially important since malaria acquired abroad could hardly be cured by mosquitoes killed at home. After implementing these two rules, what Dr. Langmuir found was that most of the cases reported as malaria were nothing of the kind, and the few legitimate cases were all in soldiers returning from the Pacific Theater, where they had been acquired in the line of duty. His conclusion was that malaria had spontaneously disappeared from the United States many years ago.

This pleased the government no end. In reporting on these results they announced that malaria had been successfully eradicated, neglecting only to mention that said eradication had occurred without any assistance from the Malaria Eradication Program. They also decided not to say anything about the DDT that they dumped everywhere. They figured no one would notice.

"Well done," said the government. And they gave Dr. Langmuir a Certificate of Appreciation.

"Thank you," said Dr. Langmuir. "May I go home now?"

"Not so fast," said the government.

"But my job is done," said Dr. Langmuir. "There is no malaria."

"True," said the government. "But we still have the Malaria Eradication Program."

"But without malaria to eradicate, what will we do?" asked Dr. Langmuir.

"You're a clever guy," said the government. "You'll think up something."

And he did. He changed the name to the Communicable Disease Center and requested a tenfold increase in his budget. And then, some thirty years later, when immunizations and antibiotics had reduced business from infectious diseases, one of his successors changed the name to the Centers for Disease Control and started investigating heart disease and cancer and other chronic illness, thereby guaranteeing its survival in perpetuity. And today the program to eradicate the disease that no one ever had has grown to eight thousand employees and a budget of ten billion dollars.

I mention this story in order to make it easier to understand how a world-famous laboratory studying obscure neurological diseases could be located in Hamilton, Montana. It all started in 1928, when a couple of clever researchers studying tick-borne diseases convinced the government that research on Rocky Mountain spotted fever was crucial to our national defense. It was an impressive feat to pull off, given that the disease, which is transmitted by ticks, is not a great candidate for germ warfare. Furthermore, the name gives lie to its primary location, as the mountains in which this particular spotted fever is most common are not the Rockies, but the Smokies.

"It didn't really matter," says Bruce when the subject comes up. "The fishing is better out here."

As luck would have it, he was in his office when I called. After our customary greetings and promises that we really needed to get together more often, I told him the story of Sunrise.

"Interesting," he said after I had finished.

"Oh dear!" I said.

"Not really," he said. "Remember, we are talking about *interesting* in my line of work, not yours. Generally speaking, we don't have much use for diseases in humans out here. But the question of the ability of prions to transmit from one species to another is something we have been working on for some time. We don't even know for sure that mad cow disease can be transmitted to humans. We have just assumed it can because Creutzfeldt-Jakob disease occurs primarily in countries with a lot of mad cow disease. There is no such evidence for scrapie. The closest we have gotten is to transmit scrapie to squirrel monkeys by injecting the scrapie prion directly into them."

"But no other species?"

"Not quite. We can always give it to genetically manipulated species."

"Like mice, I suppose."

"Like mice. Particularly *plt* mice."

"These are not a variety of your basic house mouse, I gather."

"Not exactly. *Plt* mice are a mutant strain that has almost no T cells."

"Kinda like a genetic form of AIDS."

"You could say that. Their immunity is virtually nil."

"Poor dears. They must be highly susceptible to everything."

"Exactly the point."

"Of course. I keep forgetting that in the eternal struggle between organism and disease, it tends not to be the organism you are rooting for."

"Not usually."

"So, refresh my memory on prions."

This was a bit of a fib, as the sum total of my knowledge of prions was that they were somehow involved in neurological diseases, and they did not come from another planet. But I knew Bruce wouldn't mind. He loved to explain things, and the least I could do was accommodate him.

"As you know," he began graciously, "a prion is a piece of protein that can infect an organism and reproduce inside it without the aid of any other living organism, unlike a virus or bacterium. As a consequence, prions are extremely hardy. They are very resistant to inactivation by both heat and cold. The prion is passed to one animal from another when an animal eats the tissue of an animal infected with the prion disease. Which can happen even if the tissue is cooked or frozen."

"How easy is it to find these prions?"

"Nowadays it's pretty easy. You take the tissue in question, lyse it with guanidine thiocyanate, extract it with phenol, do a western blot, and there you have it."

"Which tissue is that?"

"Whole brain homogenate is best."

I thanked him and hung up, but not before he extracted a promise to let him know if Sunrise developed any evidence of prion disease. Then I called Sunrise and told her what I had learned.

"This much I'm sure of, Sunrise. You don't want to know if you have scrapie."

"Oh, but I do. Even if there is no treatment, at least I'll have some idea of what to expect."

"Actually, I'm afraid you wouldn't."

"I don't understand."

"The first step in making the diagnosis is to remove the brain."

"Oh."

"However, on a positive note, when I described your case to Doctor Sherlock, he said that none of his mice with scrapie had symptoms anything like yours."

"That's some consolation, I suppose."

"It will have to be all there is, I'm afraid."

"So what is wrong with me?"

"Nothing."

"Nothing!" she exclaimed. "You think I'm a hypochondriac—or crazy—or maybe that I'm making this all up just to get attention. A whadyacallit—munchkin?"

"No, Sunrise. You are not making it up, and you are not crazy. And you definitely are not a Munchausen's."

"Well," she said. "My symptoms are real!"

"I know they are."

"Oh you're just saying that to make me feel better. How do you know they're real?"

"Because I get them too."

Sunrise was too startled to speak for a minute. "You do?" she said finally. "Really?"

"Really."

"But why?"

"We all do."

"We? Who is *we*?"

"*We* is everybody. There is not a single person on this entire planet who hasn't had, from time to time, a little dizziness or blurred vision or shakiness. And we all are occasionally inattentive, forgetful, and outright confused. We even get the wobbles."

"I don't believe you."

"Nonetheless, it's true. You don't have these troubles any more than anyone else. But the rest of us have gotten used to it as Just One of Those Things, and don't pay much attention to it. You notice them more."

"Why?"

"Because you have PAPS."

"That's ridiculous! All women get Pap smears."

"Not pap smears. PAPS is a syndrome."

"I've never heard of it."

"You have now."

"What is it?"

"The Princess and the Pea Syndrome."

"You made that up," she said.

"I did."

"Just now."

"No, actually some time ago."

"That's not fair," she said angrily. She was quiet for a minute before she spoke again, this time more calmly. "But you really believe it exists."

"I really do."

"Tell me about it."

"Certainly. First, think of your body as a machine."

"Well, in a way, it is."

"And a very complex machine at that, with hundreds of thousands of moving parts, all working constantly to keep the organism in good running order. Given its complexity, it's more of a wonder that it isn't breaking down all the time."

"Except mine is now."

"Maybe not. Come in tomorrow, and I'll put the Holbode apparatus through its paces to see just how off kilter it actually is."

She was there first thing in the morning. Without my asking, she disrobed and hopped up on the examining table.

"Okay, let's go," she said.

"First, I want you to hold out your hands, facing down."

Sunrise did as she was told.

I checked her first for tremors. In order to magnify any that she might have, I took a sheet of paper and laid it across the back of her hands. It didn't quiver so much as a hair.

"Very good," I said. "Did you know that in order for you to hold your hand steady like that, you must have perfect coordination not only between the muscles in your arm that want to pull it up and those that want to push it down, but with all the rest of the muscles in your body, every one of which is needed to maintain an erect and steady posture? There are over six hundred, and all yours are now in perfect harmony."

"Are you sure?"

"I am. Now close your eyes."

She closed her eyes.

"I want you to walk across the room heel-to-toe, as if you were walking a tightrope."

I watched her go—straight as an arrow.

"Angel Wallenda herself couldn't have done better."

"Really?" she said. Despite her reluctance to show it, she was pleased with her performance. "What's next?"

"Patty-cake."

"Oh goody!"

"Remember, you clap my hands then slap your thighs. Do it as fast as you can."

"That's easy."

"But this is patty-cake with a twist. My hands will be moving." Fast as I waved them every which way, each of her pattys was right on target.

"Okay. Here's the last test. Look at me. What do you see?"

"I see you."

"Do you see two of me?"

"No."

"Do I seem maybe a little blurry at all around the edges?"

"You look quite sharp."

"Any of my colors look faded?"

"No. Well, maybe a little grayish on the top where the hair is gone."

"Never mind that."

"You asked."

"Be that as it may. My point is that every waking minute of your day, your retina is taking pictures. It takes them at a rate of more than four per second. Now think about a camera. If you asked your camera to do that for fifty years, how many shots do you think you'd get that were a little out of focus or a little off color?"

"Oh, I get them all the time."

"But not from your brain. It gives a perfect picture every time."

"Sometimes it works better than others."

"Of course it does. And some machines work better than others.

Sometimes because they were better made. Sometimes because the owner took better care of them."

"Obviously," she said, a little impatient with the lesson. "So what?"

"So if you wanted a precision machine that ran perfectly, what would you need? You would need it to be well designed, put together by a high-quality manufacturer, and maintained by a meticulous owner."

"I suppose you would."

"And such a machine, being as precise as it is, would be extremely sensitive to even the slightest changes in conditions. Even the tiniest speck or the slightest of vibrations could throw it completely off kilter. So, although such a machine would be the best that money can buy, it would be—"

"—high-maintenance."

"Precisely. But this machine, when it is running as it ought to, would outperform by far all the other lower-quality machines."

"Like an old John Deere tractor."

"And the scales used by the Bureau of Weights and Measures."

"You mean a machine that sets the standards for all other machines?"

"I do."

"And you think I am one of those machines?"

"The very prototype."

"And you have seen others like me?"

"I've never seen anyone like you, Sunrise."

"I mean others with PAPS."

"I have seen a few."

"But you've never told anyone about it before."

"No, I haven't."

She hesitated. "So, you don't think this body of mine is falling apart?"

"Quite the contrary. I would say it's better than most bodies I see."

"But that might not be saying much. I mean . . ."

"*Far* better, Sunrise. In fact, it's one of the best. Professionally speaking, of course."

"Honest and true?"

I shrugged.

"Well, I guess, as they say—If the shoe fits."

"Wear it well, Sunrise."

"I will. And Beach . . ."

"Yes?"

"About PAPS?"

"Oh, that. It was just a way of looking at things. I thought it would help you understand what was going on."

"I was going to say, if you want to use it with other patients, it's okay with me."

"Thank you, Sunrise. I think I might."

18

Not Too Bad

···········

No one would say that Norma Lebrec is a generous person. They wouldn't call her selfish, but they would point out that she is an indifferent contributor to all those causes that spring up at holiday time, such as the ones that can trace their ancestry back to the Adam and Eve of charitable institutions, the Geneva Society for Public Welfare and the East London Christian Mission. Now better known as the Red Cross and the Salvation Army, this fertile pair has spawned such a multitude of descendants that for one to determine which among them are the most worthy is a formidable task, and on this ground alone one might excuse Norma for preferring to conduct her eleemosynary worship in the house of Charity Begins at Home.

It should be pointed out, however, that with respect to this particular church, her religious practices are rather more liberal than those followed by the orthodox believers, not a few of whom have called her heretical. Should a neighbor fall ill in winter, for example, it is Norma Lebrec who is there at the first sign of snow, shoveling the walk to clear a path for the subsequent parade of casseroles. And it is Norma Lebrec, who, long after the casseroles have stopped paying their respects, continues to stop by each week to have a bit of a chat and a cup of tea. The charity of Norma Lebrec is always like this, without notice and without credit. Which is just the way she likes it.

Nor is Norma Lebrec much skilled in the art of social graces. She is particularly weak at neighborly discourse, failing utterly to recognize the importance of relating to others the sundry ills, indignities, and injustices that may have been visited upon her, and, in so failing, depriving those with whom she converses the opportunity to prove that, however poorly things may be for Norma, they are far worse for that person. Plainly stated, Norma does not appreciate the value of complaint. I except in this two instances. The first is when another person's knowing her state of health would have some practical value for that person. Just as she might explain to someone borrowing her lawn mower that the starter cord tends to stick a bit and must be given a gentle pull once or twice before attempting a more forceful tug, she would have no hesitation about notifying a walking companion that her right hip is less compliant today and is likely to slow her pace. The second is when consulting with her doctor.

As she would expect me to be scrupulously honest in describing her character, I must make one more entry to complete this catalog of her deficiencies. Norma Lebrec is not a cheerful soul. While some would attribute this defect to her having been married for some forty years to her husband, Chet, those who have known her since childhood would counter that this is not so. It is just not in her nature to be cheerful, they would say.

Even the most meticulous of fault finders, however, of which Dumster has an ample supply, would concede that Norma Lebrec is never glum or ill tempered, or anything other than thoroughly pleasant at all times and to all people—especially those who are not similarly inclined.

Accordingly, no one who chanced to meet Norma on the street in the afternoon ever minded saying hello. For they could be secure in the knowledge that such a conversation with Norma would last long enough to demonstrate that she had a genuine interest in how you were doing, but not so long as to detain you from whatever more important business you had at hand.

"No airs about her," said some. "Matter-of-fact," said others. "A sensible woman," said all. In the court of Dumster public opinion, these verdicts confer a mark of the highest distinction. Not surprisingly, Norma dismissed them out of hand. "It's just the way I am," she said. "I can claim no more credit for my disposition than I should receive censure were I to be peevish or ill natured. We are made the way we are made, and all we can do is to try to live with it the best we can."

Norma was a Gauthier by birth. As with many French Canadians, her parents had come down from the Maritimes during the Depression in search of work. They landed jobs at Acme Tool and Die and settled in Dumster with their three children, the youngest of whom was

Norma, age two. All of the children were good students, but Norma was the best. She graduated valedictorian of her class at Dumster High and was given a full scholarship to the University of Vermont. Those who knew her said she would go far. Those who knew her well didn't say anything. After graduation from high school she took her usual summer job at Acme Tool and Die, where she worked as a sweeper on the cutting room floor. When fall came, however, she was still there, as she was four decades later, when the company was sold to a German firm that closed the plant and moved all the equipment and one executive to Hamburg.

In her first two years at Acme, she moved from sweeper to inspector to turret lathe operator, and then, three years after she started full-time employment, Norma Gauthier became the first woman jig maker. Once a year she was offered a promotion to management. The benefits were better, and the salary increase was substantial. Once a year she turned it down. "Thank you for considering me," she always said. "I like what I do now." And that was that.

Those who were surprised that she never went to college were even more so when, less than one year out of high school, she married Chester Lebrec. Handsome, affable, and a superb athlete, Chet was captain of both the football team and the basketball team. He was also the star pitcher on the baseball team. Although the Hornets had a mediocre record, Chet was undefeated in four years of pitching. "He had a buzz on that ball that sure could sting," they said when Chet took the mound. He was drafted by the Red Sox and was all set to go to Pawtucket, but he dislocated his shoulder when he fell out of the back of a pickup the summer after graduation, and never played professional ball. As you might expect, he was furiously pursued by all the eligible young women of Dumster, as well as more than a few of the ineligible. Overlooked on the grounds of the youthful sowing of wild oats was the fact that he was a budding alcoholic.

No one could recollect ever seeing Norma and Chet on a date in high school. No one could understand why he married her. "Knocked her up" was the initial explanation, the lie to which became apparent when no bundle of joy appeared in the months following their wedding. "It will never last," they then said, and I suppose they could have been right, depending on how one counts a marriage that, after thirty-five childless years, ends in divorce. Even though everyone agreed that Norma would have been more than justified in leaving Chet at any time, she stayed with him through thick, and thin. Mostly it was downright watery.

Once the glamour of his high school years had passed, those who had given Chet work out of deference to his youthful accomplishments would no longer take a chance on the lazy drunk he had become, and Chet was out of work more than in it. He became a neglectful philandering mooch. But Chet never abused Norma. Perhaps it was out of some twinge of consideration for a spouse who never gave him the slightest pretext for complaint, but more likely because he knew that if he had, Norma would have left him on the spot, and the humiliation of being left by Norma would have been more than he could bear. So it was Chet who eventually filed for divorce. "I think he still had a few wild oats in his bag" was all Norma said. Two other brief marriages and a string of briefer liaisons tended to bear out her judgment.

Norma was only sixty when Acme Tool and Die shut its doors. What little of her earnings she had managed to protect from Chet's profligacy was not quite enough to live on, and so Norma, recognizing that Chet had never been able to support himself, let Chet stay in their home, on which she continued to pay the taxes, the insurance, and the utilities. She moved into a small but comfortable two-bedroom apartment on Sycamore Lane overlooking the town pond. In the spare bedroom she set up an office and started a tax business. Nobody in town could imagine anyone to whom they would rather trust their financial matters, and the business grew rapidly. It wasn't long before it was more profitable than her salary after forty-one years at Acme. Four years later, when she started collecting Social Security, she talked about cutting back. Every one of her customers pleaded with her to make an exception for them, and, as she did not have the heart to say no to any of them, she abandoned the idea. Well into her seventies, Norma remained as busy as ever.

It was early May, a time when even the most hardy of Vermonters begins to get a bit miffed at the perennial inability of the season to live up to its obligations. Although the lilacs were beginning to bloom, and the grass had started to grow, the two inches of wet snow that had fallen during the night gave lie to the claim that spring had everything under control. I met Norma coming out of the post office. She had that tired but satisfied look of a job well done.

"Good morning Norma," I said. "Tax season finally over?"

"Just mailed off the last of my extensions."

"A nice feeling, I would guess."

"It is, indeed."

"And how is Mrs. Lebrec feeling these days."

"Not too bad, Doctor Conger."

"Really?" I said. "Shall I have Maggie call you to set up an appointment at your convenience?"

"If you wouldn't mind."

"Not at all. I'm on my way back to the office. I'll have her call you this afternoon."

"Thank you."

On Norma's scale of How She Was Feeling, the range in the thirty-odd years I had known her had been from *Fair to Middlin'* when all was well, to *Okay Considering* when it wasn't quite.

Not too bad was a distinct change.

Some years ago an enterprising doctor invented a scale for the profession to use in quantifying discomfort. It went from zero to ten, where zero represented no pain at all, and ten signified the worst pain ever. To assist those who needed help deciding where they belonged on it, he made a placard to show the patient. Down one side were the numbers zero through ten. Down the other side were a series of pictures that showed progressively unhappy faces corresponding to each number. To further help the patient, he created a standard for the Worst Pain Ever. It was gender-specific. Ten, for a woman, was childbirth. For a man it was an examination of the prostate. The system was sold to patients on the grounds that it allowed a more precise quantification of pain, and, as such, enabled the physician to dole out exactly that treatment which was prescribed by the most modern and objective principles of analgesic therapeutics.

It was a hoax. The real reason behind the scale, as everyone in the profession from nurse's aide to surgeon knows full well, is quite simply to obviate the tiresome and useless activity of talking to the patient about how she is feeling. In the old days, when one was merely better or worse and nothing much could be done about it except to wait and hope that the latter would turn into the former—or, barring this, that the end of feeling altogether would come as expeditiously as possible—there was no end to the time one could fritter away at the bedside on the subject of feeling. But now the issue is asked and answered in a single word, with the results duly recorded and promptly ignored.

At William Penn Hospital, the patients knew their scales well. Invariably, upon arriving in the emergency room, I could hear their cries as they tried desperately to get someone to attend to them. It was the auction of the ignored.

"Leven!" would shout one, opening the bidding.

"Twelf," would call out another.

"Thuhteen! Thuhteen! Hey, thuhteen!" chimed in a third.

"Fawteen!"

"Fifteen heah!"

"Nahnteen. Gonna be twenny, if I doan croak fust!"

On and on it went like this, all day and night, the room a cacophony of ever more outraged and outlandish claims.

It was all to no avail. Well accustomed to grade inflation, the harried staff worked their way methodically through the ranks according to a priority scale that was known only to them.

Although from time to time a traveling nurse has tried it in Dumster, the system has never caught on. People here prefer to stick with that to which they have always been accustomed. There is *Okay Considering*, *Fair to Middlin'*, and *Could Be Worse*. And there is *Not Too Bad*.

"I saw Norma Lebrec in town today," I told Maggie when I got back to the office. "She should have an appointment—soon."

"I'll take care of it," she said.

"Make it a ten o'clock appointment."

"Oh!"

"She says she's *not too bad*."

"I'll fit her in tomorrow."

It's not a subject you will find discussed in the American Medical Association Medical Guide or on WebMD. I'm not even sure you can find it in Wikipedia. I refer to the little-known fact that going to the doctor is very much like going fishing. There's a time when they're biting, and there's a time when they're not. The best time, I have always been told by my fishing friends, is at the crack of dawn. The way they explain it, that's when the fish are just getting up after a night's sleep and are eager for a good meal, although I have always suspected this was a convenient fiction propagated by guys who just want a good excuse to get out of the house before chores, so they can spend the whole day sitting around and drinking beer. Be that as it may, however good it may be for catching fish, first thing in the morning is definitely not the best time for your doctor to be fishing with you. Nor is the end of the day. The reason for the latter is pretty obvious. Tired, grumpy, and eager to go home—after a day of listening to tales of woe about which we invariably can do less than is expected—even the most dedicated healer will not be on the top of her game.

Less obvious are the grounds on which one should avoid the start of the day. Although it is true that, like any ordinary person, an adequately caffeinated doctor will have an eye pretty bright and a tail rather bushy first thing in the morning, you must remember one thing about doctors.

We are professionals.

The great Ruth would never step up to the plate without first taking a few swings of the hickory stick. Michael Jordan wouldn't have dreamed of taking to the court without completing his warm-up shots. And Babe Didrikson Zaharias always spent a good hour at the practice tee before addressing the ball on the first hole.

A doctor, whose actions are of far greater consequence than the mere propulsion of a ball through space, is no less meticulous. It is with good reason that we call what we do practice, for in the case of the majority of our patients that is exactly what we are doing. It is only the select few who get our best shot. My point here, to make it crystal clear to any who have not grasped it yet, is that what you definitely do not want to be is your doctor's warm-up patient.

End of the morning and beginning of the afternoon, although less objectionable, are also likely to yield a second-rate performance. No one works best with either food or a nap on her mind. In point of fact, the window of opportunity for seeing a doctor at the peak of her game is a narrow one. Midmorning is the prime time, but failing that midafternoon will do, as long as the condition is not too serious. Stray too far from those boundaries, and you are swimming in dangerous waters. Especially if the complaint is that with which Norma presented.

She had lost weight.

Losing weight, to continue the metaphor, is a bunker shot across the water to the uphill side of a very fast green, on the far side of which lies a sand trap the size of the Sahara. So before approaching the ball, one wants to have a steady hand, a tranquil mind, and one's full powers of concentration.

I exempt from this stipulation regarding the seriousness of the disappearance of pounds human that far more numerous group of patients who, because of a book they might have read, or a group they might have joined, or just because it is the start of a new year, have not actually lost, but merely misplaced, the weight in question. Dramatic as the apparent loss may be, these fortunate souls require no more than the simple reassurance that the pounds will all return in due time and, when found, will be discovered to reside in exactly the same place where they used to be.

But regarding the real losers—should one be so lucky—such loss might be accompanied by a ravenous appetite, an insatiable desire to drink, and a prodigious output of urine. Or, equally fortuitously, it could be associated with a marked state of agitation, an intolerance of heat, and a sudden increase in energy of the kind ordinarily found only after a couple of triple-shot espressos. Such cases are caused by nothing more serious than a bit of hormonal mayhem, and they can easily be brought to order by the use of insulin in the first instance, or a zap of the thyroid in the second.

Norma was not lucky.

"I'm just not hungry, Doctor Conger," she said.

For both the weight and the appetite to show up in the loss column did not bode well for how her balance sheet would look in the final accounting. And Norma, like anyone who had put up with symptoms they would rather not address, knew without my telling her what it would most likely add up to.

These days, when we want to know what someone has, the first thing we do is order tests. Then we see what shows up. It's an excellent approach, obviating, as it does, the need to think, thinking being, in my line of work, an unrewarding activity, uncompensated, as it is, by any remuneration. Tests, however, are very good for business.

We call this process of rummaging about the differential diagnosis. It is a fishing expedition. For much of my career, fishing was done with a rod, a reel, and a lure or two, but today such expeditions are carried out with great trawlers pulling wide nets that are capable of bringing in not only all that is edible, but also much that is not. So like the fisherman of today, we also troll for our catch.

Had it been first thing in the morning or the end of the day, even an old angler like myself would find it easier to forsake the accustomed ways and go with the flow, although, as I am rather clumsy at it, I invariably forget some vital piece. Fortunately, in such instances I am kindly reminded of my error by, say, the radiologist, who will point out to me in her report, "If what you are looking for is x-itis, then an ultrasound may be more revealing than an MRI." This, of course, is offered after, rather than before, the procedure I have ordered has already been performed, because, as the radiologist would say, she doesn't like to interfere with the clinician's prerogatives—or to limit herself to one procedure when she could do two.

But, as Norma was my ten o'clock appointment, I was prepared to make a diagnosis the old-fashioned way—first by talking with the patient, and then by giving her a thorough inspection from top to bottom.

Setting aside for the time being the most likely diagnosis, which I was only too glad to do, I began where I usually do, by eliminating those diagnoses that I would be chagrined to miss. They are the kind that, were I to overlook one in favor of a more popular rival, it would raise its ugly head in a fit of pique and make life miserable for both of us.

Tuberculosis is, in theory, one of the considerations. At William Penn it was not unusual, as it was a common traveling companion with HIV. But at Emmeline Talbot it was most unlikely. The only person with tuberculosis I have seen in Dumster in the last thirty years was Han Phang, who came to town as a refugee from Cambodia. He had a cough. "It must be tuberculosis," he told me, because that's what his father and grandfather had when they coughed. And he was right.

More commonly in the instance of weight loss, what one can easily pass by in the frenzied pursuit of exotica is what, more often than not, it turns out to be.

Depression.

Psychiatrists, recognizing the ineptitude of all save themselves in dealing with disorders of the mind, have tried to simplify the business of identifying depression for the rest of us by creating sets of what are called "screening" questions. These questions are associated with a point system, which is intended to make it simple enough for even the most emotionally obtuse to administer. Ask the questions. Record the answers. Tally up the score. And Bob's your uncle—there you have it. On a scale of one to five, how much do you enjoy hearing your morning alarm clock? On average, how many times before lunch have you had the urge to strangle a member of your family? (The score is weighted to assign the most points to a child under the age of ten and none at all for a male spouse.) How do you feel about rain?

I don't know how well they do at unearthing depression, but I can tell you that the mere asking of these questions does tend to make *me* feel a bit blue. I have tried them all over the years and never really bonded with any of them. So I have developed my own depression screen. It works for me.

"Are you depressed?" I asked her.

"No, Doctor Conger, I am not," she answered.

Depression disposed of, next on the agenda was the Review of Systems, an important but tricky activity in which we ask every conceivable question about every possible part of the body. The asking is easy. It is the answers wherein lies the rub. Take for example the simple question, "Are you cold?" A straightforward and sensible patient, of which there are precious few, would answer "yes" if she was cold, and "no" if she were not. There are not a few, however, who are aware of the fact the body is a complex organism, and the proper function of the whole depends on the perfect interrelation of all its parts. For them there is no such thing as a symptom taken in isolation, and the apparent absence of any one symptom is merely an illusion created by the failure to consider its broader connections. Such patients have never met a symptom they couldn't have.

I call such a patient a Yes Patient.

> Well, now that you mention it, Doc, I am a bit chilly from time to time, although not nearly so much as when I was twelve and had to walk home from school because the bus was late and it was cold as all get-out, and my toes got almost frostbit. Maybe that's why my legs ache in the morning. And last week I thought I might have had a cold, if that's what you meant. It felt like it coulda been pneumonia. And now I've got this cough that just won't go away, and a sore throat to boot. I get the shivers sometimes when I eat. And then my stomach aches something fierce. But actually, if you really need to know the truth, most of the time I feel sorta hottish—not burning hot, like with a fever, but just kind of warm, especially in my joints. And it does tire me out and makes it hard for me to get a good night's sleep. Sometimes it tires me so much that I feel I could just drop dead on my feet right in the middle of the day. And then my bowels . . .

Yes Patients can go on like that for a long time. Indefinitely it seems at times. But I can hardly blame them. Someone looked once at how long doctors wait before interrupting a patient in relating his tale. It was about fifteen seconds. At least for male doctors. Women doctors were much better. Their average was thirty seconds. Maybe it's because women are better listeners. Or maybe it's just that they like to have more time to their own thoughts.

At the other extreme is the No Patient. A No Patient wouldn't know a symptom if it bit her on the nose. Knowing which kind of patient you are dealing with is very important, if you are going to make any sense out of their answers. Take for example, if you ask the ordinary *how-are-you* question. The No Patient will say "Fine" even if she is at death's door, while the Yes Patient, if allowed to run his natural course, will give an answer lasting upward of five minutes.

I got the names Yes Patient and No Patient from my mother-in-law, Berit. Ordinarily a very coherent eighty-year-old, she became delirious for several days following open-heart surgery and exceedingly suspicious of all who addressed her. She excepted in this only her eldest granddaughter, who was the only person able to pacify Berit. She accomplished this by asking her to help with the vocabulary flash cards she had prepared for her Graduate Record Examination. Berit, a retired English teacher, was only too glad to be of assistance, particularly as she had discovered that many of the definitions provided were in need of correction. Most of them, she noted, were "utter nonsense." Nadya had the good sense not to dispute her grandmother and accepted without comment the substitutions she provided:

eleemosynary—a place where eels go to meditate
blandishment—what you put on food so it has no flavor
parameter—a device used to tell if someone is lying

With all the rest of us, any question, regardless of how innocuous, was met with an icy stare and a stony silence until the speaker had answered to her satisfaction whether the query proposed was "a Yes Question or a No Question."

The Yes Question and the No Question are an excellent means of identifying Yes Patients and No Patients. Simply put, a Yes Question is one to which a normal person would answer yes, and a No Question is one to which that person would respond in the negative. A Yes Patient, on the other hand, will always answer yes, even to a No Question, while a No Patient does just the opposite.

"When you eat strawberries, do your ears tingle?" is a good example of a No Question, but generally I prefer "Has your urine been blue recently?" A Yes Patient, after some consideration, will invariably respond along the lines of "Well, now that you mention it, it may have been a little bluish last Tuesday, although, come to think of it, it may have been more on the lavender side. Is that a serious sign?"

Now, I suppose there are some situations in which the urine can turn blue, and if you were to search online you would find at least a dozen or so listed on a Blue Urine website. What I can guarantee you is that the site is hosted by a Yes Person. But as I have yet to experience someone with this complaint, I feel confident that the risk of erroneously classifying someone as a Yes Patient is low.

"Do you ever feel tired?" is the simplest of No Questions, since all of us at some time or another have operated at less than full speed.

Norma being neither of these two types, I proceeded directly to her review in the full confidence that she would give me nothing other than an absolutely spot-on accurate answer.

"Any headaches, dizzy spells, or blurred vision?" I asked, starting at the top.

"Once a month, maybe. If I have been out in the sun too long."

"How about a persistent cough, unexpected shortness of breath, or pains in your chest?"

"None of those."

"Do you ever cough up blood?"

"No, thank goodness!"

"Any nausea, vomiting, or diarrhea?"

"I do get a little sickish if I eat too much."

"But no blood in your stool?"

"No, none."

"How about fevers, chills, night sweats, or muscle aches and pains?"

"Only when I get the flu."

And so it continued, as we went on down the list. A few now-and-thens, some here-and-theres, but nothing out of the ordinary. Certainly nothing that would account for the decline in her weight and her appetite.

Then it was time for the examination.

Each year, I host a pack of first-year students for their course on introduction to physical diagnosis. Although they come down ostensibly to learn the tricks of the trade, they usually seem far more interested in why I wear a tie than in how I examine the body, and I have long suspected that the course is less intended to help them acquire any particular skills than it is to be an anthropological experience, a chance to view the aboriginal doctor in his natural habitat. Be that as it may, when I see these eager young cubs out on their first hunt, traumatic memories of my own first physical examinations come back to me as if they were only yesterday. Which way does the stethoscope go? How do I hold the reflex hammer? Is it look, listen, and feel—or the other way around? So focused would I be on the form of what I was doing that I had not a clue about the substance of my examination. A bat with cataracts would stand a better chance of finding its way across the expanse of the body terrain than a first-year medical student.

But even on the outside chance that they might be eager to acquire from me those pearls of wisdom I have accumulated over the years, I would be unable to oblige them. When it comes to how to do a physical examination, I have nothing to say. For at this point in my career I really don't know what I am doing.

This is not to say that I do a poor job of it. It's just that after more than forty years of poking and prodding in the nooks and crannies of the human body, the process has become pretty much automatic. In truth, if I am to be allowed in this entire work a single vanity, which, I must say, I do not think is entirely unreasonable, it would be that I do a pretty darn good physical examination.

There. That's done. And now, having succumbed to that all-too-common temptation for self-congratulation that occurs when an author appears in his own work, I will now quickly distance myself from it.

In the first place, whatever skills I may have acquired are not something for which I can take credit. I have just spent more time on them than do the doctors of today, for the simple reason that in the prehistoric years of my training, there were no such luxuries as CT scans, echocardiograms, endoscopes, or MRIs to tell me what is really what. And with their arrival, the one thing we have learned about these so-called pearls—how to distinguish a leaky mitral valve from a rusty aortic one, how to identify the presence of extraneous fluid in the abdomen, how to determine if there is a blood clot in the leg, or how to identify a case of meningitis—is that most of the contents of this jewel box I have held so dear are little more than worthless trinkets, lovely to look at, but of no more value than costume jewelry from the five-and-ten.

In fact, if you were to ask me to name even one thing that could be better detected by physical examination than by a blood test or an imaging, I would be hard-pressed to do so.

But, as I was saying, although I proceed through an examination seemingly inattentive to what lies beneath my fingers, should they encounter something that doesn't belong, I would know in an instant. As one of my colleagues who has a flying license explained, we are like the experienced pilot of a jumbo jet whose eyes are constantly scanning the myriad dials and gauges that lie before him without appearing to pay the slightest attention to what they are indicating. But let one of them stray even the slightest beyond accepted bounds, and he is on the case in a flash. "Of course," he added, "that was before automatic pilot."

So there I was, cruising along through Norma from her head to her toes with nothing of note—not even as I crossed the abdominal plains, which is where I expected to find some rough going—and was just about done with my trip when I took one last swing through those cul-de-sacs that no one ever visits these days, behind the ear, inside the elbow, under the armpits, when suddenly there was a prickle in the back of my neck and a chill ran down my spine. I stopped to get my bearings. My fingers were in that little hollow that lies just above the left collarbone.

19

The Best Thing That Ever Happened

··········

It was just a little thing, no bigger than a pea.

But it was in a place where no pea ought to be.

It was Virchow's node.

From the time of Hippocrates well through the sixteenth century, it was universally agreed by all that the movement of blood followed the principles laid down by the Greek physician Galen of Pergamon. According to Galen, there were two separate circulations in the body. Dark venous blood was formed in the liver from food delivered to it via intestinal veins and then diffused throughout the body, providing cells with the nutrition they needed to grow and prosper. Entirely separate from this system was that of the red arterial blood. It provided the body with its spiritual essence, which was inhaled from the lungs. Blood could pass from one system to the other through a set of holes located in the heart. Galen never found any such holes, but he knew they must exist, because reason told him so, and if there was anything a Greek believed in, it was reason. That there was not one shred of evidence to support this theory bothered no one, because the theory had been confirmed by a far more definitive proof, the blessing of the Catholic Church, which had decreed that it was the true and only path for blood to follow.

Some fourteen hundred years later, a fellow by the name of Michael Servetus said it was a lot of malarkey. He asserted that there was only one circulatory system, in which blood traveled from one side of the heart first to the lungs, and then back to the other side. For this novel idea he was declared a heretic and burned at the stake. This put a damper on any further research on the subject for some seventy years, until William Harvey proved that Servetus was right, thereby winning considerable fame for himself, and, hopefully, salvation for the soul of Servetus.

In the excitement over the great rivers of blood, no one paid much attention to the little stream that traveled alongside, which carried a fluid called lymph. Placed at various intervals along the stream were a series of cisterns known as lymph nodes. The purpose of these nodes was to collect the wastes and dispose of them before they could enter the general circulation and wreak damage on the vital organs. Infectious materials and cancerous cells were high on the list of its priorities. The lymphatics merged with the blood circulation at the origin of the subclavian vein, just above the collarbone. The last of the lymph nodes coming up from below was situated right at the entrance.

No one paid attention—that is, until along came yet another Father of Medicine, Rudolf Ludwig Carl Virchow. (It was not until Marie Curie that the profession abandoned its version of immaculate conception and acknowledged having female parentage as well.) Virchow was a brilliant man. His knowledge was encyclopedic. He was also an egomaniac. He was determined that everything he discovered, or that someone else had already discovered but not yet laid claim to, should be named after him. So he created Virchow's cell, Virchow's angle, Virchow's disease, Virchow's line, Virchow's law, Virchow's triad, and the pea in question, Virchow's node. He also knew that he had to protect his reputation from the slander of others, particularly that most vile imposter of a physician, Ignaz Semmelweis. Dr. Semmelweis held the absurd view that it was bacteria that spread disease. Virchow used his considerable influence in the profession to expose this view to the ridicule it deserved, and to ensure that the techniques Semmelweis advocated for preventing the spread of bacteria, antisepsis and the washing of hands, would have no place in the practice of medicine.

But regarding his node—this Virchow considered a sure sign of stomach cancer, the cells of which, after entering the lymphatic circulation in the abdomen, would travel up through the chest and into the neck, where they were then caught by that last node on the line. As with many of his declarations, it was based on meticulous observation and careful reasoning. And as with many of his observations, it was wrong. For when one actually looks at the contents of Virchow's node, most of the time they signify something other than stomach cancer.

Nonetheless, this pea-where-no-pea-ought-to-be was a harbinger of Something. And it was not likely to be something good.

"What is it?" asked Norma quietly.

Despite my best efforts to conceal what I had found until I was ready to discuss it on my own terms, my fingers had lingered too long in this hollow to have come up with nothing.

"It's a lymph node," I said, hoping this noncommittal answer was sufficient to get me off the hook, at least for the time being.

"Which doesn't belong there," said Norma, reeling me in.

"There are lymph nodes all over the body, and it is not unusual to feel them here and there," I said. It was a lame answer, and I knew it.

So did Norma.

"But this particular lymph node in this particular place?"

"Doesn't quite belong," I conceded.

"Due to cancer, I suppose."

As I said before, the relationship between doctors and patients used to be a simple one. The patient took care of the illness. The doctor took care of the credit. Now, like all relationships, things have gotten much more complicated. It involves communication and trust and something called shared decision making. To make sure that doctors understand this relationship, medical schools now have a special course just on the doctor–patient relationship. The course is taught by highly trained instructors who are unbiased by ever having been either a doctor or a patient. The course covers such important subjects as what to do if you want to throttle your patient, or how to react if your patient tells you he is from Mars. A lot of time is spent on the subject of Giving Bad News. Perfectly healthy people are brought in who pretend they are patients, and the students pretend that they have just discovered that the person has some incurable condition like AIDS or herpes. Then the pretend doctors tell the pretend patients about their pretend condition, and afterward every-one sits down to discuss how it all went. The course is called On Doctoring. I taught it briefly last year, and it reminded me a lot of the childbirth classes we attended before our youngest was born. The class made me feel very good about my preparedness for the actual pains of childbirth.

Of course in actual life, what we all do when we are faced with catastrophe, no matter how much we have practiced what we ought to do, we all resort to what we know best.

Denial.

This is especially true when it comes to telling people they have cancer. While we are able to discuss it freely with our colleagues, including, in rather gory detail, the prognosis, when we sit down with the actual owner of the cancer—even though she already knows what she has for the very simple reason that, after we have listened to her story and done our testing, the first words out of our mouth were not *It's not a cancer*—we hem and haw and beat around the bush to a degree that would do even a lawyer proud. Because it is only human nature, when presented with a series of possibilities, immediately to assume the worst. Everybody knows this is true. Even doctors.

But at a time when we should be especially honest with our patients, helping them see that there is some silver lining in even the darkest of clouds, we revert to what we learned as children when faced with something that we don't want to see. We close our eyes and pretend it isn't there. And the cancer becomes transformed. It is a spot, a growth, a nodule, a something, a *probably nothing*—in short, anything but what it actually is.

Customary medical etiquette dictates that, even when both parties know full well what the score is, the well-bred patient should leave it up to the doctor to announce the cancer that both know is present. But if the patient happens to be so rash as to force the issue by asking, the doctor can rely upon any one of his ample stock of evasive answers to postpone the inevitable: "Not necessarily," "It could be benign," "We really can't say at this point."

This obfuscation was pointless with Norma.

"Yes," I said.

"Of course you will want to order tests."

"Of course."

"To establish a definitive diagnosis."

"Precisely."

"And to plan a course of treatment."

"An essential step."

"And to give me my prognosis."

"That too."

"Well," she said, getting up from the table, "lead on, Doctor Conger. I'm in your hands."

As it turned out, in Norma's case Virchow would have been right. The cancer was in her stomach.

After all the tests had come back, Norma's cancer had its coming-out party at the Tumor Board, where it was presented to all who would be involved in her care.

> N. L. is a seventy-two-year-old white female who presents
> with a gastric adenocarcinoma, clinical staging T, one, L,
> zero, M . . .

And after the biopsy and the CT and the literature had all been reviewed to everyone's satisfaction, a vote was taken and, by a majority of five to one, a plan of action was agreed upon. The sole dissenting vote was from an oncologist who favored etoposide over fluorouracil prior to surgery. I called Norma in to give her the news.

"The prognosis is favorable," I said, after I had finished explaining the plan for her oncologic trifecta, chemotherapy followed by surgery and then radiation.

"Ah," said Norma.

"In fact, it may even be highly favorable. Although we won't know for sure until after surgery."

"I see."

"The Tumor Board was quite optimistic."

Norma looked at me without speaking.

"All in all, I would consider this pretty good news."

"I suppose so," she said, and then paused before speaking again. "Although if I were the Farmer, and you were the Preacher, this 'pretty good news' . . ."

"Yes. It is all relative."

"Funny thing, isn't *it*?"

"What is?"

"*It*."

"Ah. *It*."

"Yes. *It* has that tendency."

"Of course, prognosis is a tricky thing to pin down precisely. There are many factors to consider, and it would be premature to make any definitive predictions."

"I will be safe planting winter squash this spring, however?"

"Most definitely."

"And next year also?"

"Perhaps."

"Perhaps. So you wouldn't recommend putting in an apple tree, I suppose."

"I wouldn't."

"Thank you, Doctor Conger. I won't. Which would leave, then, only the question of asparagus."

"Ah, the Asparagus Question."

"With respect to which, I suppose we will just have to wait and see."

"We will."

Her surgery went well. The surgeon was especially pleased with the results. "No visible tumor at the margins," she said, "and no palpable lymph nodes." The pathologist, falling in with the prevailing winds, confirmed that "the margins are clear."

And so the weather report predicted clear sailing.

Which it was—for the first year. And for most of the second. Around Memorial Day, Norma came in for a visit.

"I don't think I'll plant my tomato sets this week," she said.

"Let's get some blood work," I said.

"Is that necessary?"

"It could be something else."

"Like an underdone piece of pork."

"We should make sure."

Which we did.

"I'll set up an appointment for the oncologist," I told her after I got the report.

Norma didn't say no, and so I did. The oncologist said she wanted to assess the extent of the cancer, so she ordered a CAT scan and a

PET scan. Norma found the domestic animal theme of the imaging procedures intriguing.

"Do you ever wonder why?" she asked me.

"No, I don't."

The oncologist recommended a course of chemotherapy. She said it would be palliative.

"Palliative," she repeated when I told her. "Have I been troublesome, Doctor Conger?"

"Not you, Norma."

"The cancer, you mean."

"The cancer."

"Yes. Everyone has been so good and put in so much work. I suppose it is rather obstreperous of it to behave this way now."

And so Norma set sail again, this time in more turbulent waters.

About two weeks after Norma started chemotherapy, Chet came to see me. He had indigestion. Although Chet was not what I would call a regular customer, his threshold for visiting falling just slightly below crushing chest pain and loss of limb, and although the indigestion had been present for years, sustained as it was by his ample consumption of caffeine and alcohol, I was not surprised to see him. Confidentiality, according to Dumster ethics, was defined as the right to privacy with respect to anyone not living within town limits. Thus, the information about the recurrence of Norma's cancer had been general knowledge around town almost as soon as Norma knew about it. And as is common in close-knit communities, an illness befalling one tends to affect all. Thus, in the last several weeks, the town had experienced an outbreak of intestinal complaints and abdominal pains.

"It's not a cancer," I told him after a brief examination. I fully expected that this direct approach should suffice to quell his anxieties and send him on his way.

I was wrong.

"I know, Doc. It's the booze I reckon. But thanks for saying so anyway." He paused and then said, as if an afterthought, "Say, how's Norma doing?"

"You know I can't tell you that, Chet."

"Yeah sure, I know, Doc. But, well, do you think she's going to make it?"

"I'm a doctor, Chet, not a prophet. I can't tell what's in store for anyone. For all I know, *I* might not even be around tomorrow."

"No-o. I suppose not. But you must have some idea . . . Aww shoot! Never mind. Maybe I'll just pop by tomorrow and see for myself."

"I'm sure she'd like that."

"You bet. Anyway, thanks for the help." And he started for the door. I got out my pad.

"Wait," I said. "Let me write you a prescription for your stomach."

"My stomach?" he said, nonplussed. "Why would I want . . . oh yeah. My stomach. That's okay, Doc. It feels much better just for seeing you. Don't know what I'd do with pills anyway. Got all the medicine I need at home." He gave an embarrassed little laugh.

"A little less taste of your own medicine, and perhaps you wouldn't need mine."

"Taste of my own medicine, eh?" he chuckled. "Hey, that's a good one. Not a bad idea. Maybe I'll give it a try. You never can tell." And he gave me a slap on the shoulder and sauntered out.

True to his word, Chet popped by to see Norma the next day. Pretty soon he was popping by on a regular basis, mowing the lawn, raking leaves, and, when she was too exhausted by her chemotherapy, taking her to appointments and doing her shopping. Not only that, but it soon became apparent that Chet was not drinking, at least, according to Norma, "Not so as you'd notice."

For some months after her chemotherapy was finished, Norma regained most of her strength and all of her perkiness. But Chet kept popping by just the same, and on a couple of occasions they were even seen dining together at Nat's.

Then came town meeting day. Norma, who had attended every meeting since she was twelve, when the eighth-grade class was allowed to sit up in the balcony in order to observe small-town democracy, was not there. Everyone noticed. They also noticed that Chet, who had a perfect attendance record of his own, was sitting in the second row on the right side, just under the east-facing window that caught the morning sun. By tradition, the prominent citizens of the town all had their particular seats, and woe to the newcomer who inadvertently sat in one of them. The seat Chet had picked was Norma's.

I went by to see Norma the next day. "I certainly could have gone," she said. "I wouldn't say I was feeling too poorly to go. I just got the feeling that nothing that was decided would make any difference to me, if you know what I mean."

I did.

I launched into a convoluted discussion of *what next*. Norma cut it mercifully short.

"I suppose I'll get sick, and then I'll get sicker. And then I'll die. Isn't that what usually happens?"

I conceded that it was. As Norma didn't have any pain, and she was sleeping fine, there wasn't much for me to do. I suggested hospice.

"If you think so," she said, "but I do have someone helping me out now."

"Name of Chet, I believe."

"Yes. Funny, isn't it?" she said. "Same name as my ex-husband. Looks an awful lot like him too."

I explained to her that Chet would still have an important role as her primary caretaker, but the professional help of hospice nurses could eventually be quite helpful.

"You mean, *when the time comes?*"

"Yes."

"And you think that time is not far off, I gather."

I told her I didn't know when that time would be, but that an ounce of prevention being what it was, I thought a referral was in order.

The hospice team made one visit.

"It didn't work out," said Norma.

"*It,*" I said.

"Yes. So many things seem to go wrong when *It* is involved. *It* breaks. *It* gets lost. *It* spills."

"Fortunately, *It* isn't anyone's fault."

"Fortunately."

"What happened?"

"They were very earnest," said Norma.

"That they are."

"And they explained an awful lot."

"That they do."

"Including how their services were only good for six months, during which time, although they didn't actually say it, I was apparently expected to die. And they explained that what they provided was care designed to make me more comfortable, but not to enable me to live longer. I asked them what if I wanted to be comfortable *and* to live longer. They said that wasn't in their protocols. They also told me they would be taking care of all my medical needs at home, so I wouldn't need to go to the hospital. They discouraged going to the hospital, they explained, because I might wind up getting inappropriate care. At my stage, they pointed out, inappropriate care was a very bad thing.

"I asked them wasn't inappropriate care a bad thing at any stage, and they said perhaps it was, but that the other stages weren't up to them. Only when I was a hospice patient. The hospital bill came out of their budget. I asked them what if I broke my hip, and they said that was different, and it would be okay. But when I asked them what if I wanted more chemotherapy, they got very upset and said maybe I wasn't ready for hospice yet. They were very nice, but I don't think they were particularly pleased with my attitude."

"I can imagine."

"Before they left, they gave me a book on the stages of dying, and they took out a red marking pen and circled the stage I was in now, and they showed me the stage where I should call them for their services. And we all shook hands, and they left."

"I guess maybe it wasn't such a good idea."

"It just wasn't in the cards."

"No, *It* wasn't."

When Norma got too weak to take care of herself, Chet moved in.

I talked to him about the kinds of nursing needs Norma would be having and asked if he wanted me to arrange for a private-duty nurse.

"Oh no!" he said. "Don't know as we can afford one. If someone can just show me, I can figger it out. I'm some handy, don't you know?"

I talked to our head nurse, Sarah Trotter, and she talked to some of the other nurses. They agreed to give Chet lessons. When they were done, Chet could give an injection, change a catheter, do a sponge bath, and change sheets with a patient in the bed. They gave him a graduation ceremony and presented him with a diploma stating he was a Certified Caregiver. One of the nurses donated her old nursing cap for the occasion. I offered to compensate them for their efforts, but they flatly refused.

"He's so cute," they said.

"One of the nice things about being of the male persuasion is low expectations," I said.

The day before she died, I went over to the house. There wasn't really anything for me to do, but that didn't matter. Not having anything to do was why I went. I sat there with the two of them, talking a little about nothing in particular, but mostly not even talking, just sitting. Norma was sleeping, but Chet was in an expansive mood.

"You know, Doc," he said, "I've pretty much made a mess of my life."

"Until now."

"Until now. And I know I shouldn't say it, I shouldn't think it even, but you can't help what you think, and then what difference does it make if you say it or not?" He turned to Norma and took her hand. "But you know this cancer you've got, Nor." Her eyes were still closed, but she nodded slightly. "Now, don't get me wrong. I don't mean you to think I pleasure any in your sufferin'—Lord knows it pains me most as much it pains you. But back in the day, you usta keep saying to me to remember 'less we get run over by a truck or took in the middle of our sleep, we all got to go through sufferin' sometime. Anyway, I've got to say it, and I know you'll take my meaning. This cancer of yours, well, it's the best thing that ever happened to me."

Norma opened her eyes and looked at Chet. "Me too," she said.

They were the last words she spoke.

20

Just a Cough

....

I come in contact with a lot of people in my line of work. It's sort of like working at McDonald's, only the pay is better. If you were to ask one of the workers at McDonald's about the types of customers they get, she would probably tell you that there are two kinds. There are those that come in, place their order, take it, and leave, as if all they were doing were ordering cheap food on the go. And there are those who approach their order like a Middle East peace deal.

Although the people coming into my office are possessed of many backgrounds, personalities, and complaints, just like at McDonald's, there are the same two types.

The first type is the Important Person.

Note to Important People: I take you first out of respect for those of you who have been kind enough to take time out of your busy day, not only to buy my book, but also to read it, and to get this far even. Not wanting to make you waste your valuable time reading every word I have written, I just want to say right now: Thank you. I appreciate your effort. Now you can get on with your important work and not fritter away any more of your time on this.

Important people are serious people. And as serious people, they take themselves seriously. I don't expect they like it all that much. Seriosity is not a pleasant thing. But they really don't have much choice. It's the price they pay for being important.

Important people are also very busy. So busy, in fact, that an ordinary person can't imagine how busy they are. Busyness is another problem with being an Important Person. Between seriosity and busyness, you would wonder why on earth anyone would ever want to be one. The answer is, they don't. They are no more happy about being an Important Person than you are about them being one. Less, actually. But they know that someone has to be in charge, and they know they are the only ones qualified for the job. Naturally, they take the responsibility of being in charge seriously, because that's the kind of people they are. And they do it without complaining. Except for the part about being busy.

To the unimportant, an Important Person may seem immune from the ordinary worries of life. This is not true. I know a little about Important People, because I have a couple in my practice. I even have one Very Important Person that I can't mention by name, although you can probably figure out who she is if you read this book to the end. And I can tell you that even if an Important Person is more power-ful than a locomotive, or has more money than Fort Knox—and even, although I'm not speaking from personal experience, if that person is the president of the United States—he worries about his troubles just as much as the rest of us. More, if you want to know the truth.

Whenever an Important Person comes into the office, the first thing she tells me is that she doesn't have time to be sick. It is a lie. Because Important People are sick all the time. Not that they have heart attacks, or cancer, or pneumonia any more than you and I, but all the other things, like aches and bloats and blahs—those they have in spades. It is all on account of their having Seriosity and Busyness. These are not healthy conditions. So, despite the time it takes out of a very busy day to see a doctor, they are very good customers. Because whatever it is they have, they always want the works. Leave no stone unturned, they say. And I turn them over, every one. Two or three times usually.

I never have to ask them what's the matter when they come in. Because they have a list.

My ears ache, one might say, *and my toes too. I am tired all the time, and I can't sleep. And my back is stiff, and something else isn't. And my cholesterol is too high, and my sugar is too low. And the pills you gave me last time made me sick as a dog. And I talked to X, and X told me you should have given me the other pills instead, and . . . and . . . and . . .*

As they go down their list, they get more and more obsessed, until inevitably they begin to whine. So that even though I am being paid good money to listen to them, I am thinking, when will they ever be done? But they just keep on going on and on and on. Eventually I start to wonder what they would do if I suddenly did something really silly—

like stare at them cross-eyed, or break out singing "Farmer in the Dell."
But I never have. Because Important People are very high-strung, and
exposure to a little silliness might just put them over the edge.

Then you have the rest of us. The Placers of Orders. Now, I know
there are bound to be some people who will object that, by using us,
I am claiming to be just a Placer of Orders, when they know perfectly
well that, as a doctor, I certainly consider myself an Important Person,
even if I don't care to admit it. To them I would concede that for the
first few years I was in Dumster, I would have been guilty as charged.
But that is no longer the case.

It was all on account of Shorty Nutting.

Shorty Nutting was a railroad man. When I met him, he hadn't
worked the railroad for over thirty years, but that didn't matter.

"Being a railroad man is like one of those chronical things, Doc," he
told me. "Like pressure or sugar. The kinda thing that once you got it,
you got it, and can't never get rid of it no matter what. Once you been
a railroad man, that's what you are. After that, nothing else matters.
You could work at plumbin' or preachin'. Even doctorin', I s'pose. But
if you was ever a railroad man, that's what you'll be till they put you
six feet under."

Shorty went to work on the railroad when he was sixteen. It was
Missisquoi Valley Railroad then. He started as a laborer and eventually
worked his way up to stoker operator. He stayed with the line when
it became the Richford Branch of Central Vermont Railway. And he
kept staying on until Central Vermont was bought out by Railtex, and
they downsized Shorty out of their workforce. At the time, Shorty was
working a stretch of track just north of White River Junction, and as he
had no property back home, he figured he might as well save himself
the trouble of heading all the way back to Enosburg Falls. For if there
was anything important to Shorty it would be saving trouble. And on
the strength of a rumor he heard from a guy at the Polka Dot Diner, he
hitched a ride down Route Five to Dumster, where the rumor turned
out to be true, and he got a job on the town road crew.

Shorty lived in an apartment above Contremond's with his sister
Bea and Spike the cat. When he retired from the road crew, with the
few dollars he and Bea had saved up, he bought ten acres of river

bottomland south of town. He farmed the land "when he got 'round to it," as he said, for he spent most of his time sitting on the town bench on Main Street, listening to the stories that people who came by had to tell about themselves. It always seemed to me that Shorty had had an interesting life, but he never wanted to talk about himself. He preferred to listen. Ask him what it was like working on the railroad all those years, and he would answer, "Hard to say, you know. Never done nothing else."

If it were up to Shorty, I don't expect he would have ever come to see me on account of the cough, because his view of doctoring was that people only see the doctor when they are sick, which Shorty never considered that he was. This is not to say he didn't get diseases, but sick was just one of those things, like getting the haying done on a certain day, that Shorty never quite got around to.

It was just a cough when it started. When it didn't go away, it got promoted to a chronical cough. And after that, when he got the pain in his chest, he allowed as how it was a chronical cough with a pain on the side. Nothing he needed to bother the doctor about. Then he got a little winded when he climbed up the stairs to the apartment, and his pants kept slipping down. But he went on about his business, which was mostly just "dubbing around," and he would have been content to go on dubbing around until he couldn't do that even, but the cough got to the point where it was keeping his sister up at night. So she made an appointment for him to see me, threatening that if he didn't keep it she would "damn well dub him around." However reluctant Shorty may have been to put himself in my hands, mine were the lesser of two evils. And so in he came.

I told Shorty I thought we ought to get an X-ray to see what was going on. Shorty said he didn't see much point. What was going on, he said, was the cough, and it was going to keep on going on until it had got to where it was going, and we both knew where that was.

"It might be TB," I said.

"Was a Micmac on the railroad crew who had TB," he said. "Long time ago. Never knowed no one with TB 'round here. But could be, I s'pose. Guess you got me there." And he got the X-ray.

It was not TB.

I told Shorty we would need to do some blood work and get some more X-rays, and then I would refer him to a cancer specialist, so he could find out what his options were.

Shorty listened to what I had to say carefully.

"I thank you for your interest, Doc. An' I know you mean well. But if it's okay with you, I think I'd just as soon leave it at *Not TB*. 'Less you got something for the cough."

There was no point in arguing with him, so I gave him a prescription for some cough medicine, and told him I wanted to see him again in a month. Shorty said if it made me feel better, it was okay with him.

"Besides," he said, "I s'pose it'll keep the wolf from my door."

"I'm afraid I can't promise . . ."

"Not that one, Doc," he said. "Talking about Bea."

So each month he came in. And each month he got a little weaker, and each month I gave him a little stronger medicine for the cough, and each month I suggested maybe it was time for those other tests and the visit to the oncologist, and each time he said no thanks. Finally one day he told me if I really wanted to do something for him, he did have one problem that was bothering, and he'd appreciate it if I could fix it. I asked him what the problem was, and he told me. After I examined him, I told him it was something I couldn't fix. And he said that was okay, he didn't expect I could, but he thought he'd ask anyway seeing as how I was so interested in doing something.

After that, he brought up the problem at each visit. It would go something like this. Shorty would come in and sit down. He wouldn't say anything. He'd just sit there and look at me. And I would ask, "Shorty how do you feel?" And he still wouldn't say anything. He would just sit there looking as blank as the screen on an unplugged television. Anyone would have thought he hadn't heard me. But he heard me just fine. Eventually he would give a tug to his right ear. Just one quick pull, and then let go. Like he was pulling a starter cord. Then he'd purse his lips together, and furrow his brow, and then, all warmed up and running smooth, he would start to grin.

Shorty's grin was not an ordinary grin, like what you might see if you told someone a joke or offered him a hot fudge sundae. Shorty's grin was nothing like that. Shorty's grin was a giant of a grin. It started in one corner of his mouth, and then it spread across his face from one side clear to the other, until it looked like what a chocolate ice cream cone would leave on the face of a little boy.

I would try to hold off. After all, I was his doctor. But eventually I would have to give in. Because Shorty always held out longer. So finally, I had to grin back.

Once he was sure my grin was good and stuck on my face Shorty would repeat my question.

"How do I feel?"

And he would extend his hands in front of him, and spread his fingers wide, and wiggle them a couple of times back and forth. And then, impossible as it would seem, his grin would get even wider, and he would say,

"With my fingers."

And then I would ask him, knowing full well exactly the answer,

"What brings you in today?"

And Shorty would stick out his legs and move them up and down and say,

"My feet."

We would go back and forth like this for a while. I would ask him why he was here, and he said because I asked him. I would ask him what's the matter, and he would answer, "What's it matter?" I would ask him was he in pain, and he would say no, he was in Dumster.

Eventually I would have to ask him the question he had been waiting for.

"What can I do for you, Shorty?"

And Shorty would stick out his tongue.

Patients stick out their tongues *for* me all the time. And then they say *Ah*. It's a pointless gesture, but it's one of those things that doctors ask patients to do, just because they can. When Shorty sticks out his tongue, however, he says "*Ah Ha!*" Not in so many words, but because he knows his tongue is the one thing I don't want to see. Because every time I pester him long enough about what is bothering him, he sticks out his tongue and says,

"You can get rid of that hair on the end of my tongue."

And I say, "I don't see any hair on your tongue, Shorty."

The first time I tried to tell him there was no such thing as hair on a tongue, he said what I really meant was that I had never seen one before. And I told him that I had never even heard of such a thing. He said that was okay. There was a first time for everything. He knew it was there, because he could feel it, and in the right light with the mirror at the right angle, he could actually see it. And if I couldn't see it, why didn't I just tell him so and be done with it. Eventually I had to give up and concede.

"I'm afraid I can't do that, Shorty."

At the very end, when he was too weak to come dubbing in, I went out to his house. He was lying in the bed, picking at his tongue and grinning.

"Doc," he said to me after a bit. "You still don't think there's any hair on that tongue, do you?"

"No, Shorty. I don't."

And he said "That's okay. I was just kidding about you taking it off anyway."

"I thought that might be the case."

"Yeah. I wouldn't really want you to take it off."

"Because it isn't really there."

"Because I'm having too much fun picking at it."

There are those who would say, regarding this hair-on-his-tongue business, that because of all the medication he was taking for his cough Shorty was just hallucinating. But they would be wrong. It took me a while, but finally I realized that there was nothing delusional about it. That hair sprouted up the first time I wanted to do something about his cough, and, like Pinocchio's nose, each time I made another recommendation, it got a little longer.

It was a real hair. It was a hair that Shorty grew just for me, his doctor. He grew that hair in order to keep me from getting carried away with the idea that because I was a doctor, there was something I could do for him. And by growing that hair, he did more for me than I ever did for him. Because, before that hair, I would have spells where I considered myself an Important Person. But no more. Now if I feel one of those spells coming on, I just think of the hair on Shorty's tongue.

And I grin.

21

I'm No Good

....

The female of the species, being more evolved, is quite diverse. With respect to the male *Homo vermontiens*, however, there are but two varieties. This is not to say that, were you to travel about the state, especially if it included Brattleboro or Burlington, you would not see additional varieties, some of which are quite exotic. But such specimens are not native.

The first is the Land Male. The Land Male comes from the land, is bound to the land, and from the land he gets the sustenance needed to carry on each day. In the early days of Vermont, the Land Male was the dominant variety. He was, until recently, found exclusively on farms. As that habitat has diminished substantially, the population of Land Males is now much reduced, and those that remain are scattered widely throughout the state. Almost invisible to the untrained eye, he still can be found in select spots if one looks carefully—puttering about among tomato patches, pulling oxen at town fairs, and hanging sap buckets in the spring.

Accordingly, the last hundred and fifty years has seen the ascendancy of the second, a less hardy but more adaptable variety, the Machine Male. It almost goes without saying that as man has become more removed from the land, he has become more attached to the machine. Car, truck, snowmobile, motorboat, ATV, lawn mower, trimmer, chain saw, power drill, table saw: The list is endless. Most Machine Males use their machines at work or at play and tinker with them now and then according to their whim, but do not take them too seriously. Still, a few live for their machines, as if they were born to them.

Whether or not Charles Darwin would agree with this proposition, I am not sure. In *The Origin of the Species* he makes a particular emphasis about evolution being something that occurs over A Long Time, by which he usually meant thousands of years. But he does make note of exceptions, where sudden and dramatic changes in the environment can accelerate the process. Like the beak of the Galapagos finch, which, depending on the nature and quantity of the seeds available to it, changes every few years. He also points out that the owners of domesticated animals can rapidly create varieties according to their fancy by selective breeding. So I would expect that he would say it was at least possible that environmental change and selective breeding could have combined to produce the genetically altered male of which Archie Mack would be the prototype.

For with Archie Mack, machines were in his blood.

Archie's great-great-grandfather was a Scotsman by the name of Angus Macauslan. Angus was born the youngest of five sons in 1770 on the shores of the Firth of Clyde, in the town of Greenock. The family farm, though modestly prosperous, was only large enough to provide a living for four families. So, in his early twenties, Angus left home to try his luck in Glasgow. There, in a pub one night, while expounding on the plight of small family farms, he happened upon a fellow Grennockian and clansman, one James Watt by name. Being a generous man, Mr. Watt offered to share his bottle of Macallan single-malt. Angus readily agreed. As the scotch flowed, they discovered they had more in common than geography and clanship. Mr. Watt told Angus about his work at the university, where he was designing a new steam engine, one that he was sure would be an improvement over the old Newcomen engine. Angus expressed an interest in the project, and as Mr. Watt was never without his beloved drawings, he pulled them out of his greatcoat and laid them on the bar. Poring intently over the plans, Angus waxed enthusiastic about the design. Any fool could see, he said, that this steam engine would work a heap better than the Newcomen, seeing as how it made the steam to condense in a separate chamber from the piston. Impressed by Macauslan's grasp of the subject, Mr. Watt offered him a job on the spot. Angus accepted.

It didn't take long before Mr. Watt discovered that in Angus he had the perfect complement to his engineering vision, a man who not only understood what he was trying to do, but had an instinctive vision of how it could be done. Watt had to do no more than present Angus with a rough sketch for a new machine, and Angus could sit down at his workbench and turn out a working model that not only would perform exactly as Watt intended, but invariably contained at least a couple of improvements to the design. If Watt was the brain, Angus was his hands. Each depended wholly on the other. Watt asked him once how he did it. "Canna say," he said. "Ay just look at it a bit, an' then all of a sudden, there it be." He tapped his skull a couple of times. "Seems as if it's all tucked up in there waitin' to cumma out. Just like a borned baby."

It was a very successful collaboration. And when James Watt joined with Matthew Boulton to form the Boulton and Watt Engine Company, it was Angus Macauslan who became their chief mechanic. After Angus died, his son James Watt Macauslan took his father's position.

In 1892 James W. Macauslan's youngest son, Matthew, told his father that Scotland and the steam-engine life were not for him. He wanted to try his luck in the New World. With his father's blessing and his inheritance—a set of well-worn, well-maintained machine tools—he arrived in the United States at the new immigration facility on Ellis Island. From Ellis Island he made his way to Brooklyn, where he subsisted for the next year by hiring himself out to the numerous textile factories as a repairman for their sewing machines and looms. Then in 1893 he saw a posted bill stating that the Mack Brothers Company, owners Jack and Augustus Mack, were opening a factory to manufacture gasoline trucks. Able-bodied mechanics were urged to apply at the address below. Matthew knew at once this was what he had come to America for. He applied for a job and was accepted. Like Angus and Mr. Watt, Matthew and the Macks were a perfect fit. Matthew loved his work, and the owners loved Matthew. Soon Matthew became head mechanic for what would become the world's most famous truck manufacturer. On the assembly floor, they called him Mack. It was easier than Macauslan, and it seemed only fitting. When Matthew had a son, he named him Augie Mack. Augie, like the Macauslan males before him, wasn't much for formal schooling. At the age of fourteen he went to work for Mack Trucks. His father fully expected his son someday to take over the job he so proudly held.

But Augie had the Macauslan wanderlust. Two years later, only sixteen years old, he left Brooklyn and headed up the Connecticut River to New England, trying his hand first at the Colt factory in Hartford, then at the Rolls-Royce factory in Springfield. After hearing about a machinist's paradise in a place called Precision Valley, he finally came to its proverbial capital, Dumster.

In 1846 a Dumster gunsmith by the name of Richard S. Lawrence joined up with a local businessman, S. E. Robbins, and accepted an order from the government to manufacture ten thousand Springfield rifles. It was a staggering number, and Lawrence's tooling skills notwithstanding, the general opinion in town was that the pair were completely off their rocker. Everyone expected that the enterprise would quickly go belly-up. But Lawrence had an idea. Rather than tooling each rifle individually, he designed his machine tools with a degree of precision that would enable them to turn out identical interchangeable parts, thus vastly simplifying the manufacture and assembly process. It was a brilliant idea, and soon they were manufacturing rifles at the rate of over a hundred a day. In 1851 Lawrence displayed his rifles at the Crystal Palace Industrial Exposition in London, after which he was awarded a contract by the English to produce their Enfield rifles. Like prospectors to the gold rush, machinists flocked to the area, and soon other businesses looking to manufacture quality equipment on a large scale moved into the valley. In its heyday, Dumster had three machine tool shops employing over fifteen hundred people. But as the machine tool industry matured, it manufactured itself out of business. Each generation of more sophisticated machines could perform tasks that previously had been done by hand. Eventually the skills that had been honed in the valley were no longer needed, and owners looked to other parts of the country, where labor and energy costs were much cheaper. Like the textile mills in southern New England, one by one the businesses left town for more hospitable climes, and the factories shut down.

The largest of these was Acme Tool and Die. In its heyday Acme had over one thousand employees. By January 2000, though, the workforce was down to seventy hardy souls. Every one of them was waiting for the inevitable.

Somehow Augie knew when that would be. Walking in the door on March 7, 2001, he put his hand to his machine and toppled over. He was dead before he hit the floor. An hour later the loudspeaker came on announcing that the plant would close at the end of the day.

It was a portent of the end, not only for Augie, but for just about the entire Macauslan line as well. For the productivity of the family had paralleled that of the industry it served. Angus Macauslan was one of five, his son James of six. Matthew had four children, but, as a sign of what was to come, one was a girl. Augie had only his Archie, and despite fair looks, a sober lifestyle, and a steady job that made him as good a catch as could be found in Dumster, Archie remained a bachelor.

Archie worked at Acme too. When it closed, he went over to Consolidated Manufacturing, but it followed suit two years later. Then he went to work at Jones and Talbot. Archie knew full well that J&T was in its death throes, but machining was all he knew, and besides, for Archie the future never lay much beyond the next meal.

About half the time, when coronaries plug up, the outcome is that which befell Augie Macauslan. One minute the vessel is functioning reasonably well, with only a small spot of plaque on the wall, nothing sufficient to cause any hindrance to the smooth flow of blood. The next minute the spot explodes, and a clot fills the artery. The downstream myocardium, suddenly deprived of oxygen, stops in midstroke, and, unless it just happens to be on the way to the hospital to visit a friend, so does the being to which the heart belongs.

The rest of the time the offending plaque enlarges slowly, giving the heart a chance to find sustenance elsewhere, so that when the actual blockage occurs, the curtain does not descend completely. Perhaps Archie, being younger, was in better condition to withstand the blow than his father. Or perhaps he had seen the event coming from a long way out. Regardless of the reason, when J&T finally shut down, Archie did not. But he certainly looked sick enough when he came in two days later.

Entering the emergency department, I didn't need to ask which room he was in. The sickly sweet odor of engine degreaser that clung to him like manure to a farmer wafted out from Room Two. He looked ghastly. Sweating profusely and wheezing audibly, Archie was doubled over in agony. His vital signs, the nurse said tersely, were "unstable."

Blood pressure: eighty over sixty
Pulse: thirty-five
Respirations: twenty-four

By the time I arrived, she had already started an intravenous running full-bore and placed him on oxygen, neither, she reported, with any obvious benefit to his condition.

Asking him what was the matter was pointless. "Where does it hurt the most?" I asked.

He pointed to the center of his chest.

"Blew a gasket, Doc," he gasped. "Carburetor's shot too, I 'spect." Gasp. "Prob'ly need" Gasp. "New" Gasp. "Air filter." Gasp. "While you're at it."

From the looks of things, his diagnosis seemed reasonably accurate. The monitor showed not only the slow heart rate, but an electrical short circuit between the atria and ventricles. It was entirely consistent with a large heart attack, most likely in the lower region of the heart. Regardless of how it might affect his already low blood pressure, Archie needed something to relieve his pain. I ordered a judicious dose of morphine.

After the morphine, an aspirin, a liter of IV fluid, and a dose of atropine to stimulate the heart rate, he looked a bit more removed from the door through which there was no return. As he now seemed less indicative of imminent demise, I sat down to go over his story in more detail.

The symptoms had come on rather suddenly while he was cleaning the engine block on his car. At first he was just sick to his stomach. Then he felt faint. And then he had trouble breathing. The chest pain came a little later. As it was a hot day, and there was no ventilation in the garage, he thought it might have been the fumes from the solvent.

"But it didn't get better when you left the garage."

"Well, Doc. I didn't leave. Not then anyway. I was grinding the valves down, and it's not somepin' you can leave in the middle of."

"Like an operation."

"Right. The job was going slower than I expected. Maybe 'cause I wasn't feeling so good. Anyway. I sorta passed out, and when I came to on the floor, I realized I couldn't finish the job."

"A wise assessment."

"I know it was dumb. But Doc, you gotta do what you gotta do."

"Good point."

"Yeah, well." He tapped on his chest. "What's the damage? Any hope for this ol' rig? Or is it time for the junkyard, an' salvage what you can in spare parts?"

I went over him carefully. His blood pressure was in a more socially acceptable range, and his heart rate had improved substantially. He had stopped wheezing, and the sweating was almost gone. Other than small pupils from the morphine, his exam was now just about normal. Although it was still early, the initial blood tests showed no signs of a coronary occlusion.

"So far so good," I said.

"Just the warning light?"

"Could be, Archie. But we should keep you here overnight just to make sure."

"I'm in your hands."

The next day he was much better. His nausea was gone, his blood pressure was fine, and the blood tests remained normal. He didn't have much appetite, and his eyes had a dull look, but the aftermath of his inhalation could certainly account for that. He still had a faint but unmistakable odor of the solvent on his breath. The only real fly in the ointment was his heart rate. It was still hovering around forty. Now, a slow pulse is not necessarily a sign of a malfunctioning heart. Plenty of highly conditioned athletes are in this range. Their hearts are large and efficient, and they can pump out more blood with each beat than the rest of us, so they run at a pretty low idling speed. But Archie was not well conditioned. Forty was too low for him. Particularly when he stood up.

Archie watched me studying the monitor.

"En-gyne trouble, huh? S'pose it's only to be expected. Got a nineteen forty Mack under the hood. It's a good'n. But I know I ain't been quite up to the mark on my maintenance."

"That's certainly true," I said. We had discussed his blood pressure and cholesterol on several occasions, but Archie wasn't much for pills or diets.

"'Cept the oil. Yessir, I keep that up regl'r. I put the old oil to that baby ever' day, 'for I get out of bed. One whole cup—two if'n she feels a mite puny. Starts her right up. An' I don't use the cheap stuff. Extra-virgin cold-pressed. That's all she gets." He thumped his chest proudly.

"Olive oil can't hurt, Archie. But it looks to me that you actually have a pretty good engine. It's just running a little slow."

"Idle control a bit off, eh?"

"Just what I was thinking."

"Time to put 'er up on the rack and have a look, eh?"

"It is."

I ordered an echocardiogram. All four cylinders were firing just as they should, and each of the valves opened and closed smooth as clockwork. The mechanical parts of his heart were all in proper working order. I gave Archie the news.

"The motor's fine, Archie. What you have is a problem with the wiring. It's easy enough to fix. I'll set you up for an appointment with the electricians, and you'll be back to full speed in no time. In the meantime, you can go home. Just be sure to take it easy."

Archie looked doubtful.

"Don't know 'bout that, Doc."

"I understand. You're worried it might up and stop on you. That's perfectly natural, but quite unlikely. However, if you'd feel safer here, you can stay until I can arrange for a transfer to the medical center."

"It's not that."

"What is it then?"

"When I told you I hadn't been taking care of the engine . . ."

"I know. Don't worry about that. As you said, consider this a warning light on the dashboard of your life. Once you've got a pacemaker in, you'll be good as new."

Archie stared at the floor. ". . . what I meant was, I *really* wasn't taking care of it."

"I don't understand. What do you mean?"

Archie kept his gaze fixed on the floor. "I'm no good, Doc."

"That's not true at all! Why—you're as good as anyone in this town. A damn sight better, in my opinion, than quite a few. What makes you think that you're no good?"

"Just am, I reckon." He shrugged. "You don't know the half of it, Doc."

It was his voice. Something not right. Something I was missing.

I looked at Archie again. And then I saw them. And what a fool I had been. Merrily trotting down the cardiac lane without a second thought, I had completely missed the turn. I was on the wrong path. The one I should be on was right there before my eyes. It was staring me in the face.

Although it is an exaggeration, what was looking back at me was a set of pupils that go by the name of pinpoint. We say *pinpoint* when we want to indicate that the pupils are so small, they are smaller than any ordinary pupil can get, even in the brightest light. This happens when something jams the nerve controlling the iris, and the lens gets stuck at the highest f-stop. Advanced syphilis can do it, and severe brain damage. Also eyedrops for glaucoma. But none of these applied to Archie. Most commonly it is due to narcotics, but the effect wears off as the medicine leaves the body, which, in Archie's case, would have been almost twenty-four hours ago. That left only one other consideration.

"It wasn't engine degreaser, was it, Archie?"

Archie shook his head.

"What was it?"

"Roach poison."

I didn't have to ask why. He had already told me. Archie was a mechanic, not a moralist. When he said *No good* he did not mean he was a bad person. He meant useless. The skilled machinist, like the muzzleloader, the horse-drawn plow, and the rotary phone, had been rendered obsolete by the march of technology. Once he was a vital cog in the machine that drove the Precision Valley engine. That machine had ground to a halt.

I didn't know what to say.

"Ain't no need for this ol' rig no more," he said matter-of-factly. "So I figured it was time to junk the thing."

Archie wasn't actually depressed. It was just that in his mechanistic view of life, if the machine served no useful purpose, there was no point in keeping it running. I thought about his situation for a minute. And I realized what I had to do.

"Ordinarily, Archie, I'd call in Doctor Belittle. But I'm not going to do that. You would just drive each other crazy, and in his case that wouldn't be a long trip. So I'm going to let you go without a shrink. But I want you to promise me you'll do me a favor before you try another damn fool stunt like this."

"Fair enough," he said. "Worse comes to worst, I got plenty of time to be dead. What's the favor?"

"Fix my lawn mower."

"Bring it 'round."

I brought him the mower, and after a bit of tinkering he had it running good as new. "Just a clogged windpipe, Doc. Couldn't get no air. You know them filters work better if they're cleaned now and then. Just thought you might want to know, seeing as how you're so big on that maintenance stuff."

"Thanks, Archie, I appreciate that. Maybe what it should have is a regular checkup each year—motor maintenance you could say."

Archie grinned.

"Yer right as rain on that one, Doc. Every machine needs regl'r lookin' after if it's gonna run right."

"I'll put it on my schedule. Now, how much do I owe you?"

"Not a cent. It was a favor, Doc, remember? And I 'spect that in the favor-owed department, I'm still a bit behind. So we'll just say long as you keep me alive, you can bring it 'round anytime, and we'll leave it at that."

"It's a deal. You know, Archie, there's a lot of mowers in town, and I'm guessing they all could use a regular checkup now and then."

Archie nodded. "I know what you mean. The way some people treat their machines . . . like to breaks my heart."

"Yes. Abuse and neglect is always painful to watch, regardless of the victim. But you could do something about it."

"Say what?"

"Start a practice. Archie Mack, The Engine Doctor. There's no one better qualified to do it, and everybody knows it. You'd be doing the town a service. You'd be doing some *good*!"

"I don't think so, Doc. It's a nice idea, but it'd never work. Who's gonna pay for somepin' they could be doing themselves. Nobody I know."

"Me for one."

He thought for a minute. "Flatlanders you mean?"

"There's more of us every year."

"You ain't wrong there."

"I'll make you a deal. I'll stake you whatever it takes to get the tools and a shop set up. You pay me back when you can and give me five percent of what you make in the first year. Even if it's nothing, it's worth it for me, just to keep you from trying any of this foolishness again. Besides, I'm betting it's going to be a good investment."

Archie grinned and stuck out his hand.

"You got a deal, Doc."

The business was a big success. Archie paid me off in full in just a year, and in no time flat he had more work than he could handle. He was happy as a clam. And that's not all. He finally succumbed to the assault of Widow Jenkins, who lived with her three sons on a farm just south of town. After they were married, he moved in with them. The barn wasn't being used, and his shop in town was by then too small, so he converted the barn into his workshop.

And after her youngest son graduated from Dumster High, he joined the business.

22

One Out to Go

··········

I need to feel what I am reading—the heft of a book as I hold it in my hand, or on my lap, or, should the occasion demand, the weight of the tome as it sits facedown upon my chest. I like the feel of news-print between my fingers as I turn the pages and fold it precisely to expose just the column I intend to read. I learned to fold a paper from my father. He was a newspaperman, and he read seven papers a day, most of which he did with one hand, while with the other he held on to a strap on the A train. Unlike those raised in the electronic age, this sensation of touch is necessary in order for my primitive brain to engage fully in that remarkable process by which the printed word is transferred to the mind's eye.

So even though mail delivered to my computer is convenient and fast as all get-out, I still prefer the kind that arrives in my mailbox. Besides, a trip to one's inbox pales in comparison with the adventure of going out to retrieve the mail.

You never know what lies inside that black box until you open the lid and stick in your hand. It could be an unexpected treat. I have never found gold or diamonds, but on the day after Halloween, there is always a bar of chocolate from some unknown trick-or-treater sympa-thetic to my wants. One time it was my wallet, which had fallen out of my pocket, unbeknownst to me, while I was walking the dog. Then there's always the possibility, however remote, of some hidden danger—a steel trap or a poisonous snake—placed there by someone who, because of some long-ago insult you have completely forgotten, possibly even by your ancestors, is bent upon revenge. Not that this has ever happened to me, but the mere fact that it could makes even the most unwanted mail appreciated for what it isn't.

I love to get letters. It doesn't matter what kind. Admittedly, what awaits me these days is a large assortment of colorful pseudo-missives that are appealing to the eye, but not actually *from* anyone. But I open and read them all, at least up to the part that says, *Congratulations, you have just . . .*

Then there is the whole business of opening the letter. Which you may decide to do immediately upon its receipt, or, upon recognizing the sender, tuck away until you have time to savor it in your favorite private place. And when you finally are ready, the way in which the envelope's contents are exposed—by ripping or tearing or, if it happens to be your particular bent, by slitting with a knife—satisfies some primeval need that simply cannot be rivaled by the mere click of a finger.

All of this takes time, of course, though that too is an essential part of the whole business. But delayed gratification is a subject I will not belabor at this point, as I fear that once I get started, I will pretty quickly get mired in the whole business of how Things Aren't The Way They Used To Be, a subject that, since Things never really were The Way They Used To Be, gets tiresome pretty quickly.

Regardless of how you get your mail, however, the greatest pleasure always comes when you receive a missive unexpectedly from someone whom you haven't heard from for ages. Someone who, for all you know, might have died or moved to Australia years ago. Someone about whom you have fond memories, but whom you haven't even thought about for a long time.

In the case of Joyce Hergenhan, the long time was fifty years.

I was raised in the town of Pleasantville, New York. Pleasantville's biggest claim to fame is that it is the home of the *Reader's Digest*. It isn't. The *Reader's Digest* is actually located in neighboring Chappaqua. But you couldn't expect somebody like the *Reader's Digest* to admit to living in Chappaqua. At least not in public.

Joyce and I were not boyfriend and girlfriend. But she was more than someone to whom I just nodded in the hall or Hiya'd at a football game. We were co-editors of the school newspaper, and so we were together on a regular, if infrequent, basis. You could say she was a class-mate with privileges, although I gather that the extent of privileges in friendly relationships has expanded considerably since the days of my youth. Joyce and I and some one hundred and forty others graduated from Pleasantville High School in 1959. As do all who survive the high school experience together, we vowed that we would all keep in touch with one another after graduation and never forget the lasting relationships our high school years had created.

Our class had made the customary plans for a fifth reunion in 1964, but the week prior to the event, our class secretary, who was in charge of the event, committed suicide. That pretty much put a kibosh on the whole affair.

As the years went by without anyone daring to take on the Reunion Curse, it appeared that this would be a kibosh without end. And so it was until Joyce, who was one of those people that, once she decided something was a good idea, made sure it was brought to fruition, recognized that time being what it was, it was now or never for the PHS Class of 'Fifty-nine.

Dear Chip, the letter began, and as I saw the long-abandoned nickname, my thoughts were transported back to the world of that scrawny pimply-faced adolescent the title betokened. There followed a brief explanation of how she had come to the conclusion that it was imperative for all of us to get together. At our time in life, she said, we needed to connect with our roots. And although she didn't say it in so many words, she implied this might be our last chance before we were uprooted to the Great Harvest in the Sky. She had made reservations for a reunion date and place, and hoped that we all would come. She closed by asking that I fill out and send back to her an enclosed questionnaire so she could compile it in a scrapbook for all of us to see.

The questionnaire contained the basic who, what, where, and when questions, and I easily compiled a succinct and witty account of my life up to the present. At the end were two questions, prefaced by a stern warning in bold type not to ignore them under penalty of severe rebuke by Joyce.

What is your best memory of PHS? What is your worst?

I've always had difficulty with the concept of bestness. It restricts the scope of one's enjoyment. If one thing is Best, then something else that you otherwise would have liked immensely becomes Second Best. And everything after that gets relegated to Also Ran. So I prefer to stick with Pretty Good at the apex of my rating scale, or, to put it in *Lingua Dumstra*, Okay. It makes for a bigger tent.

I put down "good friends and good times" and was pleased to see, when the scrapbook came out, that most everybody else did pretty much the same, save, of course, for the few whom you knew would take it seriously, and who wrote a tiresome lengthy piece about The Game or The Night or The Trip.

It was the second question that gave me serious pause. This time it wasn't a problem with picking out the one outstanding event among a series of candidates. There was no question as to the winner. It was the See More Beach episode. What I was in doubt about was the propriety of setting it out for public viewing. I can't say it was because I was ashamed, or even embarrassed, in both of which categories I am, according to Trine, seriously challenged by my years of doctoring, but somehow it just didn't seem appropriate for the setting. So instead I related an event that was distressing only for the briefest of moments, and which made for a much better reunion story.

The date was Monday, October 8, 1956. I don't want to give the wrong impression here. My memory is not that good. I know the date because I looked it up. How it was that I could look it up, down even to the minute, will become apparent presently. It was a little after three in the afternoon, and I was in Mrs. Wright's seventh-period biology class. Biology was my favorite subject, and Mrs. Wright was a good teacher, so it usually had my full attention. But on this particular day my thoughts were miles away—twenty-three to be precise. It was the fifth game of the World Series at Yankee Stadium, and Don Larsen was one out away from a perfect game against the Brooklyn Dodgers. This I knew because of a transistor radio I had smuggled into class, which I had secreted in my desk. The volume was turned down so as to be inaudible even to my closest neighbors, but by means of a series of hand signals from me, everyone else in class knew what was going on. As the tension mounted in the ninth inning, with first Furillo and then Campanella grounding out, there was an unmistakable buzz of excitement throughout the room that was impossible to conceal. Mrs. Wright knew something was up.

The count was one and two on Dale Mitchell when she caught me. Marching down the aisle to my desk, she retrieved the offending device, returned to her desk, and, despite a howl of protests that there was *only one out to go*, and *how could she*, and *Aww Mrs. Wright*, she turned it off without a word. And then, in an uncharacteristically melodramatic move, she dropped it in the wastebasket.

There was no change in the expression on her face as she turned back to the class and said. "And now back to meiosis in *Euglena*." But the way she stood radiated self-satisfaction. Another victory had been won over the forces of adolescence. And for a brief moment I realized with remarkable clarity that this was why she loved teaching. It was not in the effort to interest us in the wonders of the natural world that she derived her sense of purpose, for this was a task that even for the Good Students was pretty much utter futility. Rather it was in her ability to demonstrate to us budding louts that in the war of the generations, the relentless determination of adulthood would always defeat the hormonal energy of youth.

Her victory was short-lived. The collective anguish of Biology One was abruptly ended when, a few seconds later, a mighty roar erupted from the Biology Two class next door. The teacher of Biology Two was the Mr. of Mr. and Mrs. Wright. More socially responsible than his Beloved Spouse, he had brought the family radio to school that day, allowing the entire class to hear that famous last strike. At the time Mrs. Wright was at the blackboard, chalk in hand, diagramming the *Euglena*'s procreative DNA. She lifted the chalk from the board and, holding it in a posture suggestive of a spear about to be launched, aimed it at the room next door. There would be words in the Wright household that night.

The story was well received by Joyce, who commented that it helped to set a "good tone" for the reunion book.

The reunion was fun. At least it was once I got over the shock of how old everyone looked. This was greatly facilitated by the simple expedient of never looking anyone in the face and keeping my eyes strictly focused on their name tag, upon which was displayed both the person's high school name and his or her photograph from our senior yearbook.

Even though the in-crowd at PHS was a fairly loose group, more inclusive than not, I was not a part of it. I managed to stay just beyond the fringes of its wide net, not so much by their exclusion as by my being inordinately shy. Thus it was a special treat for me that night to have an extended conversation with the captain of the football team, with whom prior to that I had never exchanged more than the *howsithangin–lownuf* repartee that was the standard male interchange of the day. He lived in Oklahoma where he had a thousand-acre farm and several hundred head of cattle. We had a nice long chat about the vicissitudes of cattle ranching in the era of Food Inc. Perhaps even more gratifying, I had a dance with one of our cheerleaders, a very pretty and popular girl, whom I'd always admired from afar. She was now a successful financial planner in Manhattan.

My best friends were there, and we had fun reminiscing about all those things we may or may not have done, but which we certainly remembered. My old girlfriend did not come. She had written in the scrapbook that she was now crippled by arthritis and would be unable to attend. It was a little sad, as it was hard for me to imagine her anything other than the girl I remembered from fifty years ago. Although she was not actually *my* girlfriend. That privilege belonged to the fellow whose ring she wore, but who was away at private school. She had selected me as a relatively harmless locum tenens to squire her to public events. I didn't mind. It was about as much as I could handle, and as she could pretty much have had the pick of the litter, I was honored to be chosen for the role.

There was a certain amount of that Doing the Accomplishment Rag, but not really very much at all. Certainly nothing like the interminable dance of my college reunions, where we all sat around and congratulated ourselves on what fantastic people we still were. It turned out that we were all simply glad to see one another after all these years. For the evening, we were just who we were, not what we had become.

I have played many roles in life—husband, father, friend, neighbor, and generally speaking I can do an adequate job of them. But just as Bela Lugosi, no matter what part he is asked to play, is always Dracula, so am I, finally, Doctor. We could be in the scene of Family at Dinner, a part of the performance in which all the actors and actresses are expected to adhere strictly to their assigned roles—but should the conversation happen to take the slightest turn in a medical direction, onto the stage leaps Doctor, pushing all others aside and declaiming lines such as *Actually, that's not quite accurate* or *Not how I would approach it*. As Trine has regularly pointed out, the performance invariably goes on much too long, past the stage of comic relief and well into tedium.

But at the reunion it was different. There was something about this gathering of old duffers that made us all feel, overwhelming evidence to the contrary, that we were still the same loose-limbed, hormone-laden kids we knew one another as many years ago, when the thought that we could become anything resembling a functioning adult was a possibility not even raised to the point of consideration.

So here I was again, just plain Chip. And when one of my classmates happened to bring up his recent bout with bypass surgery, my first thought was not whether he would have been better off with medical therapy, but "Wow, that must have been quite a shocker." And when he said that yes, it sure was, and raised his shirt to show the scar, though I had seen hundreds such before, I was as impressed as all my classmates. And when offered the chance to touch it, I did.

At the end of the evening we all said our long good-byes and agreed about what a good time we had, and we promised now to keep in touch for sure, and to have another reunion in five years. And we all knew that we never would. Because we all knew that by the next time the one uninvited guest we would not want to see would surely be there. And he would spoil the party.

23

Americanitis

....

"What is it, Samantha?"
"I'm tired, Doctor Conger."
"I'm sorry to hear that."
"I've been tired for a while."
"For a long time?"
"That depends."
"Of course."
"In addition to being tired, I'm not sleeping very well, and I get headaches. Also my muscles ache."
"And you are wondering—"
"If there really is such a thing as chronic fatigue syndrome."

Samantha Sticklethwaite was never one for beating around the bush. That, however, did not mean that I was so constrained. I saw no reason for being forthcoming at this early stage of the game.

"Well, that is certainly an interesting question."
"Thank you, Doctor Conger."
"For which there is no simple answer."
"I wouldn't expect one."
"In fact, it is a rather complicated subject."
"So I understand."
"You always do."
"I looked at the CDC website. That was your old stomping grounds, I believe?"
"It was. They do good work there."
"So I gather. According to the site, it was the CDC that formally gave the name to, and created the diagnostic criteria for, chronic fatigue syndrome."
"It was."
"And according to which, as I have four of the nine criteria, I would qualify for the syndrome."

"You would."

"Although just barely."

"Qualifying is qualifying."

"So I understand. But it does raise in my mind the question about this whole business of what is a syndrome."

"Also an interesting question."

"Since the syndrome concept appears to be essential to the understanding of my condition, and as I am both by inclination and profession interested in the precise meaning of words, I looked up its proper definition."

"That was most prudent of you."

"It turns out that the word comes from the Greek *sundromos—sun* and *dromos*—meaning 'running together.'"

"That's very interesting."

"Quite. According to *Black's Medical Dictionary*, a syndrome is a group of symptoms occurring together regularly and thus constituting a disease to which a particular name is given."

"And a very good definition it is."

"The *Oxford Medical Dictionary* says more or less the same thing, a group of symptoms occurring together, but it doesn't say anything about them necessarily constituting a disease."

"The British are picky that way."

"Particular, I would say."

"Yes, I suppose you would."

"They go on to give some examples. They mention syndrome X."

"I'm not sure syndrome X is the best example."

"No, I suppose not. I tried to find out what it was, but didn't succeed."

"Syndrome X is a very complex condition. Understanding it requires a thorough appreciation of the body's physiology. I'm afraid it might be a bit much for you."

"Perhaps so, but my main problem was that there appeared to be three different syndromes X, one related to the heart, one related to cholesterol, and one having to do with mental impairment."

"As I said—"

"I'm afraid it didn't do much to inspire my confidence in what it means to have a syndrome. And it gets me back to my original question. It is clear that by the rules of the profession, my collection of symptoms entitles me to a bona fide case of chronic fatigue syndrome, but what is less clear is whether I have a condition with an actual cause, or whether being such a case merely gives a name to a set of symptoms that none of you really understand, but are incapable of admitting."

"Well, Samantha, I would say you certainly have done your homework."

"I always do my homework, Doctor Conger. What I would like to know is whether you have done yours?"

Samantha Sticklethwaite always did do her homework, and she expected no less of others, whether it was the students in her high school English class or her doctor. And as always, her homework was thorough, complete, and spot-on accurate. There was not a *t* uncrossed or an *i* undotted. In Samantha Sticklethwaite's view, there were two ways of doing things. There was the Right Way. And there was Every Other Way. And incomplete homework definitely fell into the category of Every Other Way. She treated her students fairly and with compassion, but when it came to expectations, she gave no quarter. In class, she was always addressed as Ms. Sticklethwaite, but everyone knew her as The Stickler. It was a title bestowed not entirely without affection.

Experienced as I may be at covering up situations where I don't have a clue, I knew better than to dissemble with Samantha. As luck would have it, however, in this instance I didn't need to. The use of obfuscating terminology to conceal our ignorance has been a particular interest of mine. I was quite familiar with the details of chronic fatigue syndrome.

"I have," I answered. "Do you mind if we start with some history?"

"I would enjoy that very much."

"I thought so. You know, I hadn't really thought of it in these terms before, but in a way we doctors are very much like children."

"So I've noticed. As a group, you don't seem particularly burdened by maturity."

"It does tend to bog one down."

"Yes, it does. Was this merely a philosophical observation, or were you intending to make a point?"

"Well, I was thinking of children in a particular sense."

"I see."

"You know how it is if there are two children playing, and there is a toy nearby, and Child A shows no interest in it until Child B picks it up, at which point it becomes the one toy that Child A absolutely needs."

"I am familiar with that scenario."

"In a way, that's what doctors are like about how a patient feels. A patient might be hungry or sleepy or irritated or anything for that matter, and as long as the patient keeps that feeling to herself, we don't care a fig about it. But should the patient happen to mention that feeling to the doctor, then immediately the doctor wants it for her own."

"Which you do by taking that feeling and making it a symptom."

"That's very observant of you, Samantha."

"As in this instance, when you have taken *my* tired and made it *your* chronic fatigue.

"Yes, like that. The idea goes back to Hippocrates—"

"A long time back."

"—who noticed that people were different."

"An observant man."

"Those old Greeks were like that."

"Yes," she agreed.

"He noticed that some people were always on the go, while others just dragged around."

"Something in our natures, I suppose."

"Hippocrates viewed it differently."

"In what way?" she asked.

"He saw them as conditions."

"Thus creating out of human nature something with which to make a person into a patient."

"It was his specialty. The first condition he called *sthenia*," I explained.

"Meaning lots of energy."

"Correct. And the other group, by distinction had *a-sthenia*."

"No energy."

"Correct again. You do know your etymology, Samantha."

"It is part of my job, Doctor Conger."

"And having created these conditions—"

"He needed a treatment."

"Exactly. Since the sthenics needed slowing down, he recommended opium for them."

"And for the asthenics?"

"Alcohol," I said. "It was considered a stimulant at the time."

"I see. This would be the Father of Medicine speaking?"

"Well, you have to remember, that back then they didn't have any of the tools we have now. All they had to work with were their powers of observation and reasoning."

"They did have one other power, I believe."

"What was that?"

"Pontification."

"Perhaps there was some of that. Be that as it may, as it turned out, asthenia was a very durable condition. It survived for several thousand years, until eighteen sixty-nine, when an enterprising American neurologist by the name of George Miller Beard decided it was time to upgrade the condition to a syndrome. He took the fatigue, threw in a little headache, added a dash of depression, and renamed it neurasthenia."

"A catchy word."

"That was the idea. People who were afflicted with neurasthenia were neurasthenics."

"Not a very appetizing name."

"Nor was it intended to be. It was Beard's belief that the condition was caused by a total exhaustion of the nervous system. At the root of this, he felt, was urbanization and a sedentary lifestyle. He noticed it was most prevalent in the wealthy and professional classes. One wag called it *an intense desire to git thar and an awful fear that you cannot.*"

"A complication of modern civilization, you might say."

"Which he did. One of his colleagues went one step farther. He rechristened it Americanitis."

"A particularly apt name, considering the cause."

"So much so that the Rexall Drug Company made its fortune with a cure. They called it Americanitis Elixir."

"And this elixir, I suppose, contained alcohol."

"Not as much as their Sarsaparilla Tonic, but certainly enough to remove any desire to git anywhere at all."

"It's almost too bad, isn't it, that Americanitis as a name didn't survive?"

"It still does," I said, "in China."

"A wise people, they."

"Neurasthenia had a long run, right up to the middle of the twentieth century. There is an excellent summary of the condition in William Osler's textbook of medicine. In his time, Osler was the greatest man in medicine. He was the authority on all things diagnostic, and his description of the syndrome still holds today. I have it here, if you'd like me to read it to you."

"Please do. I think it would be good for both of us."

I got out my 1928 copy of Osler's *Modern Medicine*. It had been left to me by Dr. Franklin, the general practitioner whose retirement brought me to Dumster. When he gave it to me, he explained that he didn't rely on it much, but he still liked to read it, because the way Osler wrote was so elegant, it almost made you believe what he wrote was true, even when you knew it wasn't.

I opened it to the chapter on neurasthenia.

> Neurasthenia is used with both an indefinite and a precise meaning. Unfortunately, it is frequently used to designate very unlike conditions, sometimes as a cover for ignorance and sometimes as a euphemism for insanity. It is often confused with hysteria and sometimes regarded as mere laziness. It may be so severe as to cause permanent disability, or so slight as to be recovered from in a few weeks. Its symptoms are numerous, and its true primary cause is a matter of dispute. Yet it is a really existing thing. Strictly defined it includes a condition of pathological weakness without discoverable lesion, showing itself by too rapid and too great fatigue. The machine runs too slowly and weakly, rather than wildly or perversely. In the primary form of neurasthenia, this weakness is congenital. We come into the world with unequal powers of resistance to stress.

Secondary neurasthenia has a variety of causes, bad education being primary among them. One often learns unconsciously from his elders in the family to whine, grumble, and be unwisely selfish.

The fundamental symptom of neurasthenia is inability to withstand the normal amount of stress without breakdown. A great deal of neurasthenia would be prevented if people were taught to live properly.

"Well, he certainly covered all the bases with that. It's hard to find a loophole in a *pathological weakness without cause* that can be cured by *living properly* and not succumbing to *unwise selfishness*."

"Osler was very thorough. He goes on to point out the important caveat that one must be careful not to diagnose neurasthenia until one has eliminated other causes. He warned particularly not to confuse it with morphinism, about which he said:

The sense of responsibility is wiped out and is replaced by the indifference of perfect egotism. They are discontented grumblers, . . . often given to quarreling without cause, and they resent criticism.

"Interesting. In my experience, it would seem that either more people are on narcotics than would be apparent, or else the condition may not be restricted to those on morphine. At least not among teachers."

"Possibly even doctors."

"You would know more about that than I do."

"He concludes with an interesting case of his own. It is quite instructive. If I might read that also."

"Please do."

I well remember a man under my care. He complained of general weakness and nothing more. One day he told me he was too tired to get up, and I with a superior air, rather scolded him, and shamed him into the effort. He died before we had walked the length of the ward. The necropsy showed marked chronic myocarditis. He was not a neurasthenic, but died because his heart muscle could no longer do its work.

"Is this an example of what you doctors refer to when you say, *Win some lose some?*"

"Actually, this could probably be one of the first examples of a stress test."

"Which he failed, it appears."

"Yes. Inability to complete the test is one of the criteria for failure."

"That's true in teaching as well. Although death is a less common reason for incompletion."

"I would expect not. Eventually, as part of a general effort to make it sound more scientific, neurasthenia was changed to myalgic encephalomyelitis."

"Certainly a more dignified title."

"It was, and along with name, the theory was changed. It was thought to result from an infection, most likely viral. The underlying pathology proposed was that the immune system in the brain was overstimulated in response to the stress."

"Something brains are prone to."

"Exactly. So it seemed a pretty safe theory. At one point they even went so far as to name the virus responsible. Polio, they said it was."

"Based on their powers of reasoning and observation, I presume."

"Yes. In nineteen forty-eight there was a polio epidemic in Iceland, in the town of Akureyri. After it was over, a bunch of people came down with what they called *nervousness and general tiredness.*"

"Sounds familiar."

"They also had numbness, muscle pains, and trouble with their memory. When they were studied some years later, some of them still had the same symptoms."

"Which made it chronic."

"It did. The studies were so convincing that for a while neurasthenia was known as Iceland disease."

"But polio has been eradicated for almost fifty years now, hasn't it?"

"They were wrong about the polio part."

"So much for the powers of reasoning and observation."

"The debate about what caused the condition was pretty fierce after that, until nineteen eighty-eight, when the CDC, after a thorough review of all the epidemiological studies and the immunological data and the pathological samples, declared that chronic fatigue syndrome was a disorder *Of Unknown Origin*."

"Quite circumspect of them."

"It's a common cause of illness."

"I imagine it would be."

"Particularly pesky fevers. Fever of Unknown Origin is a very popular diagnosis."

"It does tend to get one off the hook for not knowing what is going on."

"We got the idea from physics, I think."

"Heisenberg's uncertainty principle?"

"Exactly."

"They are a clever lot, those physicists. Enshrining ignorance as a principle."

"They are indeed."

"Thank you for the history lesson."

"My pleasure."

"Could we perhaps address another topic?"

"Certainly, what would that be?"

"The symptoms."

"Well, as regards the symptoms, the CDC allows you pretty much to take your pick."

"That is very generous of them. But I was particularly interested in the symptoms I have picked."

"Ah. Those symptoms. Well—"

"I noticed that the CDC recommended that anyone suffering from symptoms that might resemble chronic fatigue syndrome should have a thorough evaluation, just to make sure it isn't something else."

"Quite true. We are always vigilant for the possibility of Something Else."

And so I inspected Samantha top-to-bottom and ordered the usual diagnostic potpourri, and when she came back I was pleased to report that there was no sign of a Something Else lurking in the bushes.

"I suppose that's good news," she said. "But it would depend on what the Something Else was."

"It would."

"If it had been a thyroid condition, for example, or a vitamin B_{12} deficiency, I would not have been displeased."

"Good choices both."

"They are, I gather, conditions that are amenable to treatment."

"Exceedingly."

"But unfortunately, it appears from the tests that I do not have either of them. And so we are back to where we started. It appears that I am indeed afflicted with chronic fatigue syndrome. What is not clear, however, is whether giving my symptoms that name adds anything to the therapeutic plan."

"We do have treatments for chronic fatigue syndrome."

"You have treatments for everything, Doctor Conger. If I remember correctly from my reading, although the condition is considered distinct from depression, the customary treatment for chronic fatigue syndrome is a dose of antidepressants."

"They can't hurt."

"Indeed? I've not heard of a medication that couldn't hurt."

Not being a comment that required a response, I did not provide one. We talked about her troubles a bit more and finally decided that she would carry on without medication but come back in another month to review the situation in order to see if there had been any change that might point us in a more fruitful direction.

When she returned, she brought with her a surprise.

"I've decided to leave, Doctor Conger."

"To leave?"

"Dumster, my job, and, unfortunately, Eurydice. But I have found a tenant who likes cats, and she is willing to look after her as part of the lease. This being June, the school will have ample time to find a replacement."

"You will be sorely missed, Samantha."

"Perhaps. But I will be back. And as it is merely an absence and not an abdication, we will see how much fonder adolescent hearts can grow when I return."

"If you don't, mind my asking, where will you be going?"

"As you are in part responsible for my destination, I do not at all mind. I am going to China."

"That should be an interesting and enjoyable trip. How long are you going for?"

"I'm not sure. As long as it takes, I would have to say."

"As long as it takes for what?"

"To cure me of Americanitis."

It took six months.

She came to see me shortly after she returned.

"It was quite an experience, Doctor Conger. You may remember my first step was to sign up with a tour through the National Teachers Association. There were twelve of us in the group, four teachers with their spouses or partners, three singles including me, and our guide. Emmanuel Chan was his name. He was born in China. He came here for college and stayed to become a professor at the University of Indiana. He leads these tours during the summer. It gives him extra income, and it also gives him a chance to see his family. Although his parents are now in the United States, all the rest of his relatives are in China. He was very friendly and exceptionally knowledgeable. Each day was something different—the Forbidden City, the Entombed Warriors, the Great Wall. We even went to Three Gorges Dam. In the morning we would have a lecture by Emmanuel on the place we were going to see, and in the afternoon we would have a discussion about it over tea. The accommodations were all very nice, and Doctor Chan was a treasure. He even took us to visit one of his uncles who lived in Beijing.

"It was fascinating, of course, but, too much so, I'm afraid. By the end of the tour, I was totally exhausted. My chronic fatigue syndrome had taken its revenge."

"A little too much *gittin' thar?*"

"I'll say. But I discovered something about the chronic fatigue syndrome that might be of interest to you."

"What was that?"

"I think it's contagious. You see, we spent a lot of time together on the trip, and so we got to know one another pretty well, including even our afflictions. And I was surprised to discover that despite our academic background, we spent more time discussing those issues than our experiences of the day.

"Of course, I told them about my chronic fatigue syndrome. They wanted to know all about my symptoms and what made them worse and what I did for them, and of course about my doctor. And then, when we were saying our good-byes at the end of the trip, two of the teachers came up to me and thanked me for sharing my story with them, and although they had had a wonderful time, they were afraid that, well you can guess what. They had contracted chronic fatigue syndrome, every single symptom! Needless to say, at that point I was pretty discouraged about the whole experience. Then, the day before we were to leave, I was having tea in our hotel when I happened·to see a young man wearing an Oberlin College T-shirt. Well, Oberlin was my alma mater, so I went over and introduced myself. He told me he was in his second year at Oberlin. He had taken a course on Chinese history, and found it so engrossing that he decided what he had to do was come to China to find out about the country for himself. They do this, you know, the young people. It has to do with one's space.

"Anyway, he was very pleased, because he had succeeded in his quest, and the way he did it was by hiking the entire Great Wall of China—at least the parts that were still intact. It was eighteen hundred miles, and it took him four months. It was, he said, the greatest experience of his life. Although I suppose at his age, there probably wasn't a lot of competition in that area.

"He was very eager to talk about his trip, and, as I·am a good listener, we got along famously. That night, I got to thinking. The next morning I called and canceled my return flight home and made a reservation for a flight to Lanzhou for the following day. Then I went to the tourist office and talked to a very nice man about my plans. He explained that it would not be a problem as long as I stayed away from 'sensitive' areas. I told him I certainly didn't want to upset any sensitive areas. He said that was good, and he showed me where they were on a map. I thanked him for the map, and after we had finished, I went out shopping. I bought a backpack and a sturdy pair of hiking shoes, and a warm jacket. Then I went to the bank and used my credit card to get a supply of yuan.

"When I got to Lanzhou, I had to take a train to get to my starting point, which was the city of Jiayuguan. Jiayuguan marks the western-most portion of the Great Wall. It is also in the Gobi Desert. It was a hundred degrees when I arrived. And me in my warm jacket. By the time I got to my room, I felt absolutely awful. My head was pounding, I was sick to my stomach, and every fiber of my being ached to fury. I could hardly get my head off the pillow, let alone get out of bed. All I wanted to do was cry. I didn't leave my hotel room for three days, and then it was another week before I could walk to the nearby restaurant without wearing myself out. I was so discouraged, I almost gave up the whole idea.

"But then one afternoon, I met a young Tibetan man who worked in the charcoal factory. He was studying English and was very eager to talk with me. I told him about my plans and that I wasn't sure I could do them. He looked at me for maybe a minute as he tried to formulate what he wanted to say. Then he smiled. 'No plan,' he said. 'One step.'

"That was all I needed. The first day I walked less than a mile. But I was on my way. After that, I got a little stronger and walked a little farther each day. I didn't bring a watch, and I had thrown away my maps, so I didn't know how far I had walked or where I was. I just followed the wall. I would get up with the sun and walk until I felt like stopping. Most of the time I stayed at someone's house—everywhere I went, people were very eager to put me up, and the only price was listening to them try out their English. No one would take money. As I eventually found out, having me stay in their home was a very high honor to my host family. It accorded them great stature in the commu-nity. It was of far more value than any monetary recompense I could make. In the larger towns I stayed in hostels. Then one day, when I felt I could walk forever and not get tired, I decided I had had enough. So I came home."

"How far did you walk?" I asked.

"Pretty far, I'd say."

"And you were gone for quite a while."

"Almost six months."

"It was a long time for a walk."

"I'm not so sure about that."

"Seems long to me."

"To you maybe. But chronic fatigue syndrome is a chronic condition. Many people suffer from it for years. For some it is incurable. Six months for a cure might not be all that long. I would say it all depends on that to which it is relative."

"It always does."

24

A Matched Set

....

Who is a Vermonter? It would seem such a simple question to answer. Like who is an American. But it isn't. One of the peculiar things is that the less time you have been here, the more important it is. Not that this is surprising. Anytime you have been something for a short period of time, such as a king or a spouse, it seems so much more important than when all is just old hat.

The tricky part is it all depends on where you are in the state. Unless I had been born in Dumster, for example, I could never be considered a true native. In Burlington, after two or three years, one is dyed-in-the-wool and part of the woodwork. In Brattleboro, all it would take is two months at the Latchis Hotel. Of course, if you want to bypass the waiting period altogether, all you have to do is shake a politician's hand.

It wasn't like that in Philadelphia. In Philadelphia, they didn't make much fuss about who was a Philadelphian. And in Other Philadelphia, they didn't make any at all. It wasn't that they thought less of where they were from. They just didn't think it was a big deal. If you were there, you were there, and if you weren't—well, then bully for you.

Right from the start, everyone went out of their way to make me feel at home. It was very nice. But, after a while, a bit odd. It wasn't that they were pretending or putting on. Their friendliness was real enough. It was just that—well, you know how it is when you meet someone for the first time. You are all smiles and just as polite as can be. But then after a while, once you get to know each other, it changes, so that should the occasion strike, or should the mood arise, you might, from time to time, be a bit short with that person, or even so far as to be miffed. Just as you would with anyone, even, and here I am speaking only hypothetically, as I have never experienced it personally, with your Dearly Beloved. Well, in Philadelphia that never happened. From the first day I arrived until the day I left, I heard not a sharp or discouraging word. Not a one.

It was almost as if we were all in a great hotel, and they were the staff, and I was the guest.

I asked Shirley Covington about it.

"Two different teams," she said.

"Teams?"

"You're on the A team."

"And you?"

"I'm B team."

"B?"

"Yes. We *B*e here before you come, and we *B*e here after you leave."

She was exactly right, of course. Unlike Dumster, our actual lives outside of work had nothing to do with each other. Our children didn't go to school together. We didn't shop in the same stores. We didn't even get our haircuts in the same place.

I tried, once, getting a haircut at the barbershop on Germantown Avenue next to the hospital. They greeted me in a most friendly manner, but even though there were several empty chairs, no one made a move to offer me one. I had to wait the longest time until finally a fellow came in the front door and called me up. He apologized profusely for the delay but explained that it was his day off. I didn't say anything, but I was puzzled why neither of the other unoccupied barbers could help me. He must have noticed the expression on my face. "I'm the only one knows how to cut white hair," he explained.

What little hair I have left is gray.

If you asked somebody born and raised in Dumster if he was a Vermonter, he would have to think a bit before answering. Then most likely he would say something like, "S'pose so" or "Must be." Because Vermonter is a bit too grand a concept for someone whose sense of place does not extend much beyond the town line. Whether you come from Saigon or San Francisco, once you have shopped at Contremond's and eaten at Nat's, your place of origin is usually overlooked. Except for people from New Hampshire and New York.

I come from New York, but I am exempted, because, as Maggie explained to me, "You're a doctor." New York, like Philadelphia, is not one of those places that, if you are from there, you think has anything to do with who you are. So the whole fromness business is puzzling to me. As she was an official foreigner, I asked Trine about it. She said it was only natural.

"It makes perfect sense," she said, "It's the same way for us with Denmark and Sweden. It all has to do with our history. Because Norway was owned for a long time, first by Denmark and then by Sweden, when we finally became independent, it was especially important for us to distinguish ourselves from Swedes and Danes. To avoid confusion, you know."

"And since back in the day, both New York and New Hampshire owned large chunks of Vermont, you think that's the reason?"

"I'm sure of it."

"Even though our most famous Vermonters are three guys from Brooklyn?"

"That just makes it even more so."

"But there was a time when the French claimed part of Vermont for Canada. What about if you are from Canada?"

"Canada?!"

"There is that about Canada."

Now, it's pretty easy to tell if someone is One of Those People from New Hampshire. All you have to do is get up first thing in the morning and head toward the sun until you reach the Connecticut River. Anyone you see coming at you from the other side is one of them. But New York is another matter. It's not a problem if you are anywhere north of a line from White River Junction to Fair Haven. What you do in that case is turn around one hundred and eighty degrees and head due west until you reach Lake Champlain. New Yorkers will be coming from across the lake. But if you are down around West Rupert or Bouplon Hollow, you're out of luck. Because all you've got on the boundary there is trees. And even though none of us would like to admit it, a Vermont tree and a New York tree look just about the same. So you really can't tell where the one ends and the other begins.

And this is the point I wanted to make. Think about a set of Siamese twins joined in the middle. Or a pair of Republicans and Democrats. It's easy to tell that the right hand of one is different from the left hand of the other, but as you move toward the middle, it gets harder to distinguish which is which, and eventually you get to where it is just about impossible to tell them apart.

This is the way it is with Muriel Goode and Olive Best. Muriel and Olive are sisters. Muriel is ninety, and Olive is eighty-six, and except for one year when Olive was married, they have lived their entire life together on the family farm. Why Muriel agreed to marry Wilbur Goode no one is entirely sure, least of all Muriel, but at least Wilbur had the sense to realize that it was a foolish thing to try to separate the two, and so he went off to France to war and obligingly got himself killed.

Their farm is located at the river's edge on Best Road, a short dirt road coming off Route Five about three miles north of town, just below Sumners Falls. It was settled in 1809, when Jeremiah Best joined the land-hungry emigrants who came up the Connecticut River from Hartford. He purchased five hundred acres of prime river bottomland from Oliver Willard. Willard had acquired the land from Governor Benning Wentworth as one of a series of land grants totaling some eight thousand acres. The grants were a token of gratitude from the Crown to Wentworth for his successes in the war against the Abenakis and the French.

Mr. Best promptly commissioned a large brick two-story federal in the style made popular by Benjamin Asher. It is a testament to the quality of Asher's workmanship that the house, except for the addition of indoor plumbing in 1850 and electrification in 1900, remains unaltered to this day.

The same, unfortunately, cannot be said for the five hundred acres. Sold off in various parcels large and small, sometimes to support the education of a child with greater aspirations, sometimes to allocate an inheritance to one who didn't get the farm, once, in 1880, to support an ill-fated investment by Jed Best, a younger brother who thought that farmwork involved too much work for too little profit. On the strength of a fast-talking engineer who came to town with slick reports about the burgeoning demand for industrial copper and a sheaf of figures showing, beyond any reasonable doubt, that just beneath the surface Abenaki Mountain held a wealth of ore, Jed convinced his father to purchase one hundred shares in the Mt. Abenaki Copper Mine. The mine actually did produce a little copper for two years, but when the price of copper went south in 1883, so did the engineer and with him, the investors' money. A small piece of ore from the mine still sits on the mantelpiece in the sitting room as a reminder to all of the implications of looking for more than that to which you are entitled.

Mostly, however, land was sold when the price one could get for a hundredweight of milk fell below the cost to produce it. Which, in two hundred years, was all too often, so that today the farmhouse sits at the head of a narrow strip of land, from the road to the river totaling not much more than fifteen acres, just enough to feed the current herd, which consists of one elderly Guernsey.

The farm was run by a series of sons until 1940, when Alan Best, predeceased by his wife, Ellen, died and left as his procreative capital a pair of young daughters: Muriel, twenty-four, and Olive, twenty. It was widely assumed that the girls would sell the farm and move on. The assumers were wrong. Without much help from hired hands, the two sisters kept the farm up and, with a thrifty philosophy and a shrewd head for the value of land, managed to keep the place afloat. That they were down to one cow and a pair of laying hens bothered them not in the slightest.

"We live *on* Social Security," they said. "We live *for* the farm."

Even now one or the other can be seen on the old Farmall, plowing the drive in winter or haying the field in summer.

The bond between mother and daughter is usually acknowledged as the strongest of family ties in the animal kingdom. And there is considerable evidence to support that claim, particularly when compared with that between father and son, or husband and wife. But it is no match for that which links a pair of sisters who have lived together all their lives. And with the mother and the daughter it is usually possible, barring visits by one to the plastic surgeon, to determine that one has lived a part of her life without the other, enabling one to distinguish which is which. But so much will such sisters come to resemble each other over time that eventually they will take the form of a single sentient being inhabiting two bodies. So that when Muriel and Olive came to see me, which *they* always did, it was impossible for me to determine whether a complaint with which they presented had originated in the body of one or the other.

They are a sprightly pair—the picture of health even for someone with a score of years less to her credit. Upon my entering the room, they greeted me in turn as usual.

"Good morning—"

"—Doctor Conger."

"And good morning to you also," I replied. "How are we feeling today?"

"We are fine, thank you."

"Just dandy, in fact."

"That's good to hear. There has been no weakness or dizziness then, I gather?"

"None."

"Whatsoever."

"Not even, let's say, for Olive, first thing in the morning when you get out of bed?"

"No," said Muriel. "Not even then."

"Only there has been, perhaps," said Olive, "a bit of a cough."

"Which one—?"

"Doctor Conger!"

"Excuse me," I said. "I forget things sometimes these days."

"Happens to all of us."

"The cough has not been too bothersome, I hope. The new medication can be troublesome that way."

"Not at all."

"It is barely noticeable."

This was a relief to hear. Over the years, they both had been extremely healthy, only requiring treatment for those minor ailments that really require no treatment at all, save the usual prescription of fluids and rest, a regimen with which it was easy enough for both to comply even if only one was ill. There was a bladder infection in one of them once that, in order to treat, both had to take antibiotics, but that was only for three days, and in the category of unnecessary prescriptions was a minor enough indiscretion on my part that I felt it was a small price to pay.

But last month, when they had come in for a routine visit, Muriel's blood pressure, which had been sufficiently borderline that I could ignore it in good conscience, had risen to one seventy-five over one hundred. Olive, on the other hand, was a lovely one twenty-five over seventy. I worried about the possible effects of lowering it further, but the risk of stroke that her sister's reading portended made it impossible to defer treatment.

I discussed at length the potential side effects, focusing particularly on what might happen if a blood pressure got too low, and that this might limit our ability to treat the condition effectively. They said they understood and were confident that I would do what was best for them, a confidence that I was not entirely sure was justified.

"Well," I said, after we had finished with the preliminaries, "let's see how the blood pressure is doing today. Remember, I will have to check it twice. As I told you before, it is important to know the pressure in both arms, as sometimes there can be a significant difference."

"Of course, Doctor Conger."

"We remember."

Olive promptly rolled up her right sleeve, Muriel the same with her left. I took the respective pressures.

"One hundred over sixty on the right, and one forty over eighty-five on the left," I reported when I had finished.

"That's not too high, is it?"

"Or too low?"

"No. Not really. It is perhaps a tad high on the left arm and a smidge low in the right one, but under the circumstances, I would say it is just where it should be."

"Goody."

"And now, we have—"

"—a question."

"We want to get your advice."

"About exercise."

"Certainly," I said. "Regular exercise is very important in maintaining health—at any age."

"We know, Doctor Conger."

"You've told us that before."

"What we are interested in is which particular form of exercise you would recommend, for us."

"For the winter."

"Ah," I said. "Ordinarily I would recommend walking, as it is the simplest form of exercise, and with our hills here, it can keep you quite fit. But in the winter—"

"It would not be a good choice."

"No, it wouldn't."

"We figured the choice would be snowshoeing—"

"—or cross-country skiing."

"Snowshoeing and cross-country skiing. Well," I said, "those are definitely activities for the winter. It's not an easy choice, however. Particularly—"

"Yes, Doctor Conger, we know."

"Which is why we decided—"

"—to ask your advice."

Both possibilities gave me pause. A broken limb is a broken limb, and I shuddered to think what would happen to one if the other broke a hip. To treat them both for one heart attack, however, boggled even my imagination.

"On the one hand, the risk of falling is greater when skiing, and at your age that could mean a broken arm, or worse. But on the other hand, the exertion of snowshoeing can be considerable, especially in heavy snow, and that could perhaps be a bit too much for a heart of the . . . let's see, nineteen eighteen to nineteen twenty-two vintage, I believe?"

"Yes, but sometimes the old models—"

"—are more reliable—"

"—than the new."

"Quite true. And the new aluminum snowshoes are quite light. If you pace yourself carefully, you should be perfectly safe."

"We're not interested in safe."

"Which is more fun?"

"That would be skiing."

"Then it's settled."

"Skiing it is."

"A wise choice," I said, not at all certain that it was. But the *alea* certainly had been *jacta*, and there was nothing for it but to make it the best experience possible. "In that case, I think you would be well advised first to take some lessons."

"Oh yes!"

"That's an excellent idea."

"Whom would you recommend?"

The answer to that question was easy. I knew who would be the perfect instructor for Muriel and Olive. It was a person experienced in introducing the joys of cross-country skiing to students of all ages— from two to eighty-two. It was the person who had taught all of our children how to ski. And although the person had been retired from teaching for a number of years, I considered it more than likely that I might be able to use my persuasive powers to get that person to return to the profession in this special case.

"That would be Trine," I said.

"Your wife?"

"My wife."

"Oh goody!"

"That's wonderful."

"When can we start?"

"Well, there are a few things that must come first."

"Like skis—"

"—and snow."

"And a checkup from you."

"Yes, that, of course."

"And just think."

"Here we are."

I got out my stethoscope. First I listened to Muriel, or maybe it was Olive, I can't remember. Her heartbeat was like the drumroll of a precision marching band—strong and regular as a metronome. Just as it should be.

The other heart, however, was playing a somewhat different tune. It would be hard to define exactly, but if pressed, I would have to say it most closely resembled a cross between "Tutti Frutti" and "Whole Lot of Shaking Goin' On." What the tune was most definitely not, however, was one that any respectable heart was supposed to be playing. Especially not an aged heart about to embark upon a sortie into major oxygen consumption.

Atrial fibrillation in a young and otherwise healthy person is no big deal. Even in the senior set, it is not necessarily a serious condition. But it does reduce the efficiency of the pump, and it can represent the outward and visible sign of an inward and serious malfunction. If not treated it can lead to faintness, shortness of breath, congestive heart failure, and worst of all a stroke. Accordingly, the Standard of Care dictates that, regardless of age, it is a condition for which Something Must Be Done. And more than likely that something, with all its accoutrements, would be such as absolutely to preclude precisely that activity upon which their collective hearts were so ardently palpitating.

Statistics abound for a rational decision-making process in the treatment of atrial fibrillation. There is even a simple scoring system, where one adds up points for blood pressure and diabetes and age and determines whether the benefit of treatment outweighs the risk. All of which is very informative in the usual case. But the usual case has nothing to do with the conundrum I faced in deciding how to treat Muriel and Olive. Because the benefits are always half of what they should be, and the risks double. And in this instance, the risks are serious. Depression, fatigue, hypotension, and hemorrhage—the last being especially awful when the place the hemorrhage occurs is the brain, thereby causing the very condition it was designed to prevent. All of which just goes to prove yet again that the whole idea of risk–benefit analysis very quickly becomes moot when you are one of those whose benefit has become the risk, and you have been sacrificed for the greater good.

Take, for example, an aneurysm of the abdominal aorta that has grown to a size ripe for picking. If you fix the aneurysm, it is with the idea that you can forestall the Untimely Demise that could occur if that vessel at some future point decided to rupture without so much as a by-your-leave. Should, however, the operation itself bring about that very event it was designed to avoid, the fact that it was performed according to Best Evidence is not much consolation to the Dearly Departed.

Nonetheless, according to our Rules of Evidence, it is acceptable to adopt a win some, lose some, philosophy, as long as the former exceeds the later by a *significant* margin. Significant as defined in medical terms, not necessarily meaning significant at all. In fact, it can be as insignificant as one in a thousand. Just as long as the statisticians bless it.

However, doctors, when it comes to making decisions, turn out to be no different from any other human being. Our attraction to the rational choice of what we *ought* to do is dependent less on the strength of the facts of the matter than on the degree to which it coincides with what we have already decided we *want* to do. And what we usually want to do—financial considerations for the moment aside—is determined not by what we have most recently read in our journals or been lectured to by a recognized expert in the field, but rather by what happened the last time we were in a similar situation. Statisticians scorn such behavior. They call it Last Case Bias.

Clinicians prefer to call it Experience.

It does not actually have to be the last case. Most are not. They are cases so burned in the doctor's memory as to be unforgettable, and they remain forever a powerful force in her decision-making process, even when she should know better.

The plight of Muriel and Olive reminded me of just such a case. Although it occurred a long time ago, I can still remember it as if it were only yesterday.

25

What the Doctor Did

···········

It was the winter of 1973. The patient was not someone whom I attended in the hospital. Nor was he one who came to my office. The site of our encounter was a snow-covered meadow in Yosemite National Park known as Crane Flat. The occasion was a cross-country ski lesson.

At the time, Trine had largely abandoned her profession as a ski instructor to pursue a career in the law. It is a decision she still revisits every winter with not inconsiderable regret. She was at the time, however, still giving classes at Yosemite on weekends, and I accompanied her on these expeditions. It was partly for companionship, and partly for the skiing, but it was also because these lessons were the seminal event in our relationship.

Despite having spent much of my youth and early adulthood in New England, I had never strapped on a pair of skis. So when a classmate of mine, who was also at the University of California Medical Center in San Francisco, suggested we should take up the sport, I agreed to give it a whirl. Our plan was first to take a week of lessons in alpine skiing at Lake Tahoe, and then a weekend of cross-country at Yosemite National Park. The alpine experience was a dismal failure. Our instructor was using a technique called the graduated length method, whereby we started on very short skis, and were given a longer pair to work with as we progressed each day. At the end of the week, I had the distinction of being the only person in the history of the ski school to be on shorter skis than when he started.

I hoped to do better with cross-country skiing. We went to Yosemite on Washington's Birthday weekend, 1972. As we were getting our equipment before the start of classes, I was quite taken with the young woman handing out boots and more than a little impressed with how well someone from California could speak

Norwegian. There were some seventy of us in all, and the head instructor explained that cross-country was not difficult to learn, but that going down hills on the skinny skis could be tricky. Those with alpine experience would pick it up quickly, however, as the balance issues were the same. Accordingly he would divide the class up according to its alpine skiing abilities, with Trine taking those who were expert downhill skiers. When he asked for a show of hands, mine shot up. "What are you doing, you fool?" whispered my classmate, who had correctly classified himself as novice. "You are an utter klutz on downhill skis." I told him to shut up. I was determined to be in Trine's class.

The first day of lessons was uneventful, as we paddled around harmlessly in the flat meadow. At break, I learned that Trine, despite her long hair and Valley Girl speech, was actually from Oslo, Norway. She was over here on an Essential Worker visa, at the time there being not a sufficient supply of American citizens to instruct in the national sport of her own country.

The second day was a disaster—from the point of skiing that is. She took us to what looked to me like the edge of El Capitan, although in truth it was no more than a slight dip in the meadow, and told us just to use our alpine turns for the descent. We all got to the bottom. The only difference was that for me each time it was flat on my face. Trine did compliment me on the fact that my falls were forward, which, she explained, was the honorable way to fall. She was impressed also with the bloody nose and split lip I got as a result of my efforts. I can't say that the wounds were incurred intentionally, but the concern she showed and the tender ministrations she applied to them did make me feel they were but a small price to pay for the result. It was only after we were married that Trine explained that her concern was not out of any regard for my well-being, but solely for her potential liability in the matter. But it did get her attention, and as she turned out to be living in Berkeley, it was an effective, if unorthodox start to our relationship.

Although I still had no real skiing ability, I did serve a useful purpose as her assistant. Born, as she was, virtually on skis, Trine was singularly deficient in the ability to perform that maneuver so essential to those for whom the long strips of wood resembled more a pair of toothpicks than a mode of transportation: getting up after a fall. So while she introduced her students to the finer points of diagonal stride, step turns, and the double pole, I would demonstrate the technique of plop, prop, and up.

On this particular day, one of the new students was a man by the name of Otmar Frieze. To say that he was elderly might not be quite fair, as that could imply a lack of sprightliness, which would not be at all true, so I will simply say that he had been young for a long time. Just how long can perhaps be best judged by the fact that in outfitting himself for the occasion, he had taken the unusual measure of tightly binding with duct tape the pole attached to his left hand in order to improve his grip. During the war, a grenade had partially detonated in his hand and taken with it three fingers. The war in which this happened was World War I.

Trine looked at Otmar. Then she looked at me. She nodded in my direction. I got the message. She wanted him checked out.

Absent any diagnostic accoutrements, and with Otmar bundled up like a mummy, my evaluative options were rather limited. Blessing him by sight would have been my preference, but I was sure that would not pass Trine's muster. There was no hope for it but to do some laying on of hands. At least I could check his pulse. Although not as well versed in the subtleties as were the ancient Chinese, who claimed to be able to tell from it everything one needed to know about the body's health, I could at least confirm its presence, which seemed to me under the circumstances about the best that one could do. Check the pulse, look thoughtful, and declare Mr. Frieze fit for duty. That should suffice.

I took his wrist. I checked his pulse. I looked thoughtful. I *was* thoughtful. The pulse I felt was not the pulse I expected to feel. It was not the pulse I had wanted to feel. In my office, or in the hospital, I would have known exactly what to do with a pulse like his. I had done it hundreds of times before. But never before had I dealt with atrial fibrillation in the mountains.

That morning before the start of the lesson, as a way of getting acquainted, we all told one another who we were and where we came from. Otmar had come from Gdansk, although he explained that wasn't strictly accurate, since when he left in 1937, it was still the Free City of Danzig. But that was before the German occupation and the subsequent ceding to Poland. He was a practical man, he told us, and although he had always wanted to try skiing, he feared that with his handicap it would not be practical. And so he had not tried. But now he had reached the age where practicality had lost its appeal, and what he looked forward to most was precisely that which he had so long avoided: indulging in the impractical.

Otmar looked at me expectantly. He was eager to get on with the lesson.

"Okay," he said. "I can go now, yah?"

What I should have said was, *No, I don't think you should, Mr. Frieze. You have a heart condition.* But I couldn't.

"Yes," I said. "Just be sure to pace yourself . . . and be careful on the hills. However, you should be sure to have a checkup as soon as you get home. Just to make sure everything is okay."

Otmar promised he would and went off to join the rest of the class. The lesson went uneventfully. After the lesson, I reminded him about the checkup, and we said our good-byes. We didn't see him again that year, or the next, and I had forgotten all about Otmar and his erratic heart.

At the end of each season there is a nine-mile ski race. Skiers like Trine and her compatriots zip along lickety-split. And then there are the rest of us. We plod along enjoying the scenery. It was our last winter in Yosemite. Some time after what appeared to be the last plodder had finished, and it was starting to get dark, one more skier hove into view. The duct taped ski pole in the left hand left no doubt who it was.

There was a big cheer from the crowd as he crossed the line. Afterward I went up to offer my congratulations. I asked Otmar how he was doing.

"Fine now, but before, not so goot," he said. "I vent to ze doktor ven I got home, joost like you sett. He tolt me heart very batt. Put me in ze hospital. Stuck in me many toops. Gafe me lots of pillz. Sett no ski. No do nuffink. Only rest. Pillz mate me tiret, depresset, unt veak as ze kitten. Hartly even valk could I. It vas awful."

"Well," I said. "You looked pretty spry today. The doctor must have done something right. What did the doctor do?"

"Yah," he said. "Ze doktor dite."

"Doctor Conger?"

"Yes?"

"Is something wrong?"

"You had a kind of look."

"As if you weren't sure about something."

"No. I'm quite sure."

"About the skiing?"

"Yes. Everything is fine. Go out and get your skis. I will talk to Trine."

"Oh goody."

"We will."

26

The Stork at the Window

···········

There is something comforting about a farm. Take, for example, the Stedrock farm. It sits atop a hill. The barn is red. The house is white. The cows are brown. And the fields are green. Everything is just as it should be. Sabra Field herself couldn't have done better. It is the kind of farm the Preacher had in mind when he marveled at what God and man could do when working together. Hardly a day goes by, rain or shine, summer or winter, when someone from somewhere else doesn't stop by to admire it and to take a picture. In the fall the traffic is very heavy, and on weekends there are so many cars parked along the side of the road, and so many people tramping through his pastures, that finally Hiram put up a sign saying BEST PICTURE HERE and put it as far out of the way as he could.

To Hiram it is just a farm. He keeps it in good order, with or without the help of God, not so much out of pride or vanity, but because keeping it up is less work than not.

"A farm is always working, Doc," he told me once in one of his rare philosophical dissertations. "You gotta make sure it's working *for* you, not against you."

Although it is uncertain to what degree the hand of the Almighty set itself to till the fields of the Corless farm down the road from Hiram, there is no disputing that it would benefit substantially should the hand of man do a bit more. No one ever stops to take a picture of the Corless farm. It has never been on the pages of *Vermont Life*.

For many years after Abraham, the first Corless, came to Steddsville and cleared the land, the farm was kept up as well as that of its neighbor. But then, through numerous spells of misfortune, misadventure, and not quite being up to the task, first one Corless fell a bit behind, and then another Corless was not quite able to catch up, until eventually things reached the state where even the most diligent was forced to say "Owell" and try to make the best he could of it. So the barn sags on one side, and the house is shedding a few shingles. Here and there the carcasses of decaying farm implements dot the land. Next to the house is an ancient school bus that from time to time serves as winter dwelling when there isn't quite enough stove wood to last the season. The cows are often seen gazing across the fence at the greener pastures on the other side, but they are clean and sleek, giving testimony that the occupants, if they can't quite care for the inanimate as they ought, do not stint with their herd.

The current Corless household consists of three persons: Minnie, a cousin named Wayne, and Minnie's only child, a son known as Uptah.

Uptah, now in his forties, is of uncertain parentage. He was born just ten months after Minnie's husband, Frank, overturned his tractor on the steep hillside and broke his neck. Some months later when her condition became apparent, neighbors commented upon the fact that her husband was dead. "But I ain't," said Minnie. It has been said by the less charitable in town that Uptah was a bit off plumb, to which I would say only that there are worse things to be. But being a Corless, and under suspicion of being inbred, there has been, consequently, on the part of those whose business it is to dispense it, no doubt remaining of which he could receive the benefit.

The origin of his name is a matter of some controversy. Some say it is a modification of the more formal Upton. Others say it derives from his propensity as a youth perpetually to be up to no good. But in truth it dates back to his first day at the Steddsville School, when the teacher asked him where he was from, and he answered, "Upta Corless."

Fortune has not shown its best light on Uptah. Struck with measles encephalitis at the age of three, he was left with a speech impediment. Most of the time it is only slightly noticeable, but when he becomes agitated, it becomes so pronounced as to render him almost unintelligible. When he was eight years old, a tine from the hay rake broke off and impaled Uptah's right eye, leaving him blind on that side. At age fourteen he developed diabetes. Say what you will about how full his pitcher was, Uptah has managed his illness as well as anyone. He is strict about his diet except during sugaring season and on those occasions when he gets himself blind staggering drunk, and he is religiously meticulous about his insulin. One day he told me he wanted an insulin pump. I explained to him that the pump was a complicated device that required frequent adjustment and strict monitoring of the blood sugar. I thought it might not be the best thing for him. "It's just a pump, ain't it?" he answered. "I can figger it out." Which he did, and before long his sugars were the best in my practice. But the years of diabetes took their toll, and by the time he was forty he had lost the other eye to a vitreous hemorrhage and had developed a painful neuropathy in his legs. But he carried on without complaining and continued to do his share of the farmwork by feel, feeding the cows, mucking the stalls, and operating the milkers almost as well as when he had his sight.

He has tolerated his disability with the patience of a man who long ago learned the value of low expectations, but he has no use for those who are more bothered by it than he. So I was not surprised when I got a panicked call from a new nurse in our emergency room, because there was a Mr. Corless there who had burned his leg, and the patient was blind and couldn't speak and was in such a state that she was afraid the patient might become violent, so would I please come right away.

It took only a moment to see the problem. Uptah, obviously in severe pain, was unable to sit still, while the nurse was doggedly trying to restrain him in a futile attempt to apply the bags of ice to his right leg that protocol demanded for the occasion. After a shot of morphine settled him down, Uptah became his usual dour self, and I was able to examine the limb in question. There was a nasty second-degree burn running from just below the knee to the top of the ankle. It was heavily blistered, but fortunately his sensation was intact, and the burn did not cross either the ankle or the knee. Some skin grafting would be required down the road, but it should heal without difficulty. I asked him how he got burned.

"Blowtorch," he said.

"Not a good tool to have an accident with."

"Weren't no accident."

I was surprised. Self-mutilation was the last thing I would have expected from Uptah. Still, if I had learned anything in the last forty years, it was that the last thing I expected was not infrequently exactly what happened.

Nonetheless, I wanted to make sure I had heard him correctly.

"You did this on purpose?"

"Yup."

"Why?"

"Had to."

"You *had* to?"

"Said yup, din't I?"

"But why on earth would you have to burn your leg with a blowtorch?"

"Onliest way I could get rid of the snakes."

"You had snakes on your leg?"

"What I said."

"And you used a blowtorch to burn them off?"

"Tried pulling 'em off. But they kep' a-comin' back. The torch done good though. They gone now."

"How did you get snakes on your leg?"

"Dunno for sure. The barn I 'spect. In the foundation. Milk snakes they was."

"But . . . how could you be sure they were milk snakes?"

"Saw 'em."

It was as I feared. Hallucinations were a sign of several possible conditions. None of them was very good.

Although he was much more lucid than I would expect for a full-blown case, given Uptah's propensity to liquor, DTs had to be a first consideration.

"How much have you been drinking, Uptah?" I asked.

"As much as I can git."

"And how much would that be . . . in bottles, let's say . . . each day?"

"Wouldn't be any. Last time I was drunk, I went and busted up the dining room table for kindlin'. Ma didn't take any too kindly to it. So she done hid my bottles. These"—he put each index finger up to his eyes—"ain't no good for finding likker. Nor these." He touched his nose. "And these"—he put out his hands—"ain't a whole lot better."

"I see."

The fact that he had lost his supply made perfect sense. For it is the stopping rather than the drinking that brings on withdrawal symptoms.

"Exactly when was it she hid your booze?"

"Jus' afor Christmas."

"Hmmm."

The time course of DTs after withdrawal from alcohol is variable. In some cases it can be as little as a day. Usually it is about a week to ten days. But it can be as long as two. As it was now the middle of April, I had to bark up another tree.

I rolled up the other pant leg. Sure enough, it sported similar burns in various stages of healing. Some were a few days old, some at least several weeks.

"Yup," said Uptah as he felt my examination. "They allus come back."

So that was it.

Uptah was crazy.

For any of you in the mental health field, please excuse my use of this lay term. I ask you to take into consideration that most of my readers are not as well versed as you in the intricacies of the *DSM IV*, according to which the correct diagnosis would most likely be a 295.7: schizoaffective disorder, subtype somatic delusion. If pressed, I might concede to a 297.1 delusional disorder, but I would draw the line at 292.89 hallucinogen persisting perception disorder. The idea that Uptah had ever taken LSD or any of its relatives just didn't seem possible. His poison of choice had always been alcohol.

It wasn't all that surprising. Uptah had always been a bit peculiar. And his recent vicissitudes could certainly have been enough to tip him over the edge. But something about the picture didn't quite fit. There was something I was missing. Something in what he had just told me.

"The snakes, Uptah. What kind did you say they were?"

"They was milk. Thought they was copperheads at first, but a course they eyes gave 'em away. They was nice and round, not like them copperhead slits."

"Interesting. I didn't know that about snake eyes. I'd say you're pretty good at identifying snakes, being able to tell them apart just by the eyes."

"I guess." He shrugged. "Never thought much of it."

"Especially for a blind man."

"Yeah," he said after a period of silence. "I thought a that. But I know what I seen."

"Everyone always does."

Uptah thought about this for a minute before he spoke again.

"Doc?" he said uncertainly.

"Yes."

"I ain't goin' off my deep rocker am I?"

"No, Uptah. You're not."

And he wasn't. He was just seeing snakes where no snakes were. The brain is a funny thing. Like a farm, it's always working. Sometimes it's working for you. And sometimes it's working against you. Take the back of the brain, the occipital lobe. The job of the occipital lobe is to take the electronic signals that come in from the retina by way of the optic nerve and convert them into a visual image, so the frontal lobe can watch them and then decide what the rest of the body should do. It's a bit like a television set. Except in one respect. When you turn a television off, it knows that its work is done, and it takes a nap, or goes for a smoke, or whatever televisions do when they're not displaying pictures. But the occipital lobe doesn't ever shut off. So if it doesn't have any pictures coming in, it makes them up. Like at night, when your eyes are closed. We call those pictures dreams. And if it can't get anything from the Vision Network, which is the case for a blind person, it will surf the other sensory channels to see if it can find something out of which it can create a picture show.

In the spinal cord is a collection of nerves called the lateral spinothalamic tract. The lateral spinothalamic tract is a kind of neurological garbage collector. It collects all those impulses—pain, touch, vibration, temperature—that other nerves don't have any use for, and it dutifully trucks them up to the noggin, where the frontal lobe looks them over. Most it throws away, but some it hands out to the other lobes, particularly those that are looking for something to do. In Uptah's brain, the conversation between the frontal and occipital lobes might have gone something like this:

Frontal Lobe: Hey, got something for you.
Occipital Lobe: About time.
Frontal Lobe: Not my fault. I gotta deal with what they
    give me.
Occipital Lobe: So what's up?
Frontal Lobe: Something on the leg. Feels like crawling.
Occipital Lobe: Crawling, you said?
Frontal Lobe: Yeah. Whatcha got that crawls?
Occipital Lobe: Lemme see. Well, I got ants.
Frontal Lobe: Naw. It's bigger than ants.
Occipital Lobe: I got mice.
Frontal Lobe: No good.
Occipital Lobe: How come?
Frontal Lobe: Mice don't crawl.
Occipital Lobe: How 'bout snakes?
Frontal Lobe: That's a crawler.
Occipital Lobe: Snakes it is.
Frontal Lobe: What kinda snakes you got?
Occipital Lobe (rummages through Uptah's photo library
    and takes the first snake it finds): Milk.
Frontal Lobe: Okay. Milk snakes on the leg. Roll 'em.
Occipital Lobe: I'm on it.

Back in 1759, there lived in Switzerland an old man by the name
of Charles Lullin. One day, while his grandson was visiting him, he
looked out the window and said to the grandson, *"Regardez là-bas."*

"Qu'est-ce que c'est, Grand-père?" answered the grandson.

"La cigogne," said the grandfather.

The grandson didn't bother to look out the window for the stork.
He knew there wasn't one. In the first place, it was in the middle
of winter. And in the second, his grandfather was totally blind from
cataracts.

The grandson was a curious man, so he asked his grand-père if he
ever saw anything else out the window. *"Oui,"* he said, *"beaucoup de
choses."* He saw beautiful women, he saw elegant carriages, and he saw
a whole menagerie of animals. And quite often he saw a large blue

handkerchief covered with orange spots. Most of the time the visions were quite pleasant, and the grandfather was happy to see them. But not always.

The grandson's name was Charles Bonnet. He was a philosopher and writer of some renown. He wrote a paper describing the hallucinations of his grand-père, who, he assured the reader, was of a perfectly sound mind. And probably he was right. But it should be pointed out that before Charles Bonnet became a philosopher, his major interest in life was the mating habits of the aphid. So you have to wonder about the pair just a bit.

Although it took almost two hundred years, eventually he got credit for his discovery, and in 1937 it became an official condition: the Charles Bonnet syndrome. Blind people seeing things.

I explained all this to Uptah. Then I told him that regardless of the cause, there were medications that were quite effective at ridding a person of hallucinations. I suggested that he give them a try.

"You telling me you got a pill to get rid of snakes?"

"I got a pill for everything, Uptah. Try it for a couple of weeks, and we'll see what happens."

Two weeks later he came back. He was all smiles.

"The snakes is gone," he said. "For good."

"I guess the pill worked."

"Mebbe so. Kin I ask you a question, Doc?"

"That's what I'm here for."

"That pill you gave me—is it the kind that you gotta take to make it work?"

"That would be the usual plan. Why do you ask?"

"Well, I got the bottle a'right. An' I brought it home. An' I put it in a particul'r place. So's I would know just where it was, don't ya know. But then I plumb forgot about it for a bit. An' when I remembered, for the life of me, I couldn't find that place where them pills was at."

"So I guess the snakes just went away on their own."

"Nope."

"What else would account for it?"

"'Twer them kittens."

"You mean you got some kittens to keep the snakes away?"

"Yup. Pair of tabbies they is. Cutest little things you ever seen. Got the idear on account a we us'ter have an' ol' tom tabby lived in the barn. Didn't care much about mice or even birds, but, lordy, how he loved them snakes. Grabbed 'em back a the jaw he would, an' then he'd snap the head right off. Like it was no more'n a string bean. Then he'd play with it a bit till it stopped wrigglin'. Yessir. That tom was a snaker, a'right. So I figured: Mebbe kittens would work. An' they sure did. 'Course they crawl all over my legs now. But I don' mind. They a lot softer than them milk snakes. Friendlier too."

I was sure I knew the answer, but I had to ask.

"Where did you get the kittens?"

Uptah smiled. "I thought on what you told me t'other day 'bout that old Switch fella. An' so I thought and I thought an' I thought. Real hard I did. An' one day, there they was."

"I'd say that's quite a testament to the Power of Positive Thinking."

Uptah smiled. Then he bent over and, with his hand hovering about six inches above the leg, slid it down toward his ankle with a slow back-and-forth motion. Like he was stroking something.

"Sure 'nuf is."

· 27 ·

Unnecessary Care

···········

The examination room is a sanctuary. Protected from intrusion by the outside world and insulated from distractions, the place it most closely resembles is the confessional, excepting, of course, the need on the part of the confessor to maintain the illusion that his identity is unknown to the confessee. But the fundamental principle is the same. It is inviolate to interruption. There are exceptions, I expect. A fire in the church or a call from the pope would qualify, but these are extraordinary circumstances.

Likewise is the exam room for doctors. Barring a natural disaster, a cardiac arrest, or the arrival of Harriet Washburn's fudge brownies, the doctor and the patient in consultation are not to be disturbed. Thus it was with no small degree of interest that I awaited the news portended by the knock on my door, as I was in the midst of curing a particularly nasty case of the flu.

"Come in," I said. "We're decent."

Maggie opened the door. She stuck her head in partway and silently mouthed the letter *P*. Once. Twice.

"Excuse me," I said to the patient. "There is an emergency, and I must go. I will be back as soon as I can."

Although Emmeline Talbot Memorial Hospital has never been considered divinely blessed, should the case ever be successfully argued that we have received assistance from On High, there is no doubt as to who would be its purveyor, our Blessed Saint Preserver.

It would be The Honorable.

If it had been told on *This Is Your Life*, the story of Pauline Pontifact most likely would have been titled Against All Odds. Orphaned at age five, when both her parents were killed in an auto accident, she was taken in by an aunt who, although very well meaning, being childless herself and well on in years was utterly useless in the department of parenting. Pauline was unfazed. She simply took on the task herself. A voracious reader, she discovered early on the wonders of Astrid Lindgren, and at age seven declared to all that henceforth she would be known as Pippi. The choice was a perfect fit. As strong-willed and independent as her namesake, Pippi did a good job of raising herself. And although she never went to the South Seas, and her socks always matched, she did favor pigtails. She had a pet dog that followed her wherever she went. His name was Mr. Nilsson.

In her youth, it was on the playing fields that Pippi showed she was a cut above everyone else. Leading scorer on the Dumster's field hockey and basketball teams, she led the latter to four straight state basketball championships, which accomplishment alone would place her high in the annals of Dumster mythology. But substantial as they were, these accomplishments pale before what she did at the 1977 Division III Girls State Track Meet. Outraged that the school board, in the throes of a series of budget rejections by the voters, had eliminated the girls' track team on the grounds that there wasn't enough interest, she entered the state meet as Dumster High's sole competitor. On the strength of four firsts and a second—the latter coming in the two-mile, which she entered because, as she said, "it was the last event, and I needed the points"—she won the meet. Her achievement remains notable to this day, not primarily because two of the state records she had set in the high jump and the four hundred meters remain the longest unbroken records in Vermont competition, but because of the rule that was passed after the meet. Known as the Pippi Rule, it states that a competitor may not compete in more than three individual events in any one meet.

Pippi graduated at the top of her class at Dumster High and went to the University of Vermont on a full scholarship. Despite fervent pleas, from not only the coaches and the athletic director but even the president of the college herself, she refused to have anything to do with competitive sports. "That is child's play," she said. "I have more important things to do now."

She graduated summa cum laude in three years with a degree in political science. Then, to the surprise of all, she returned to Dumster and ran for selectboard. Her opponent was Tom Comstock. Tom had held the seat for as long as anyone could remember, as had his father before him. In fact, so long had it been in the Comstock family that the position was jokingly referred to as the Comstock Bottom.

Tom didn't bother to campaign against Pippi. "I stand for election" was his favorite expression come election time. "I don't run for it." But Pippi did. She didn't spend a dime, but she visited every house in Dumster to make her case for change, and when the votes were counted, she had beaten Tom by a margin of two to one.

"It's only the beginning," said people after her victory. And they were right. Three years later she was Dumster's representative to the State House, and four years after that one of the two state senators from Abenaki County. After serving eight years in the senate, the last four as president pro-tem, she ran for Vermont's congressional seat and won handily. After two terms she announced that she was not running for reelection. Everyone assumed that she was leaving her seat in order to run for governor. She was considered such a certainty that no other candidate came forth. Even the Libertarians held back. The political wisdom in Vermont was that whatever Pippi wanted, Pippi got. But once again she surprised everyone. "I'm done with elected politics," she said. "It's just another game, and the competition isn't that good. Besides, all the important decisions are made by staff." And she went to work as chief of staff for the senator.

As always, she was right. Particularly for us. Which is why, despite her renunciation of public office, she is still known in town as The Honorable.

Many people have given generously to Emmeline Talbot. A few have been sufficiently munificent to have their names given to various appendages and accoutrements. However, without the contributions of Pauline Pontifact, the Hospital That Never Should Have Been never would have.

Year after year, she worked for us behind the scenes. "Most of what legislation accomplishes is under the radar," she explained to me once. "And Congress has some pretty high fliers, so there's a lot of room down there." She would slip into an amendment here, or an earmark there, those little clauses and codicils that have guaranteed that our little hospital on the hill would be equipped with all the amenities

of one many times its size. As a result of Pippi's nurture, Emmeline
Talbot has not just survived, it has thrived.

Under the Traumatic Brain Injury Act we got an MRI machine
and a state-of-the-art radiology suite in which to house it. Under the
Clean Water Act we got an Olympic-sized indoor heated therapeutic swimming pool. Under the National Institutes of Mental Health
Budget, we received funds for a rehabilitation unit, complete with
physiatrist, therapists, and a board-certified neuropsychophysiolo-
gist. Art is his name. He is a very nice fellow, and he is exceptionally well qualified. Nobody is exactly sure what he is supposed to
do, so he spends most of his time either in the pool or the cafete-
ria. And under the Katrina Emergency Relief Act, we were declared
a Critical Access Hospital with the associated guarantees of extra
reimbursement for all our charges. All we had to do was ask, and The
Honorable provided.

There was one thing Pippi always provided without even asking.
When it came to whatever it was she wanted, she saved you that
trouble.

I picked up the phone, ready to do her bidding.

"Hey, Peachie Beachie," she said. "I hope everything is going well
down there at my favorite hospital."

"It sure is. Thanks, as always, to you."

"Just doing what I can to pay back Dumster for all it's done for me.
Listen. I'll be in town in half an hour. There's a couple of things I need
from you. I know it's short notice, but any chance that you might be
free?"

"No problem. My schedule is completely open."

"Great. See you soon."

I looked at my watch. It was quarter to twelve. I called Maggie in
and told her to notify Kathy Ducharme that the quarterly meeting of
the medical staff would have to be canceled, and I asked her to move
my first two afternoon patients to the end of the day. Then I went
back and quickly dispensed with influenza. When Pippi arrived, I was
ready and waiting.

She didn't waste any time with niceties.

"First," she said, "I want a referral to Doctor Skinner so he can get rid of this—" She pulled up her shirt to expose a half-inch flat brown spot that might be described as resembling a freckle on steroids. "—*disgusting* thing."

"That's a solar lentigo, Pippi. It's . . ."

"I know. I know. You're going to tell me it's perfectly harmless. Don't waste your breath. Lentigo schmigo. Call it what you want. I know what it really is. It's an *age* spot! And I am not ready to start having anyone or any*thing* remind me of my age. So as the lady in the play said, 'Out, out, damn spot.'"

"I think Florence Nightingale would be a more apt role model than Lady Macbeth."

"There are more than a few in Montpelier and Washington who would disagree with you," she said with quick grin.

"Their error," I said. "Anyway, no reason you have to see Skinner. I'll have Maggie get the liquid nitrogen, and I can take care of it right now. It won't cost you any time or money. If you go to Skinner he'll want to use his brand-new laser toy, and it will run five hundred dollars easy, maybe more."

"Not with a referral from my primary care physician. No offense, Beachie baby, but I'd just as soon have a specialist take care of it."

"Consider it done."

"Next, I got your letter about my cholesterol," she said, pulling out the paper. "It says:

> Your cholesterol is within the desirable range for your age, and as your good cholesterol level is adequate, this means that you have a lower than average risk of coronary disease. Nonetheless, it would be prudent to maintain a diet that is low in saturated fats.

"Leaving aside the bit about *adequate* and *desirable for my age*, I'll tell you this about that. First, as to a prudent diet, forget about it. I can't remember the last time I saw a home-cooked meal. I eat whatever I can, whenever I can get it. Fast food? It's what I eat on a *slow* day. And Beach, do you really think that I am going to accept even for a minute being *better than average?*"

"Of course. It was silly of me. Nothing but the best will do for Pippi."

"Correctamundo, Beachie boy."

"That should be easy enough. There are several excellent choices—"

"Had a visit the other day from one of the boys at Big Pharma. He told me that Supertor was the hottest thing on the market right now. Promised it would melt my cholesterol like butter on the burner."

"As it were."

"Yup. So serve me up and get it down."

"I would rather do it with a generic medication that, unlike Supertor, has a proven safety record. Furthermore, it will only cost a fraction as much. Supertor will run you in the neighborhood of three hundred dollars a month." I thought this would seal my argument as Pippi, at least where her own expenditures were concerned, was a thrifty as any Dumsterian.

I was wrong.

"Wrong-o, fish face. Won't cost me a penny. Congressional health insurance provides one hundred percent reimbursement on all medications, generic or brand name. So take out your pad and scribble away."

I did as instructed.

"Last, I want a CT of my heart. The one they do for coronary calcium deposits."

"Really? You know that there isn't any—"

"Proof that the test can actually improve prediction of a person's *risk* of heart attack? Yes. I know. You gave me that same *evidence* business last year with my whole-body CT scan, and the year before that with the MRI of my breasts. You're quite cute when you talk all that Evidence Based, Prior Probability, Risk Benefit stuff. It's as if you actually believed in it. But we both know better. Anyway, I'm not talking about medical science here. I'm talking about what I want."

"And I would love to accommodate you, naturally. There is, however, one slight difficulty."

"You mean the fact that the test requires an electron beam CT scanner, and Emmeline Talbot doesn't have one?"

"Or the medical center. In fact there isn't one within one hundred miles."

"Heh heh," she cackled. "There is now."

"Oh? Where?"

"Right here, at little old Emmeline T. At least there will be. I got the money for it inserted into the Omnibus Appropriations and Defense Authorization Act. It should be arriving next week. And the construction funds will be coming from the stimulus bill. Which makes it a rush order. They estimate the whole shebang will be up and running in no more than a month."

"And you will be its first customer."

"If you insist."

"It's only fitting. I must say, Pippi, I don't know how you do it all. Don't you ever get tired out?"

"Well, I must admit that these last few months have been rough sledding. Especially getting the health care reform bill passed. There were a lot of tough choices to make."

"So I gathered."

"We had to extend coverage to the uninsured without busting the budget. That meant somehow reducing our current health care costs. It involved a lot of burning of midnight oil, believe you me."

"I can imagine."

"We started with malpractice reform."

"Always best to pick the low-hanging fruit first."

"We wanted to protect you doctors from having to practice defensive medicine."

"Be good to get back on offense again."

"And avoid having to do all those tests just so you won't be sued."

"Yes. That is what we preach. Although it's funny, I've never heard of a doctor being sued for not ordering a test for a condition that a patient didn't have."

"Of course by itself, that wasn't nearly enough. In the end, we had to do some trimming of our current health expenditures."

"Like Medicare."

"Yes." Pippi frowned. "I didn't like that. But by placing an emphasis on primary care and eliminating unnecessary services, I think we came up with something that will fit the bill without having a negative impact on the quality of care."

"Ay, there's the rub."

"Quite the literati today, aren't we? You mean quality of care, I suppose?"

"Actually, I was referring to unnecessary services."

"I know. Without the unnecessary, many of you—"

"Would be out of a job."

"We intentionally avoided being specific."

"Always a good idea."

"We figured that should be left up to the doctors who knew best, you primary care folks."

"We appreciate that. It is always difficult deciding what really needs to be done and what doesn't. But over the years, I've found an approach that works pretty well. And I think my patients like it as well."

"Which is what?"

"Unnecessary care is that which is provided to someone else."

· 28 ·

On Doctoring

···········

There was a picture window in the waiting room. A large tree dominated the view. It looked like a maple, but without the leaves I couldn't tell. It ought to have been a sugar maple, the only tree worthy of the place. Through the branches of the tree I could see sky. There were a few bits of blue, but mostly it was gray. Next to the tree were some bushes.

Ordinarily I would not notice such details, but I was practicing the art of looking. It was an activity recommended to me by Anton Chekhov. I had been reading a collection of his short stories, and in these stories the protagonists spend a considerable number of pages doing nothing but looking, glorying in the majesty of the world around them, and becoming inspired with a greater appreciation of life. In the end, all his characters either die or go mad, but as Chekhov doesn't blame this on the looking, I thought I'd give it a try.

I should hasten to say that I don't want to give my readers the mistaken impression that my literary tastes are superior to theirs, me reading one of the great masters of all time and they reading, at least presently, this meager work. It was really by accident that it came about. I was clearing out our bookshelves to make room for the spate of grandchildren books that were arriving on a weekly basis when the volume fell to the floor and split in half. It was a relic of my college days, and as it lay there more or less pleading to be read, I didn't have the heart to throw it out.

Ranging alongside the spot it had vacated were an equally distinguished set of companions, *War and Peace*, *Anna Karenina*, *Dead Souls*, *Crime and Punishment*, along with a smattering of works by lesser-known Russian authors. They were artifacts of my college days. I was a Russian major. It was not a course of study I chose out of a burning desire to study great literature. Rather it was upon the advice of a classmate, who told me, after we had finished a rather indifferent performance in Physics One, that the best way for us to ensure a place for ourselves in medical school at that point was to show that we had something called *broader interests*. Why it was so he had no idea, but he knew personally of two fellows who had actually failed organic chemistry and still succeeded in their quest, one by becoming an expert on medieval music, and the other by mastering the history of the Ming dynasty. It was not clear why such endeavors would qualify one to be a doctor, but then, to this day, I am unable to understand how Physics One and organic chemistry would do that either. Be that as it may, the ploy succeeded. Maybe that was why I couldn't throw the book out. Or maybe it was because Chekhov started adult life as a doctor before he turned to writing. But most likely it was simply that a book in hand is worth, well, you know the expression.

To say that I liked the stories or that they were very well written would be a bit silly. They were, after all, by Chekhov. But his observations about observing did give me something to do when I was waiting. In this instance I had opportunity to sharpen my powers of observation for a little over an hour.

"The dean will see you now," said one of his emissaries, interrupting my studies.

"So good to see you, Beach," said the dean after we shook hands. And so heartily did he say it that, despite myself, I believed him. Which, presumably, is one of the things you have to be able to do in order to be dean.

The dean is a handsome man. Tall and slim, with clean spare features, he has clear blue eyes and a thick shock of white hair. He wore a pale blue shirt and dark blue tie patterned with the university crest. Over it he wore a freshly starched immaculate white coat with the letters DEAN embroidered in gold cursive just above the right breast pocket. A gold-plated stethoscope protruded neatly from the left hip pocket. I have never quite understood what use a dean would have for a stethoscope, unless it was perhaps for eavesdropping on what his staff were saying behind his back, although that would seem rather below a dean's dignity. But every dean I have ever met had one. And all the pictures of deans past that graced the halls outside his office showed them similarly outfitted. It was their scepter, I suppose.

"I can't tell you how much we appreciate all the effort you've put in for our students over the years," he effused. "Let's see . . ." He paused to consult the sheet on his desk. "It looks as if it's been—my goodness, yes, it seems that—well, in fact it has been . . ." He hesitated. Perhaps the math was too difficult or, more likely, my inception antedated the computerized record upon which he would be relying.

"A long time," I ventured helpfully.

"Yes." He smiled. "A long time indeed."

"And I wanted you to come in so I could thank you personally on behalf of the medical school, and of course on behalf of all the students who have benefited from your wisdom."

"It was nothing," I said. Which was true—at least from the point of view of compensation.

"Nonsense!" he beamed. "The opportunity for our young doctors-to-be to see an old experienced hand plying his trade is invaluable."

"Generous of you to say," I said, waiting for The Rest of the Story.

"It's nothing but the truth, the whole truth, and nothing but the truth." He said, pleased with this turn of phrase. "And that's why I wanted to talk to you about the new directions we are taking, particularly as it involves the course you have been so generous as to help us with over the years."

"Introduction to History and Physical Diagnosis."

"Precisely. And again, let me say, I just can't thank you enough for your contribution."

"Er . . . it's a pleasure," I stammered, embarrassed at this plethora of encomiums and wondering what it was leading up to. "I enjoy working with the students. And learning how to take histories and perform examinations on the people they will care for is such an essential component in the making of a good doctor that anything I can do to pass on whatever tidbits I have acquired over the years is the least I can do to pay back for the privilege of being a doctor."

The dean nodded. "An admirable sentiment. As it turns out, we've decided to eliminate the course."

"Ah. Well, yes, I suppose the obtaining of histories and the performing of examinations is rather subjective, and now that we have such a battery of sophisticated tests at our fingertips, they have become rather old hat. Testing is much more objective."

"Exactly. I'm glad you can see it. Quite frankly, some of our other older—excuse me—*senior* physicians have been quite resistant to the idea."

"Subjectivity is rather hard to give up. It does give one a bit more flexibility in planning one's action."

The dean looked pleased with my answer. "But not for you, I see. Not that I am surprised. And that is precisely why I asked you to come in today. I was hoping you would help us out with the new course we have designed to replace it."

"I'd be delighted. I assume on the same terms as before?"

"Naturally. I'm sure you will find it an even more satisfying experience."

"I'm sure I will."

"We call the course On Doctoring."

"*Doctoring?*"

"Yes. We chose that name to emphasize the much broader nature of the course. It will address the entire spectrum of what a doctor does in the course of his work."

"That's quite an ambitious undertaking. Somewhat akin, I suppose to what Plumbering would be for plumbers, or Carpentering for carpenters."

"Still the same sense of humor, I see. I like that in a man—as long as it doesn't interfere with the serious nature of our work."

"Perish the thought."

"I should say at the outset that On Doctoring will include some aspects of History and Physical Diagnosis from the old course, although the format will be different. We want to ensure that all of our students have a uniform experience. Uniformity of experience is the principle on which all of our medical education is now based. We consider it essential."

"Yes. The old way was rather hodgepodge."

"Hodgepodge. Yes. Hodgepodge describes it perfectly. And as

you so obviously have realized, the major source of the difficulty was patients."

"They can be unruly."

"*Actual* patients certainly can," he said. "Being as by definition they have to be, different, they are rather . . ."

"Inconsistent?"

"Precisely. Thank you, Beach. You know, I can see that I really shouldn't have to explain any of this to you. You really grasp the issues quite well."

"But you need to ensure that all of us preceptors are treated uniformly."

"Indeed we do." He chuckled. "Just like the patients."

"But how can you do that with patients? They tend to be a rather heterogeneous lot."

"We use only healthy ones."

Now I was on more familiar ground. Taking healthy people and converting them into patients was a familiar concept. It was the bread and butter of primary care.

"Of course! How stupid of me not to think of that. As a strategy for creating patients out of whole cloth, Health Maintenance can't be beat. But I'm puzzled. Even in Health Maintenance, you get variable results. Some people have high blood pressure, others high cholesterol, still others osteoporosis or abnormal PSAs or spots on mammograms. How can you standardize that?"

The dean frowned. "We don't use Health Maintenance, Beach. Although we did consider that approach. But as you said, even starting with healthy people, there is simply too much variability. No. We realized that using real patients in any form just wouldn't do at all."

"I suppose not."

"And as you so correctly pointed out, we'd wind up in just the same pickle, wouldn't we?"

"You're right, of course. Silly of me to think otherwise."

"Not at all," said the dean, smiling. "You must remember, Beach, we have committees to work on these issues."

"Whereas I have only myself."

"Yes. Perhaps we could . . . Well, let me explain to you how the program works. What we do is create patients out of whole cloth, as it were. The applicants are all in perfect health."

"To prevent any contamination with real conditions."

"Exactly. We take the best-qualified and enroll them in a course that teaches them how to be the kind of patient who meets our specifications. We call them Standardized Patients, or SP for short. It works quite well."

"Sounds as if it should."

"Then we train our SPs to have exactly the right symptoms for the condition we wish them to portray, so that when the students ask the standard questions we have taught them, they will get predictable answers."

"Gee!" I said. "What a great idea. I wonder if . . . I mean—well—er—have you thought about enrolling *real* patients in this type of training? It would be such a help—so much easier, as I am sure you can imagine—for those of us who still have to work with them if they could learn to behave the way the Standardized Patients do. I guess you'd call it On Patienting."

"On Patienting. Hmm. That *is* an interesting idea. I like it. In fact, I'll bring it up at our next committee meeting. You may have something there."

"Well, it's just a thought."

"But a good one. And I believe it has great potential. There's no intrinsic reason, I suppose, to limit the classes only to those involved in our On Doctoring course. Yes, it's definitely worth looking into. But let me explain to you the details of how the course works. It's really quite elegant. For example, take chest pain."

"Please do. Chest pain is one of the banes of my existence. There are so many possibilities, and it is always so hard to sort them all out."

"That's the beauty of using SPs. They have only those symptoms that correspond either to the classical presentation of angina, or that of reflux esophagitis—depending on which we are deciding to use on a particular day."

"Angina or reflux esophagitis. Does rather simplify the whole business. But you don't think it's at all limiting? I mean—"

"Of course it is. We are planning to add a pulmonary embolus module. It should be available by the next semester."

"So that would make three possible causes."

"We figured that was as much as they could digest at this stage of their careers."

"I understand. You wouldn't want to get them in over their heads with a patient whose problem remained vague or unclear after the dust had settled."

"Heavens no! Each patient, if questioned properly, will lead the student to exactly the right diagnosis, and only to that diagnosis."

"I see. A kind of a Stepford Patient, you might say."

"And it's not just physical complaints we address," he said, choosing to not comment on my remark. Perhaps he didn't know about the Stepford Wives. You never can tell with deans. "We have also trained our SPs to present with broader issues. Ones that we have determined are important for any doctor to be able to address."

"What kinds of issues?"

"Oh, you know, the usual," he said. "Sexual abuse, suicidal ideations, eating disorders—and how to convey bad news."

"Those certainly are important issues."

"We felt it was important for all physicians, regardless of what career choice they might eventually choose, to have the ability to address them."

"And in the first year of medical school at that."

"Exactly. So we can be sure they are well grounded before they get involved with real patients."

"Or choose a career path where they might not have an opportunity to experience them later."

"Not necessarily. All of us have to deal with them at some time or another, even we deans, you know. We are often the bearers of bad news."

"I'm sure you do it quite well."

"We do our best."

"Funny thing. I've been passing on bad news all these years, and I didn't know it made that much difference what *I* did. It always seemed to me that it was about the message, not the messenger."

"Not so, Beach. How you pass the message is very important."

"Kind of like getting things off on the right foot, I suppose."

"Exactly."

"Even when the journey is one you don't want to take."

"As I said, we feel this is a wonderful addition to the curriculum. And we would love to have you on board."

"I'd be honored to help out. But I'm not sure how qualified I am for this. I haven't really had much experience with Standard Patients. Mine have tended to be mainly of the nonstandard variety."

"Of course you haven't. None of you clinicians has. Which is why we have created a course for the teachers. So that you can learn how to play your assigned role."

"As a Standardized Proctor."

"A good way of putting it."

"Uh—you know I want to do whatever I can for the school, Dean," I said. "But I'm still not sure how well I'd fit into this curriculum. You know, old dogs and new tricks being the problematic combination that they are."

"Nonsense!" he exclaimed. "It really isn't that difficult. Someone of your intelligence will pick it up in no time. Besides, we start slowly with very easy issues. We want to be sure to build success upon success."

"That makes sense."

"We think so. Which is why the first topic is Handwashing."

"Handwashing. Certainly a most important subject."

"Indeed it is."

"So I am reminded regularly by my grandson. As well as to be sure to cough into my elbow. I suppose that's part of the course also."

"No-o, it isn't. That would be more of a *patient*-related skill. But now that you mention it, perhaps we should include it in the module. Teaching patients, after all, should be one of our roles. You know, Beach. You really have some interesting ideas. Perhaps you might like to be on our committee. I think you could make a real contribution."

"I'd be honored, Dean. But maybe I should try the course out first, just so I get a better feel of things."

"Good idea. We have a training course starting next week. It's with one of our most experienced SPs. I'll sign you up."

The training lasted three sessions. I have included the notes I took for each of the classes thinking, erroneously as it turned out, that I would be using them for future reference, as I taught the course. More than likely, they are not representative of the course as a whole, but they are all that I have. Anyone who is truly interested in how On Doctoring prepares the doctors of the future will have to look elsewhere.

SESSION 1: INTRODUCTION TO DOCTORING

I think this course is going to be fun after all. We all took turns introducing ourselves and where we came from. The students are a lively bunch; most are from Vermont. There was even a Windsor girl, Patty French, whose parents were patients of mine. Three were from out of state, one from California, one from Massachusetts, and one from New York. Since I had lived in all three places I was interested in exactly where they were from, but no one else seemed to be, so I didn't ask. One student was older than the rest and spoke with an accent that sounded Slavic. Her name was Azra. She said she was from Winooski.

The SP asked her was she really from Winooski.

Azra admitted that it all depended on what one meant by from. "I was born in Bosnia," she said. "But it was Yugoslavia then. I came here during the war."

The SP said that was very interesting, and that she should tell us all about it sometime. Azra didn't say anything.

I learned something else today. The course is actually run by the SP, and pretty strictly at that. I am there mainly as a "resource." She explained this to me before class so there would be no misunderstanding. I am encouraged to make contributions whenever I feel like it, but the actual management of the lesson plan will be her responsibility. It is no reflection on me, she told me. It's just that they need to ensure uniformity, and their experience is that doctors sometimes have difficulty with following the rules, especially senior ones like me.

It should be an interesting challenge. Not being in charge is a new role. Trine says it will be good for me.

SESSION 2: EXAMINATION OF THE SKIN

I got in trouble today. Twice. It wasn't my fault, but I'm going to have to be more careful if I want to continue.

My first mistake was with handwashing. The SP gave a demonstration of proper handwashing techniques. She explained that it was particularly important for the patient to see that you had washed your hands, because it helped to cement the doctor–patient bond. We all practiced several times and everything was copasetic until one of the students asked about Purell. Without thinking I piped up that I used Purell all the time, especially in the hospital, where it was more convenient, as the sinks weren't in the patient's room. The SP said Purell was not part of the course. Handwashing was what would be on the exam. And that was that for Purell.

Then the students practiced examining the skin of the SP. She had a few moles on her chest, which she said were benign, and a small pimple on the side of her nose. She told the students that pimples on the nose were very common and also were harmless. Then she asked me if I had any comments. I knew we would be covering the skin, so I had brought in some slides I had used during my physical diagnosis teaching. The slides showed various types of skin cancers—melanomas, squamous cell carcinomas, basal cell carcinomas—which I pointed out can look a lot like a pimple if you don't look closely. I also showed them a slide of Kaposi's sarcoma. I explained it was the lesion that led us to the discovery of AIDS. I told them they would probably never see a Kaposi's sarcoma here in Vermont, because AIDS was quite rare around here, but if they ever went to the inner city for their residency, for example, which I said I thought was a good idea as it would broaden their experience, they would need to know what it looked like. Then I told them the story of how I discovered my own melanoma. It was on the top of my foot, and I thought it was just a blister, but when it didn't go away, I looked at it with my magnifying glass and realized that it wasn't a blister at all. I told them I always used a magnifying glass to examine the skin, and I showed them mine. It is a large round glass with a long black handle. It looks like the kind Sherlock Holmes used. I told them there were newer ones now, more high-powered and with their own light, but they were quite expensive, and besides, this one made you look very clever. The SP said that was very interesting, but for now the students were to use the naked eye only. I said that was too bad because I had brought one for each of the students. Well, there wasn't much the SP could do about that, and pretty soon they were all examining one another with their magnifying glasses. I could tell she wasn't happy with me at all.

Afterward she told me that she could understand my motivation, seeing as how I was a Melanoma Survivor, but that this kind of thing wouldn't do at all, as it provided a different experience to my students. She also told me that my remarks about inner-city medicine, although well intentioned, were not appropriate for first-year students, as it was especially important that at such an early stage of their education, they not develop any feelings of inadequacy, especially with regards to their experience here. Furthermore, she explained, the Curriculum Committee had stated quite clearly that they wanted to ensure that nothing about their education here would discourage them from seeking a residency at the medical center when they graduated. I apologized and promised I wouldn't do it again. I'm not sure she was satisfied.

Session 3: Chest Pain

Well, I did it again. I spoke out of turn. I'm afraid SP is pretty much fed up with me. I wouldn't be surprised if she reported me to the dean. It was the first Chest Pain day, and the SP was scheduled to have a heart attack. Each student in turn was expected to ask three questions in a prearranged order assigned by the SP. If all went according to plan, it would lead them to the correct diagnosis. Everything started out swimmingly. The first students performed just as expected. They asked the right questions and got the right answers. The SP had been in good health all of her life, although she used to smoke a pack of cigarettes a day. She had quit two years ago. For three weeks SP had been having chest pain whenever she walked her dog up the hill, but she didn't think anything of it, because it went away when she rested. Then yesterday evening she had the same pain, only it was stronger, and it didn't go away for quite a while, even after she rested. It was right in the middle of her chest, and it radiated up to her jaw. She thought it was indigestion. Today it came back again and didn't go away at all.

Then it was Azra's turn to ask her questions.

Perhaps it was because she was older, but whatever the reason, Azra was usually much more at ease when talking to SP than the other students. She managed to give the feeling that she really cared about the answers, probably because she did. So it was a bit of a surprise when she just sat there looking at the floor with a disinterested stare, as if her thoughts were anywhere but where she was.

"Your colleague was asking about my chest pain, Doctor Kovac," prompted the SP.

Azra started slightly at her name. She looked blankly at the SP. Then she appeared to remember where she was. "My name is Az-ra-Ko-vac," she said mechanically. "On a scale of one-to-ten-how-bad-is-your-pain?"

"Six," said the SP. And she accompanied the remark with a grimace appropriate to the rating.

Azra nodded slightly but asked no more questions. She appeared to have lost all interest in the proceedings. For a brief instant the SP registered displeasure. Then suddenly her expression changed. The grimace disappeared. She started to cry.

I asked her what was the matter. She gave me a funny look and said, "Nothing." But clearly there was. I asked her again, and was about to say there was no need for her to continue with this session if she was upset—at which point she shot me such a glance that I almost jumped back. Too late, I remembered. All SPs have in their historical repertoire an emotional trauma that the student is expected to unearth by drawing her out, and about which the student should then demonstrate an appropriate empathy.

The tears seemed to work. Azra looked at the SP and asked if something had happened to her to bring on the pain. The SP told her that her sister had recently been killed in an automobile accident, and today was her funeral.

Azra said "Oh." Then she paused. Finally she said. "I'msorryforyourloss." It sounded just the way they say it on the crime shows.

The next student asked his three questions. He determined that the pain was a pressure, that it was like an elephant sitting on her chest, and that it squeezed, which the SP demonstrated by taking her hand, making a tight fist, and clutching it to her chest. It was a pretty classical story for a coronary. Then the SP said we were finished. She asked the students what was their diagnosis. They all agreed that she was having a heart attack. The SP said very good. She complimented each of them on their interviewing skills, which she said were coming along nicely. She mentioned to Azra that she might benefit from working on her empathy, and Azra said she would. Then she dismissed the class, and they all left.

Except Azra. She had some papers on her desk. She kept shuffling them aimlessly. She was stalling. I asked her if there was anything she wanted to go over from the day's lesson.

"It wasn't like that," she said.

I asked her what it wasn't like.

And she told me.

29

Endangered Species

....

"I was born in Bratunac. It's a small town in eastern Bosnia that lies in a valley along the Drina, the river that forms the border between Bosnia and Serbia. My family had lived there for as long as anyone could remember. We owned a grocery store that was started by my great-great-grandfather, who was a sausage maker. His *sudzuk* was very famous in the area. People came from all over to buy it, even from across the river. The recipe was a big secret. It was passed down each generation from father to son, when the son was old enough to run the store. We lived in an apartment above the store. You could see the river from our window. It was very pretty. When I was growing up we all got along together, Bosnians, Croats, and Serbs. Nobody cared who you were or what church you went to. When the big split came in 1991, nobody cared much. Sarajevo was a long way away.

"In 1992 I was home from the university. My grandfather still owned the store, but mostly he just made *sudzuk* and talked with the old folks who came in. My father was the manager. My brother worked in the store. He expected someday he would be the manager and then the *sudzuk* maker. I had finished university and was going to be starting at the medical school in Sarajevo in the fall.

"In April the JNA came into town and told everyone they had to turn in their guns. They said it was for security reasons. People were nervous, but our police chief said it was okay, he would make sure we were all safe. A week later the bodies of all the men in one of the leading families of our town were found in the river. The chief blamed it on Croats. We heard stories about the killings in other places, but nobody wanted to believe them. After all, we all agreed, we all got along so well. Nothing like that could happen in our town.

"At the beginning of May a JNA army man was shot and killed. The next day they started rounding up the men and taking them to the elementary school. My father joked that they wouldn't touch us. 'They would lose their *sudzuk*,' he said.

"That night the police chief came to the house with two men. They were wearing uniforms I didn't recognize. The chief wanted my father and brother to come with him to the station. He had some questions, he said. My brother started to go, but my father said no, there was no need. The chief said okay, no problem. Then he took out his gun and shot my father. They took my brother outside. We heard some scuffling and then a shout and then a shot. My grandfather said he felt tired. He wanted to sit down. He asked for a drink of water. Then he got this look. And then he died, right there in the chair. The men came back in. They way they were looking at me, I knew what was coming next. The chief looked at my grandfather, and at my mother, who was still holding the glass of water to his lips. He turned to the men and said *dosta*. And they went away.

"We left that night for Srebrenica, to live with one of my mother's sisters. I told my cousin, who was a doctor, what had happened to Grandfather. He said it was a heart attack.

"In 1995, when the Serbs attacked Srebrenica, we left for Tuzla, where there was a UN refugee camp. I started medical school at the university there. I met an American soldier who was with NATO. Pretty much the only men you could meet were soldiers from other countries. All the Bosnian men were gone. He was from Iowa. We went out together. I got pregnant. He said he would marry me and take me back to Iowa when his tour of duty ended. He kept his word.

"The first two years of the marriage were good, and the next three were pretty good. After that it was not so good. When it ended, I knew I didn't want to stay in Iowa. I had a friend from back home who had been placed in Winooski by the Refugee Resettlement Program, and she invited me to come live with her. I got a job housekeeping at the Radisson and went to night school at UVM to get an American college degree. When I finished, I applied to medical school, and here I am."

"Your grandfather didn't complain of any chest pain."

"No. He just said he was tired."

"And he didn't put his hand on his chest with a clenched fist."

"No."

"But he had that look."

"Yes. I don't know how to describe it exactly, but . . ."

"You don't have to. I've seen it. Once I had a patient who came in complaining of a pain in her toe. She had that look."

"And she was having a heart attack."

"Yes."

"Do they always get that look?"

"No."

"So sometimes they do get chest pain?"

"Sometimes. Sometimes they get indigestion or dizziness. I had a patient once whose only symptom was hiccups."

"Oh."

"You never can tell with patients."

"I see. Thank you, Doctor Conger. I think I understand better. And I'm sorry I wasn't more empathetic during the class, it's just that . . ."

"It's hard for you to pretend."

"I guess it is."

"That's understandable. But you'll have to learn. Pretending is a large part of what we do."

"I will."

A few days later I got a call from the dean. He wanted to know how the course was going. I said it was having its ups and downs. He said so he had heard. Then he said maybe the format as it was currently structured wasn't well suited to my skills. I allowed as how maybe it wasn't. And we both agreed that it would be best if I didn't continue.

I was a little sad. After all, I had been teaching in one way or another for all of my forty-two years as a doctor, and it always made the work more fun. But, as we had said, I was an old dog. I did get one compensation from the course, however. Every Wednesday afternoon is free time for the medical students, and Azra comes down to my office. We see patients together, and she practices pretending. She has gotten to be quite good at it. I told her if she wanted it, she had a job with me when she finished her training. She said she would like that. That's a long way off, however.

But the handwriting is on the wall. After Azra there won't be anyone else. The old ways I have learned are just that. It reminds me of what one of my colleagues said, just before he retired: "You know, Beach, we old internists are like the gray wolves. We cover a lot of territory, and we're finding it harder and harder to find a suitable habitat. We are an endangered species."

He was right about endangered. And I liked his choice of species. Better than the wag who compared us to those lumbering behemoths that once ruled the earth but, as a result of an inability to adapt to a changing environment, were gradually reduced in numbers until they were unable to find mates with whom they could reproduce, so that today they exist only as fossilized remains in a museum.

But like every other living thing, we too are evolving, and already the next breed of doctors is leaner, fleeter, stronger, and in every way fitter for survival in today's world. Which is only as it should be in a profession where what we know and what we can do is advancing at such a rapid pace that being older doesn't make one wiser, it only makes one more out of date.

There is one thing, however, that I would wish to pass on to the new generation if I could, because I know it would make them better doctors. But it is one of those things that if you can't figure it out for yourself, no one can teach it to you.

I am happy in my work.

30

The Value of Convenience

....

I was sitting at my desk, slogging my way through the mounds of paperwork that greeted me each morning, test results, prior authorization forms, referral requests, and the like. It is tedious work, but not always tiresome. The unexpectedly improved test result or the encouraging consultant's report often makes up for the mountain of forms just requiring my signature, which, as I never read any of them, do not really present a significant burden.

The phone rang. I looked at the number on my caller ID. I picked up the phone.

"I wonder if you could come over sometime," said the voice on the other end of the line.

"I can stop by at noon," I said.

It certainly wasn't an emergency. More than likely it wasn't even necessary. It didn't matter. I was desperate to get out of the office. And a house call was the perfect thing to escape from the drudgery of modern medicine.

Besides, I liked to visit him.

C. Frederick Selkirk, Freddy as he was called by those who visited him, had been, in his day, a writer. Mostly he was a journalist. He preferred newspaper writing, because writing for the paper you had to say your piece without dawdling.

Some time ago he bought the Marcotte farm up at the top of Killdeer Hill and moved to Dumster. He lived alone there now. His wife had died a few years back, and all of his three children had predeceased him. Although it never seems right when children die before their parents, in Freddy's case it is perhaps understandable. In deference to his contention that talking about age was a conversation of fools, I won't mention his, but I will say this much: Once, when I was attempting to sympathize with a particularly unpleasant flare-up of his arthritis, I made the mistake of telling him I knew how he felt.

"No you don't," he said. "Not in the least."

I started to explain I only meant that all of us get aches and pains now and then, but he wouldn't hear any of it.

"Stop," he said. "This is how I feel. If I could be in the same condition I was when I was ninety, I'd be satisfied."

He was right. I didn't know how he felt.

His only regular visitor was Millie Webster. She considered herself his housekeeper, and he was willing to maintain this polite fiction. Millie came every day to "tidy up," she said. The tidying consisted of a small bit of puttering about and then sitting with him for a bit in silence while he read and she had a cup of tea. "For a man," she said, "he's pretty tidy. Quiet too." Millie had outlived three husbands, and in her opinion tidy and quiet were the primary virtues one should seek when selecting a spouse.

Millie and I were two of a handful of visitors. And although he was perfectly able, he did not go out much. It was not because he disliked people. It was just that he had no tolerance for fools and phonies, and he would rather stay at home than run the risk of meeting up with one.

He went to the bank, and he went to Contremond's, and he went to Nat's. And when he did, he was pleasant to all he met. He treated the townspeople with respect and courtesy. He had no airs about being better than they were. People liked him for that. Even Nat. "Not a bad customer," she said. It was her highest compliment.

Despite his years, he still had a sense of humor as sharp as two-year-old Cabot cheddar, and it was a pleasure to listen to his scalpel-like dissection of any issue, from our international policy toward China to the paving of Killdeer Road. But it wasn't for his wit that I liked him most. It was because of his respect for authority. He had none. Endowed with an unflinching belief in the equality of all persons regardless of title or status, he abhorred condescension from any quarter—be it religious, judicial, or medical.

Whether it was because he was a true believer, or just to prove a point, I never could tell, but he would regularly reject whatever advice

I had to offer, rebutting it with a well-reasoned mixture of Christian Science and Eastern philosophy. "Keeps you honest," he said. In which regard he felt doctors needed a lot of keeping.

Accordingly, I was someone whose skills he appreciated, but no more so than Millie or Nap or Will Contremond, the carpenter who made his bookshelves. And to all of us, in appreciation thereof, he was civil and expressed a polite, but not excessive, personal interest.

He was quite deaf. Although in most people this would be considered one of the vicissitudes of old age, in Freddy's case it was more of a fringe benefit. He refused to read lips or wear a hearing aid, and so all communication on the part of the speaker had to be done in writing, to which end he provided an erasable slate, a little smaller than an ordinary sheet of paper. Anything one wanted to communicate to him had to be done in no more than one slate, which was about fifteen words for me, although Millie could get in a few more because her handwriting was smaller.

I told my daughter about this, and she said it sounded like Twitter, which I guess would be the best analogy for her generation. But I prefer to think of it as haiku. For each slate had to be carefully crafted. When you gave it to him, he would read it word by word, slowly and methodically. If you failed to express your meaning clearly, he would just shrug and hand it back without comment.

It was a short drive up the hill behind the hospital to his house. When I arrived, he was sitting in his favorite chair. Next to him was a dark brown bottle with a straw sticking out of the top. The label was pretty much worn off, but the ridges circling it gave it away. It was an Orange Crush bottle, the kind they didn't make anymore. Freddy would buy the soda in the ordinary aluminum cans, but he would drink it out of this old bottle. With a straw. Contremond's sold Orange Crush. So did the supermarket in White River Junction. But Freddy didn't buy his soda there.

Once a month he would drive over to Penobscot, Maine, to Hathaway's General Store and get a case of the beverage. I asked him why Penobscot. He told me Penobscot was where he spent summers as a child, and Hathaway's was where he had bought his soda. Orange Crush was his favorite.

"Long trip for a soda," I wrote.

"Convenience is overrated," he said.

On his lap was a well-fed calico cat. He had a soft spot for cats. It was an appropriate pet for Freddy. Independent and without any sense of obligation, even to those who provided room and board, cats' personalities were similar to his. At the time, he had two, Cat *Cuatro* and Cat *Seis*. Cats *Uno* through *Tres* and Cat *Cinco* had used up their allotted supply of lives. Freddy had a thing about Spanish names. His mother had been Venezuelan.

"*Playacita*," he said as I entered.

After the war, he was stationed in Madrid for *The New York Times*. The Madrid bureau chief for Associated Press was a guy named Beach Conger. He had a son also by the name of Beach. He called the father *Playa Grande*, and the son *Playacita*. Big Beach, Little Beach. When we first met, he reminded me about that. He said he remembered me as a rather obstreperous young man. The war in question, however, was World War I, and the Big and Little Beaches he referred to were my grandfather and my father. I had explained this to him several times, but it made no difference. Whether it was his idea of a joke, or whether his memory refused to adapt, I never could tell. It didn't matter. I liked the name.

After I had reviewed his current list of complaints, and he had rejected my suggestions for each of them, we fell to talking about other things. He wanted to know what I was doing these days when I wasn't doctoring. I told him I liked to be outdoors, I enjoyed grandparenting, and I was writing a book.

He wanted to know which I liked best.

I have discovered
having children
is the price
you pay
for the way
you treated
your parents

"Oh?" he said

> And that having
> grandchildren
> is the reward
> you get
> for the way
> your children
> treated you

He nodded.

He asked me what I was writing, and I told him. He wanted to know who the characters were.

> A bit of a jumble
> Partly people
> I have met
> Partly people
> I would like
> to have met

He shrugged.

> But mostly people
> I didn't meet
> Until
> they showed up
> on the page

"Usually that's the case," he said.

He told me that he was working on a book. I asked him what it was about.

"Books are not about."

He said it would be short. Then he asked me if I thought he would have enough time left to finish it. I told him time left wasn't my department, but it might be prudent to check the regulations regarding carry-on luggage for trips to the next reincarnation.

He smiled. Then he walked over to his bookcase and picked out a slim volume. He handed to me.

"Read this," he said.

The author was Penelope Fitzgerald. I had never heard of her.

"You probably haven't heard of her," he said. "Too bad for you. She's good."

I read the book. He was right. She was good. About halfway through, I found a small piece of paper with some writing on it. This is what it said.

> Don't you think you were planted here to write about all this and other things—to expose the world to these minds you love so . . .

And below that,

> You might want to pick up the pace.

Although the note wasn't meant for me, it was still pretty good advice. If he had asked, I would have told him I'd done the best I could. And I think he would have accepted that.

Around here, that's all anyone asks.

ACKNOWLEDGMENTS

••••••••••

Their patients are too sick, and their resources are not enough. But the doctors at Temple University Hospital do their job without complaining—not much anyway. They do good work for little credit. And they made me feel welcome. My thanks to all of them, particularly the basement gang: Bizath Taqui, Keith McNellis, Giuliana De Francesch, Jean Miller, and Emmanuel King. Also Darilyn Moyer, Larry Kaplan, Andy Roberts, and Gary Cohen. And to Joel Richter, a most tolerant boss, who bears no resemblance to any chief in this work.

And to my agent, Colleen, who got me started in all this.

ABOUT THE AUTHOR

· · · · · · · · · · ·

Beach Conger, MD, was born in New York City and graduated from Harvard Medical School. He has practiced general internal medicine at Mt. Ascutney Hospital in Windsor, Vermont, taught hospital medicine at Medical College of Pennsylvania and Temple University Hospital in Philadelphia, and served as chief of hospital medicine at the latter. He is a member of the Dartmouth Medical School faculty, where he precepts medical students in their primary-care rotations.